JUMP-ROPE RHYMES

A DICTIONARY

Publications of the American Folklore Society
Bibliographical and Special Series
General Editor, Wm. Hugh Jansen
Volume 20   1969

JUMP-ROPE RHYMES

A DICTIONARY

EDITED BY
ROGER D. ABRAHAMS

PUBLISHED FOR THE AMERICAN
FOLKLORE SOCIETY BY THE
UNIVERSITY OF TEXAS PRESS
AUSTIN & LONDON

TO ARCHER TAYLOR

FOREWORD

We live at a time when older boundaries between work and play seem less formidable than they once were; when much of the work of the world is carried on through mathematical games theory, probability theory, and computer and educational game simulation, and yesterday's work—hunting, fishing, archery, and boating—has become today's play. At a time of reformulation it is "fair" that one of the most persistent of children's play activities be introduced into this changing intellectual stadium.

For centuries jump-rope rhymes, along with riddles, jokes, superstitions, games, and graffiti, have been held behind a "triviality barrier," which only in more recent years has permitted the sober psychological intrusions of play-therapy, the analysis of dreams, cartoon analysis, and the study of projective blots and pictures. Yet they are all part of the one world, The Psychology of Childlore. The systematic, scholarly study of the developmental phenomenon in this world, along with the study of the larger set of related expressive phenomena (art, dance, music, mime, and drama), offers revolutionary promise for understanding the ways in which children are committed to their experience. Children who will not otherwise talk cannot be silenced on the subject matter of their own art and jump-rope rhymes. Here at least life is vivid. Here is an enrichment program and a pedagogic advantage that only an esthetic of uselessness can prevent us from grasping.

When esthetic and loristic expression become the focal point of new and more vivid understanding in education, then this collection of rhymes may well become both a bible and a source of advice to our blinkered perceptions, crying to our teachers: "Lady, lady, drop your purse."

Teachers College   Brian Sutton-Smith
Columbia University

ACKNOWLEDGMENTS

I am indebted to a number of persons who helped order the chaos I faced in preparing this dictionary. Archer Taylor has given a great deal of encouragement to projects of this sort both by words and by example, and my decision to see the project through was made because he argued so strongly on the importance of collecting and arranging materials so that they can be noticed and worked with, no matter how fallible the arrangement might be. Kenneth S. Goldstein provided further incentive by his enthusiasm on seeing the first draft of the manuscript; since then he has helped track down recondite sources, spending much time when he had little to spare. To the reference staff of The University of Texas, and especially to Charles Lee Dwyer, I owe many thanks for help in locating materials. After compiling a bibliography incident to the completion of the first draft, I sent copies to a number of interested scholars asking for suggested additions. Ben A. Botkin responded heartily with some important inclusions. Herbert Halpert spent many hours of his valuable time going through his notes, digging out a carload of supplementary references. For these, my thanks. Edith Fowke sent copies of three out-of-the-way Canadian articles, which were helpful in filling in the repertoire of that country. I am indebted to the staff at the School of Scottish Studies in Edinburgh, who allowed me to browse through and copy some of the materials in their files, and to C. A. Gardiner, Esq. M.A., for permission to print some of the unique rhymes from his collection lodged at the School. Dorothy Mills Howard discussed my project with me near its inception and subsequently sent a mimeographed collection of rhymes from Maryland, an act typical of her kindness. Carl Withers contributed a great deal of important data concerning his own collections, along with encouragement and good suggestions. William Hugh Jansen has exercised firm and benevolent editorial direction, offering many helpful hints for rewriting, both in the Introduction and in the text. Brian Sutton-Smith read the manuscript and sent on important ideas, especially on increasing the scope of the comments about the historical dimension of the playing of the games. Roger Pinon has helpfully discussed the problems of studying children's games and texts. Finally, my appreciation to my students at The University of Texas who provided so much original collectanea on the subject, to my colleagues here who encouragingly inquired about my work when I needed to joke about it, and to my family, who patiently sat and wondered what in hell I was doing.

CONTENTS

INTRODUCTION

Until relatively recently the ancient pastime of jumping rope was exclusively a boys' activity and had no rhymed games associated with it. Joseph Strutt, in his *Sports and Pastimes of the People of England,* mentions that rope skipping "is probably very ancient. It is performed by a rope held by both ends, that is, one end in each hand, and thrown forward or backward over the head and under the feet alternately. Boys often contested for superiority of skill in this game, and he who passes the rope about most times without interruption is the conqueror."[1]

Rope skipping of this description is still encountered among both males and females, but with men it is now part of the training program for some athletic activity such as boxing rather than a game. Jumping rope as a boys' game persisted well into the twentieth century, however, a fact recently attested to by the folklorist William Hugh Jansen. He says:

I can testify that at least in one region of the U.S. in the 1920's the boys' games still prevailed. Primarily they were competitive solo performances for speed, for altitude, and for tricks. And there were recognized terms for particular techniques, most of which I cannot recall. I do remember "cross-hands," "double-rope" (the jumper actually spun two ropes), "pepper," "Double-" and "Triple-skip" (in which the spinning rope passed under the jumper's feet twice or thrice in one skip—or more accurately, one jump), "one-handed" (in which the jumper spun with one hand a weighted rope rather like a trick lariat and skipped over it), and there were competitions which were not solo or which required assistants: Two in which the assistants served as high-jump standards; one in which a single assistant swung a rope close to the ground for the jumper to skip over (maybe called "whip"); one in which two assistants spun two ropes in opposing directions (called "Dutch rope"?);

---

[1] London, 1845, p. 383.

one, "High Water, Low Water" (the progression was from *low* to *high*);
and one called "Snake," in which the rope was undulated from side to
side so sharply that if it caught the jumper's toe he was likely to be sent
sprawling face down unless a kindly or weak rope-holder released his end
upon contact."[2]

Most of these games are still in active use, often called by the
same names, but they are now performed by girls. Just when this
change-over occurred is difficult to say, but it seems to have been
during the last generation of the nineteenth century. James Ritchie
in the *Golden City*[3] quotes R. L. S. (Stevenson?) from a work en-
titled *Notes on the Movements of Young Children* (1874), which
describes the activities of "a mistress in the art of skipping . . . in
the familiar neighbourhood of Hampstead. . . . There were two
sisters from seven to nine perhaps. . . . The elder was just and
adroit in every movement; the rope passed over her black head and
under her scarlet-stockinged legs with precision and regularity that
was like machinery; but there was nothing mechanical. . . . There
was one variation favorite with her, in which she crossed her hands
before her with a motion not unlike weaving. . . . And then the two
took the rope together and whirled in and out!"

Clearly we have here an early example of the activity of rope-
skipping as performed by girls, and much in the same manner as
played by boys. But as the activity has been taken over by girls the
focus of the games has changed. Now it is the jumping games calling
for two "turners" or "enders" and for one or more jumpers that are
the most common, and these rope-turning games present the proper
milieu for most of the rhymes included in this compilation. Such
games are played throughout the English-speaking world by girls
from the ages of six to thirteen, and the prevalence of the games
seems to be a twentieth-century phenomenon that grew out of play
activities in the city. The oldest recorded rhyme in this dictionary
comes from William H. Babcock's study of Washington, D.C.,
children, published in 1886.[4] The earliest large compilations, such
as Norman Douglas' *London Street Games*,[5] come from urban areas.
Commenting on the growth of jump-rope activities, Brian Sutton-
Smith notes:

[2] From personal communications, July and November, 1967.

[3] Edinburgh and London: Oliver & Boyd, Ltd., 1965, p. 111.

[4] "Carols and Child-Lore at the Capitol," *Lippincott's Magazine*, 38 (1886),
332.

[5] London: St. Catherine Press, 1916.

It appears probable that the girls of the nineteenth century were not as skilled as their modern counterparts in the art of skipping. Their clothing and the rough playgrounds of the day would certainly have militated against a superior performance. Skipping was the major winter game of girls before 1900, and it still rivals basketball for that position today. It continues to be the major winter game of the younger girls. Both in New Zealand and in England, few rhymes were used in skipping games before 1900. After that year, however, rhymes appeared in ever increasing numbers . . . suggesting that they are both a twentieth-century and a metropolitan phenomenon. They are certainly a play form that has thrived in the cramped play space and playgrounds of the modern age.[6]

Though he is discussing rope-skipping practices in England and New Zealand, his description also fits the other parts of the English-speaking world, to judge from the materials here assembled.

Just why this activity should have been taken up by girls and dropped by boys is difficult to ascertain; however, some important factors are pointed out by Sutton-Smith: the change in girls' dress, the improvement of playgrounds and the gravitation of children toward such areas, and the movement of the population to the cities. Elsewhere he notes that during this period girls were encouraged to play more, and more actively.[7] Jumping rope, especially jumping in groups to the accompaniment of the game-rhymes, *is* essentially an urban phenomenon. I have questioned a number of persons born in various rural areas of the United States around the turn of the century, and there is general agreement that they did jump rope (both boys and girls) but not with the virtuosity nor the number of rhymes that city children exhibit today.

Another factor that must be considered is the changing fashion of girls' play activities during this period. It is clear that along with the movement to the cities there occurred a drift from ritual-like play such as singing games to activity that emphasizes the play process and individual adeptness in movement. In most singing games, for instance, the focus is upon the dramatic enactment and repetition of a basic story. In jumping-rope and other presumably recent activities of girls the emphasis is instead on agility; story elements, if present, are secondary. This may reflect a changing attitude toward movement in general, for agility and gracefulness have attained high value for girls, witness the growth of ballet

[6] *Games of New Zealand Children* (Berkeley and Los Angeles: University of California Press, 1959), pp. 73–74.

[7] *Ibid.*, p. 75.

and modern-dancing courses for children. Thus, jumping rope may have been taken up by girls not only because of their shortened skirts and their need to play in the street or on the playground, but also because of a change in the focus of games, from dramatic enactment to skill activity.

This change can be seen in the development of "Teddy Bear, Teddy Bear," one of the most popular rhyme games. To surmise from the earliest British reportings of this piece, the rhyme developed from a chant used in the game "Drop the Handkerchief." This widely found game is a semiritualized contest activity in which a ring is formed, one person drops a handkerchief behind the back of another, and the two of them race around the outside of the ring attempting to be the first to return to the place where the handkerchief was dropped. This game is found with a number of accompanying chants, including "Itisket, Itasket," and "Lady, Lady, drop your handkerchief." Both of these rhymes are still found not only in connection with the game of "Drop the Handkerchief" but also with a jump-rope game in which the focus is on the performance, or imitation, of these commands ("drop the handkerchief," "pick it up," and so on). But much more common is the rhyme beginning:

> Teddy Bear, Teddy Bear, turn around;
> Teddy Bear, Teddy Bear, touch the ground.

The development of this rhyme can be clearly seen by comparing its various reportings. The earliest forms simply refer to "Lady, Lady" and utilize the dropping of the handkerchief as an indicator of the imitational activity (whereas it had been incidental in the game, serving only as a signal for the race around the ring). The Douglas text (1916) shows clearly how the transition took place:

> Lady, Lady, drop your purse,
> Lady, lady, pick it up.
> Lady, lady, touch the ground,
> Lady, lady, turn right round,
> Lady, lady, show your foot,
> Lady, lady, sling your hook.

With the establishment of the pattern of imitational movements as a demonstration of the jumpers' agility, new tricks were inevitably added. Furthermore, the similarity of "Lady, Lady," and "Ladybird, Ladybird, fly away home" led to a confusion of the rhymes ("Lady*bird*" is really easier to jump to). Finally, with the fad of the "Teddy Bear" doll (supposed to have been a compliment to Theodore Roosevelt), the dominant form of the rhyme evolved. And with the growing emphasis upon agility, this easily expandable game has remained at the center of the repertoire. (In the text, 125 reportings of the game are noted, plus seven for "Lady, Lady" and two for "Itisket, Itasket.")

The example of "Teddy Bear" is not unique. A similar development might be traced for that other ubiquitous group of rhymes, "Ice cream soda with a cherry on top" and "Strawberry shortcake, huckleberry pie," which seems to have developed jointly from the singing game of "Rosy apple, lemon, pear," and the "Hide-and-seek" rhyme beginning "Apples, peaches, pumpkin pie." However, many of the rhymes in this volume come from traditional sources other than singing games. Counting-out rhymes are the most common source, in fact, because so many jump-rope games involve counting and invoke player elimination of the "out-goes-she" sort. Similarly, many games are used for divining husbands, marriage dates, and so on, and often these rhymes have been adapted from earlier divination devices like button-counting rhymes.

Commentary on jumping rope has been done primarily by journalists and recreation experts. In the case of the former, the approach all too often has been of the "isn't this cute" sort; and the latter usually have been concerned with encouraging the playground use of the activity. Folklorists, on the other hand, have generally been content simply to present the rhymes and the games, sometimes annotating from other collections. Little beyond the work of Sutton-Smith quoted above relates rope skipping to any historical perspective or to the ways in which it fits into other patterns of play activity. Catherine Ainsworth's study[8] does rest on a broad geographical base, but she does little more than present her texts.

Though Britt and Balcom call their article "Jumping-Rope and the Social Psychology of Play"[9] and mention that "Jumping rope is a play activity for children [that] involves group participation in which . . . the physical activity of jumping, running, and skipping is involved," they do not follow up on this aspect of the activity. Rather, they devote themselves to a gratuitous examination of how

---

[8] "Jump Rope Verses Around the United States," *Western Folklore*, 20 (1961), 179–199.

[9] Stewart Henderson Britt and Margaret M. Balcom, *Journal of Genetic Psychology*, 58 (1941), 289–305.

certain rhymes maintain the proper rhythm of the game (in conjunction with the slap of the rope) while changing "thought and
content with the times." They do say at one point that "the play of
jumping-rope is regarded as a socializing force," but this premise
is never investigated.

The only work encountered that tries to account for this activity
in theoretical terms is Marion Sonnenberg's doctrinaire Freudian
article "Girls Jumping Rope." The argument here is that "The girl
in jumping rope acts out the to and fro movement of the man during sex intercourse. Her own body takes the part of the active man,
while the swinging rope *imitates* her own body *in adjusting* to the
movement of the man's. Thus, in this game, the girl acts both the
role of the man and of the woman."[10] The far-fetched nature of this
argument undermines what might have proved to be an important
technique for considering the sociopsychological dimension of this
play activity.

Though previous scholarship has provided us with few insights
into the social and psychological functions of rope-skipping, a number of observers have made meaningful attempts to analyze and
categorize the games. Sutton-Smith's primary purpose is to study
the historical dimension of children's play, but his description of
jump-rope games is helpful in establishing a classification system.
He divides the games into those in which the turners attempt to trip
the jumpers, those skipped through in turn, those calling for special
jumping skills, those using multiple ropes, those calling for divination, and those calling for imitation. These are presented not as
mutually exclusive categories but simply as the basis of discussion
and description.

A similar analysis is given by Sue Hall in her article "That
Spring Perennial—Rope Jumping!"[11] She proposed the following
game categories: Fundamentals (turners are also jumpers, singly
or in concert); Combinations of Play Jumping (turners are distinct
from jumpers—games are subdivided into those with a full turn of
the rope and those without); Counting (and other formulaic pro-
gressions); Hot (Pepper); Verses with Pantomime; and Single
Line Chants. The various games associated with specific rhymes are
then fully described as she had observed them.

Bruce Buckley's recent informative study "Jump-Rope Rhymes

[10] *Psychoanalysis*, 3 (1955), 59–60.
[11] *Recreation* (March, 1941), pp. 713–716.

—Suggestions for Classification and Study"[12] also classifies rhymes by their style of jumping. His self-explanatory categories are: Plain Jump; Endurance Jump; Call-in/Call-out; Speed Jumps; and Action Jumps. He had access to a large number of rhymes and provides an index to the frequency of the game-types in terms of percentage of repertoire.

Ruth Hawthorne's classification system, in "Classifying Jump-Rope Games,"[13] attempts to spell out the variables of jumping rope, rather than establish categories. She says:

It seems that four possible criteria stand out above the rest as a basis for classifying jump-rope games: (1) the position or action of the rope; (2) the position or action of the jumper; (3) the pattern of the verse (if one is given); and (4) the purpose of the verse (if one is given).

Her arrangement allows for a wide range of descriptive differentiations:

Under the first classification, the position or action of the rope, number I could be the most frequently used type. The grouping follows:

  I. One rope used, turned at regular speed.
  II. One rope used, turned at fast speed (Hot Pepper).
  III. One rope used, goes from regular to fast speed.
  IV. One rope used, held stationary at varied levels.
  V. One rope used, held stationary in unusual ways.
  VI. Two ropes used, both turned at regular speed.
  VII. Two ropes used, one turned, one stationary.

Under the second classification, the position or action of the jumper, letter A could be the most frequently used type. This grouping follows:

  A. Jumping on both feet.
  B. Jumping on both feet, other action involved (touching the ground, shoes, turning around).
  C. Jumping on both feet, eyes closed.
  D. Hopping on one foot and jumping.
  E. Unusual foot patterns.

Under the third classification, the pattern of the verse, a position would have to be available for those containing no verse. For making things simple, this could be placed first:

  1. No words.
  2. Words used, no verse.

[12] *Keystone Folklore Quarterly*, 11 (1966), 99–111.
[13] *Keystone Folklore Quarterly*, 11 (1966), 113–126.

3. Spelled out word.
4. Single-line verse.
5. Short rhyming verse.
6. Short partially rhymed verse.
7. Short unrhymed verse.
8. Longer rhymed verse or several verses.
9. Several partially rhymed verses.
10. Several unrhymed verses.

In the fourth classification, which states the purpose of the rhyme or game, again space must be left for the one which has no verse. When words are left out, the purposes will be entertainment or skill.

a. No words, entertainment or skill only.
b. Attempts to predict, by counting out or spelling.
c. Counting to answer non-prediction-type question.
d. Used to eliminate as many jumpers as possible.
e. Tells a story (only; no questions).
f. Call another person into the game.
g. Gives a command or asks for a specific action.
h. Counts (without answering any question).

Using these four classifications, a rhyme like "Teddy Bear" would be coded IB5g.1.[14] [The .1 refers to example one of this configuration.]

Hawthorne's system thus attempts to provide a description of both game and rhyme.

In another recent work, *Chansons Populaires de la Flandre Wallonne*,[15] the distinguished Belgian folklorist Roger Pinon outlines a classification system that also focuses on both games and rhymes. His categories, by game-type, are:

A. Apprentice formulae (techniques to learn how to jump rope, mostly those involving individual jumping).
B. Formulae for playing "Low Waters" (rope passed under feet but not over head).
C. Formulae for the turned rope
   (a) counting
   (b) enumerative
   (c) nonsense rhymes
   (d) divination
   (e) thematic formulae.
D. Miming or imitational formulae.

---

[14] *Ibid.*, p. 118–120.
[15] Brussels, 1965, pp. 78–79.

The four categories refer to discrete techniques of performance. The subcategories of *C* are essentially ways in which the rhymes are constructed. This becomes more evident in his breakdown of subcategory *Ce*:

1. infancy
2. forsaken infancy
3. school or convent
4. apprenticeship
5. clothing
6. eating and drinking
7. the gluttons
8. dwellings
9. heating
10. gymnastics
11. sports
12. dance
13. love
14. household life
15. rural professions
16. transport
17. shops
18. the smaller crafts (vending, etc.)
19. military profession
20. health
21. faith
22. history
23. the foreigner
24. taunts
25. nature
26. weather
27. plants
28. animals
29. diverse

Essentially these are descriptive terms for the content of the rhymes and are not mutually exclusive categories. The list gives good insight into the content of Belgian jump-rope rhymes and is interesting in comparison to the subjects explored in this volume. Many of Pinon's themes, such as eating and drinking, infancy, school, dance, and taunts, are present in abundance in English-language rhymes. Others, like the foreigner, the smaller crafts, the rural professions, are not found at all. This reflects different cultural backgrounds rather than different preoccupations of the children.

The content of the jump-rope rhymes in English is similar to that of rhymes used in conjunction with other play activities. Often a strong antitaboo and antiauthoritarian tone is assumed. This is reflected in the fantasy themes expressed in rhymes like "Fudge, fudge," in which the new baby in the family is wrapped in tissue paper and dispatched down the elevator. It is also evident in the numerous taunts and parodies throughout this volume and in the attachment to clown figures (Dagwood, Charlie Chaplin, Happy Hooligan), that is, to adult figures that children can at the same time both identify with and make fun of. Parents, when they appear, are portrayed more often than not as ridiculous, more to be laughed at than feared, and the same could be said of other authority figures such as policemen, doctors, judges, even movie stars.

A great deal more work needs to be done on the content of children's rhyme—and on all aspects of both the games and the rhymes. One potential area of investigation emerged as these rhymes were brought together: it becomes clear that, although many rhymes are found throughout the English-speaking world, there are also regional repertoires. For instance, the repertoire of rhymes in Scotland seems significantly different from those in other English-speaking countries, even England; the repertoire of the West Indies too is both different and much smaller. While England and the United States have a number of rhymes in common, a close scrutiny of the provenience of the rhymes in this collection will reveal equally pronounced differences. The nature of regional differences and how to account for them is obviously beyond the object of the present work, but I hope that this dictionary will serve to stimulate studies of these problems.

JUMP-ROPE RHYMES

A DICTIONARY

A GUIDE TO THE DICTIONARY

RHYMES

Texts

A representative text has been chosen for each rhyme and is given completely except where the rhyme is essentially repetitive. Spelling and punctuation are occasionally altered to aid understanding. Common variations are provided within parentheses in the text. Names marked with an asterisk are identified in Appendix B.

Alphabetization

The arrangement of the rhymes is alphabetical. Punctuation is ignored in the alphabetizing, and contractions are treated as though they were spelled out. Numbers and "Dr." are spelled out; "Mr." and "Mrs." are not. When any name could serve as the first word of the rhyme, the rhyme is alphabetized according to the second word, as are rhymes beginning with articles and "O" or "Oh."

Comments on the rhymes

Some rhymes are found in connection with other play activities. The identification of such activities, and general comments on the texts, appear in italics beneath the rhymes. The inclusion of a rhyme in *The Oxford Dictionary of Nursery Rhymes*, edited by Iona and Peter Opie, is also noted here. Appendix A lists jump-rope games and terms and provides information on sources that discuss them.

CROSS REFERENCES

The first line of a variant rhyme, if unlike the first line of the representative text, is included in the alphabetical arrangement of texts, with cross reference to the representative text. These variant entries are not numbered.

NOTES TO THE RHYMES

Sources for each rhyme are listed beneath the rhyme. In the

source entry, year of publication is given in parentheses. Provenience, where ascertainable, is provided in brackets, together with the year the rhyme was recorded if this date is known and differs from the year of publication. Notation on substantive variations from the representative text, if any, follows.

When a text has been reprinted, the additional source is joined to the original source by an equal sign. "Listed" indicates that only the first line of the rhyme was printed in the source.

Sources are in chronological order by year of publication or, if a rhyme is assigned a significantly earlier date in the source, by year of collection.

Publication information on sources can be found in Works Cited, at the end of the *Dictionary*. The abbreviations used in the notes for titles of periodicals are as follows:

AA: *American Anthropologist*
CFQ: *California Folklore Quarterly*
GMW: *Green Mountain Whittlin's*
HF: *Hoosier Folklore*
HFB: *Hoosier Folklore Bulletin*
JAF: *Journal of American Folklore*
J Gen Psy: *Journal of Genetic Psychology*
KFQ: *Keystone Folklore Quarterly*
MF: *Midwest Folklore*
NYFQ: *New York Folklore Quarterly*
NCF: *North Carolina Folklore*
SFQ: *Southern Folklore Quarterly*
TFSB: *Tennessee Folklore Society Bulletin*
WF: *Western Folklore*
WVF: *West Virginia Folklore*

(1)   **A,** b, c, d, e, f, g,
H, i, j, k, l, m, n, o, p,
Q, r, s, t, u are out.

Abrahams, *SFQ*, 27 (1963), 202 [Texas].
Buckley, *KFQ*, 11 (1966), 102 [Indiana]. Listed.

(2)   **A** bottle of pop, big banana,
We're from southern Louisiana.
That's a lie, that's a fib,
We're from Colorado.

Ainsworth, *WF*, 20 (1961), 192 [Colorado].

(3)   **Acca,** bacca,
Boom a cracka,
Acca, bacca, boo.
If your daddy chews tobacco
He's a dirty-do.

> *Often found at the end of "My mother, your mother."*
> *Usually collected as a counting-out rhyme.*

Nulton, *JAF*, 61 (1948), 57 [North Carolina]. Ends with a fragment from
    "Mother, mother, I am ill" rhyme.
Evans (1955), 7 [California] = Evans (1961), 31.
Abrahams, *KFQ*, 8 (1963), 11 [Pennsylvania, 1959].

(4)   **A**-hunting we will go,
A-hunting we will go,
We'll catch a fox,

Put him in a box,
And then we'll let him go.

Common nursery rhyme.

Randolph, *MF*, 3 (1953), 81 [Arkansas, *ca.* 1930].
Musick and Randolph, *JAF*, 63 (1950), 431 [Missouri].
Leventhal and Cray, *WF*, 22 (1963), 235 [California, 1959]. Begins "Chase the fox."

Albert, Albert.
See "Tommy, Tommy."

(5)   Ali Baba and the Forty Thieves
           Went to school with dirty knees.
           The teacher said: "Stand at ease."
           Ali Baba and the Forty Thieves.

                                    Cf. "Robin Hood."

Ritchie (1965), 119 [Edinburgh].

(6)   All in, a bottle of gin;
           All out, a bottle of stout.

Holbrook (1957), 58 [England].

(7)   All in together, (girls)
           How is the weather, (girls)
           January, February, March, *etc.*

           *The Douglas variant indicates a relationship to
           the sea chantey "Blow Ye Winds Westerly."*

Gibbs, *NYFQ*, 14 (1958), 313. Two variants: one from *ca.* 1890, one from *ca.* 1900.
McCormick (1912), 91 [Galloway]. Ends "I espied Peter,/Hanging out the window,/With his gun:/Slap! bang!! fire!!!"
Douglas (1916), 88 [London].
Goddard, *Word Lore*, 2 (1927), 128 [England]. Ends "I spy Peter hanging out the window,/Shoot, bang, fire."
Wood and Goddard (1938), 814 [New York].
Park, *CFQ*, 1 (1942), 377 [California].

Treneer (1944), 119 [Cornwall]. "All in together,/This frosty weather."

Halpert, *JAF*, 58 (1945), 350 [New Hampshire].

Withers (1948), 60.

Daiken (1949), 71 [Great Britain].

Frankel (1952), 62.

Browne, *WF*, 14 (1955), 14 [California]. "All in together,/Rainy, rainy weather."

Evans (1955), 17, 18 [California]. Two variants, the second begins "Sunny, sunny weather."

Godman, *Folk-Lore*, 67 (1956), 173 [Sussex]. Ends "Put your paint and powder on,/Tell the boys you'll not be long:/Shoot, fire, bang!"

A. W. Smtih, *Folk-Lore*, 67 (1956), 248 [Sussex]. Two variants.

Holbrook (1957), 56 [England].

Abrahams, *KFQ*, 8 (1963), 8 [Pennsylvania, 1959].

Sutton-Smith (1959), 75 [New Zealand]. Three variants.

Ainsworth, *WF*, 20 (1961), 194 [New Mexico], 195 [Utah].

Worstell (1961), 38.

Heimbuecher, *KFQ*, 7, No. 4 (1962), 5 [Pennsylvania].

Abrahams, *SFQ*, 27 (1963), 198 [Texas]. Two variants.

Butler and Haley (1963), n.p.

Ritchie (1965), 113, 128, 129 [Edinburgh]. Four variants: one, with "frosty weather," ends "All out together"; two end "January, February, . . ."; one with "Like a bunch of feathers" as second line.

Those Dusty Bluebells (1965), 13. Ends "I see a picture hanging on the wall,/When I count twenty, the rope must be empty."

Buckley, *KFO*, 11 (1966), 102 [Indiana]. Listed.

Hawthorne, *KFQ*, 11 (1966), 116, 123 [Delaware]. "Two in together," ". . . I spy Peter,/On a heater;/Ding Dong! The fire bell!" Ends with "Up the ladder" rhyme.

       All last night and the night before.
       See "Last night and the night before."

(8)   All over Italy
         The Kings are playing leap-frog.
         One, two, three and over . . .

Ritchie (1964), 42 [Edinburgh].

(9)   All the boys in our town, eating apple pie,
         Excepting (Georgie Groves), he wants a wife—
         A wife he shall have, according he shall go
         Along with (Rosie Peters), because he loves
            her so.

He kisses her and cuddles her, and sits her
   on his knee
And says, my dear, do you love me?
I love you, and you love me.
Next Sunday morning the wedding will be,
Up goes the doctor, up goes the cat,
Up goes the little boy in a white straw hat.

> *Cf. ending to "Mother, mother, I am ill."*

Douglas (1916), 59–60 [London].

(10)   Amos and Andy,* sugar and candy,
        I pop in;
        Amos and Andy, sugar and candy,
        I pop down;
        etc.

> *Comes from the nursery rhyme "Handy
> Spandy, Jack a Dandy" (see Opie, DICTION-
> ARY, 232). The radio program "Amos 'n'
> Andy" occasioned the change. See also
> Gomme, 1 (1894), 189.*

Gomme, 2 (1898), 204 [England]. "Andy Pandy, Sugardy Candy."
Gillington, *Old Hampshire* (1909), n.p. [Hampshire]. "Handy Pandy."
Sutton-Smith (1959), 73 [New Zealand]. Two variants from 1910.
Douglas (1931), 88 [London]. "Handy Pandy."
Wood and Goddard (1938), 813. "Handy Wandy."
Ashton, *JAF*, 52 (1939), 120 [Iowa]. "Handy Spandy."
Speroni, *CFQ*, 1 (1942), 247 [California].
Sone (1943), 198 [Texas].
Opie (1947), 79 [England]. "Handy Pandy."
Withers (North) (1947), 83 ("Andy, Nandy") = Withers (1964), 97.
Ashby, *Christian Science Monitor Magazine* (April 9, 1949), 8.
Haines, *Daedalian*, 17 (1949), 26 [Texas].
Harris, *Evening Bulletin* (May 30, 1949), 10 [Pennsylvania]. Mentions
   "Amos and Andy had a piece of candy."
Evans (1955), 2 [California, three variants] = Evans (1961), 14.
Holbrook (1957), 57 [England]. "Andy Pandy."
MacColl and Seeger, Folkways 3565 (1962) [Durham, England]. "Hanky
   Panky."
Abrahams, *SFQ*, 27 (1963), 198 [Texas]. Two variants.
Butler and Haley (1963), n.p.

Ritchie (1965), 129 [Edinburgh]. "Andy Pandy/Sugaralie Candy."
Buckley, *KFQ*, 11 (1966), 107 [Indiana].

(11) Amy Johnson* flew in an aeroplane
      Away to America and never came back again.
      She flew in an old tin lizzy
      Enough to make you dizzy.
      Amy Johnson, away in an aeroplane.

Those Dusty Bluebells (1965), 10 [Ayrshire].

      Anda Panda.
         See "Teddy Bear, Teddy Bear, turn around."

(12) Andy Gump* sat on a stump.
      He fell off and got a bump.

Botkin (1947), 906 [Connecticut].

      Andy, Nandy.
         See "Amos and Andy."

      Andy, Pandy.
         See "Amos and Andy."

(13) Angel, devil, angel, devil.

                    *Keep jumping until you miss to see
                    which you are.*

Student oral collection (1964) [New Jersey].

(14) Anna Banana,
      Play the piano.
      All she knew was "The Star Spangled Banner."
      Banana, banana split.

              See "Policeman, policeman, do your duty."

Harris, *Evening Bulletin* (May 30, 1949), 10 [Pennsylvania].

Abrahams, *KFQ*, 8 (1963), 10–11 [Pennsylvania, 1959]. Two variants,
one "Banana, banana."
Ainsworth, *WF*, 20 (1961), 195 [Utah].

(15)   Anna girlie, Anna girlie, come and take a swim;
          Yes, by golly, when the tide comes in.

                              Usually a taunt, "yellowbelly."

Haufrecht (1947), 64.

          Ann, Ann, took a trip.
          See "I took a trip around the world."

(16)   Annie cum banny,
          Tee alligo skanny,
          Tee-legged, tie-legged,
          Bow-legged Annie.

                         Usually a taunt; see "Johnny Maloney."

Butler and Haley (1963), n.p.

(17)   Ann is angry;
          Bob is bad.
          Helen is hateful;
          Sam is sad.
          I'm in love
          And love is bliss.
          How many times
          Do I get a kiss?
          1, 2, 3, 4, *etc.*

                              Usually an autograph album rhyme.

Mankins, *WVF*, 12 (1962), 55 [West Virginia].

(18)   Anthy Maria jumped in the fire;
          The fire was too hot, she jumped in the pot;
          The pot was too black, she jumped in a
              crack;

The pot was soon over, she jumped in some
  clover.
Clover's too sweet, she kicked up her feet.
Feet was soon over, she cried 1, 2, 3,
  jumped in a tree.
The tree was so high she couldn't go higher.
'Long came a breeze and blew her away.

Other versions give different particulars.

Evans (1961), 23 [California].
Worstell (1961), 10–11.
Abrahams oral collection (1962) [Nevis, B.W. I.].

Apartment to rent.
See "A house to let."

Apple, jelly, my jam tart.
See "Ice cream soda."

(19)   Apple on a stick
          Five cents a lick,
          Every time I turn around
          It makes me sick.

Musick, *HF*, 7 (1948), 11 [West Virginia].
Withers (1948), 63.
Butler and Haley (1963), n.p.

(20)   Apple, peach, pumpkin pie
          How many days before I die?
          1, 2, 3, *etc.*

Cf. rhyme for "Hide-and-Go-Seek" game.

Douglas (1916), 83 [London]. "Appletree, peartree, plumtree pie."
Heck, *JAF*, 40 (1927), 41.
Evans (1955), 18 [California].

Apples, peaches, cream of tart (creamery butter).
See "Ice cream soda."

Archie-ball-ball-ball.
See "Nebuchadnezzar."

Apples, pears, peaches, plums.
See "Ice cream soda."

(21)   As I was going to Strawberry Fair,
        Singing buttercups and daisies,
        I met a maiden taking the air—
        Her eyes were blue and gold her hair,
        As she goes on to Strawberry Fair.

Douglas (1916), 70 [London].

(22)   As I was in the kitchen
        Doing a bit of stitching
        In came a bogy man
        And I walked out.
        I saw a lark shining in the dark.

Douglas (1916), 68 [London]. Begins "I-N spells in"; ends with "Old Father Nimble/Came and took my thimble,/I got up a great big stone,/ Hit him on the belly bone."
Daiken (1949), 63 [Great Britain].
Musick, *WVF*, 2, No. 3 (1952), 5 [West Virginia]. Ends "In came Boo/ And out I flew."
Evans (1955), 15 [California] = Evans (1961), 34.
Holbrook (1957), 57 [England]. "Mother's in the kitchen."
Bluebells (1961), n. p. [Ayrshire]. "Polly in the kitchen."
Daiken (1963), 33 [Dublin].
Ritchie (1965), 114 [Edinburgh]. "Grannie in the kitchen."
Those Dusty Bluebells (1965), 12 [Ayrshire]. "Polly in the kitchen."

(23)   As I was walking by the lake,
        I met a little rattlesnake.
        I gave him so much jelly cake,
        It made his little belly ache.
        1-2-3, out goes she.

          Often found as a counting-out rhyme and taunt.

Brewster (1952), 172 [North Carolina]. "As I went up silver lake."
Abrahams, *SFQ*, 27 (1963), 202 [Texas].

(24)   As I was walking through the city,
Half past o'clock at night,
There I met a Spanish lady
Washing her clothes at night.
First she rubbed them, then she scrubbed them,
Then she hung them out to dry,
Then she laid her hands upon them,
Said: I wish my clothes were dry.

Douglas (1916), 34 [London].

(25)   As I went down to my grandfather's farm,
A billy-goat chased me around the barn.
It chased me up a sycamore tree,
And this is what it said to me:

Speroni, *CFQ*, 1 (1942), 248 [California]. Ends with "Down by the river" rhyme.
Haufrecht (1947), 63. Ends with "I love coffee" rhyme.
Haines, *Daedalian*, 17 (1949), 24 [Texas]. Begins "I went down to Grandpa's farm," ends with "I like coffee" rhyme.
Evans (1955), 21 [California]. Begins "When I went down . . . ," ends with "Down by the river" rhyme.
Buckley, *KFQ*, 11 (1966), 103 [Indiana]. "I was born on Grandpa's farm." Listed.

As I went up silver lake.
See "As I was walking by the lake."

(26)   A tisket, a tasket,
Hitler's* in his casket;
Eenie, meenie, Mussolini,*
Six feet underground.

Parody of "Itisket, Itasket."

Britt and Balcom, *J Gen Psy*, 58 (1941), 294 [Maryland, District of Columbia].

(27)   At the Battle of Waterloo
This is what the soldiers do:

Left, right, left, right,
All the way to Timbuctoo!

Ritchie (1965), 129 [Edinburgh].

(28)   Away down East, away down West,
Away down Alabama:
The only girl that I love best,
Her name is Susy Anna.

I took her to a ball one night
And sat her down to supper:
The table fell and she fell too
And stuck her nose in butter.

The butter, the butter,
The holy margarine,
Two black eyes and a jelly nose
And the rest all painted green.

Ritchie (1964), 26 [Edinburgh].

Baby in the cradle.
   See "Wavy, wavy."

(29)   Baby in the high chair
Can't sit still.
Ma! Pa!
Whoops-a-la!
Wrap her up in tissue paper,
Send her down the elevator.

                              Cf. "Fudge, fudge."

Gibbs, *NYFQ*, 14 (1958), 315.

Abrahams, *SFQ*, 27 (1963), 198 [Texas].
Buckley, *KFQ*, 11 (1966), 105 [Indiana]. ". . . in the bathtub." Listed.

(30)   **B**ake a pudding,
         Bake a pie,
         Did you ever
         Tell a lie?
         Yes, you did,
         I know you did,
         You broke your mother's
         Teapot lid.
         O-U-T spells out
         And out you must go,
         Right in the middle
         Of the deep blue sea.

                        Usually a counting-out rhyme.

Sutton-Smith (1959), 76 [New Zealand].

         Baker, baker,
         Bake your bread.
         See "Salt, vinegar, mustard, and pepper."

         Banana, banana.
         See "Anna Banana."

(31)   **B**anana, banana, banana
         Split!

Schiller, *NYFQ*, 12 (1956), 205 [New York].

(32)   **B**ean porridge hot,
         Bean porridge cold,
         Bean porridge's best
         When nine days old.

                Usually a hand-clapping rhyme (see Opie, DIC-
                TIONARY, 345). See also "Coffee hot, coffee cold."

Haufrecht (1947), 63.
Hawthorne, *KFQ*, 11 (1966), 114, 121 [Delaware]. "Porridge hot, . . ."

(33)   **B**een in Grandad's garden,
         Turned on the hose;
         How many times will he
         Punch me in the nose?
         1, 2, 3, 4, *etc.*

Mankins, *WVF*, 12 (1962), 55 [West Virginia].

         Benjamin Franklin* went to France.
         See Charlie Chaplin went to France.

         Beryl Grey* is a star, S-T-A-R.
         See "Spanish dancers."

         Betty, Betty.
         See "Teddy Bear, Teddy Bear, turn around."

         Betty, Betty, Betty Jo.
         See "Ice cream soda."

(34)   **B**etty, Betty stumped her toe
         On the way to Mexico;
         On the way back she broke her back
         Sliding on the railroad track.

                        See also "Cowboy Joe."

Brewster, *SFQ*, 3 (1939), 178.
Botkin (1944), 795.
Buckley, *KFQ*, 11 (1966), 101 [Indiana]. Listed.

(35)   **B**etty Boop,* isn't she cute?
         All she can eat is vegetable soup.

Emrich and Korson (1947), 137.
Abrahams, *SFQ*, 27 (1963), 198.

         Betty Grable* went to France.
         See "Charlie Chaplin went to France."

(36)   **B**ig Ben strikes one,
         Big Ben strikes two,

B

Big Ben strikes three,
etc.

Douglas (1931), 26 [London].
Opie (1959), 4 [London].
Ritchie (1965), 140, 141 [Edinburgh]. Two variants.
Those Dusty Bluebells (1965), 6 [Ayrshire].

> Black currant, red currant, gooseberry jam
> (raspberry tart).
> *See "Ice cream soda."*

(37)   The Black man said (My mother said)
That you are A.,
If you do not want to play,
You can sling your hook away.

Douglas (1916), 63 [London].

(38)   Black Pig, Black Pig went to the house.
Up on the top he went and he fell,
Single, single, Blackie Pig went.
Father told him to get in the corner
Because he said, Shut up.

Seems improvised.

Fife, *JAF*, 59 (1946), 322 [North Carolina].

> Black sugar, white sugar.
> *See "Ice cream soda."*

(39)   Blaw, blaw my kilt's awa',
My kilt's awa', my kilt's awa',
Blaw, blaw my kilt's awa',
Bring me back my troosers.
Meg, Meg, I broke my leg,
I broke my leg, I broke my leg,
Meg, Meg, I broke my leg,
Sae bring me back my troosers.

Cf. the ballad burden best known in
"The Elfin Knight" (Child 2A).

Bluebells (1961), n.p. [Ayrshire].

B-L-E-S-S-I-N-G.
See *"Roses red, roses white."*

(40) Blondie* and Dagwood* (Toots and Casper*)
Went downtown.
Blondie bought an evening gown,
Dagwood bought a pair of shoes,
And Cookie* bought the Daily News.

See also *"........... went for a ride" (under W)*.

Mills and Bishop, *The New Yorker* (November 13, 1937), 36 [New York, 1934] = Botkin (1944), 802.
Britt and Balcom, *J Gen Psy*, 58 (1941), 294 [Maryland, District of Columbia].
Emrich and Korson (1947), 136.
Haufrecht (1947), 63. "Jack and Jill."
Musick and Randolph, *JAF*, 63 (1950), 431 [Missouri].
Browne, *WF*, 14 (1955), 21 [California].
Abrahams, *KFQ*, 8 (1963), 11 [Pennsylvania, 1959].
Ainsworth, *WF*, 20 (1961), 181 [Maine].
Abrahams, *SFQ*, 27 (1963), 198 [Texas]. Three variants, two with "Fred and Wilma."*
Butler and Haley (1963), n.p. "Dagwood, Blondie went downtown."
Buckley, *KFQ*, 11 (1966), 104 [Indiana]. Listed.
Hawthorne, *KFQ*, 11 (1966), 114, 124 [Delaware].
Fowke, *Hoot* (September, 1966), 42 [Canada]. Two variants, one with "Maggie and Jiggs."

(41) Bluebells, cockleshells,
Eevy, Ivy, Over.

See also *"Wavy, wavy."*

Douglas (1916), 92 [London]. "Erie, Ivy, over,/The kettle is boiling over ...."
Winifred Smith, *JAF*, 39 (1926), 83 [New York]. "Tinkle bells," ends with "Mary Mack" rhyme.
Davis (1949), 215 [Florida, 1938].
Ashton, *JAF*, 52 (1939), 120 [Iowa].
Rudy, Mills, and Sone, *Jack and Jill*, 4 (March, 1942), 7. With "I love coffee" rhyme.
Sone (1943), 198 [Texas]. With "I love coffee" rhyme.

Halpert, *CFQ*, 3 (1944), 154 [Alberta].

"Jump-Rope Rhymes," *WF*, 23 (1964), 258 [California, 1944]. Ends "Mother's in the kitchen; Frying egg an' ham;/Baby's in the cradle; kickin' up his legs;/Father's in the hallway/Doin' arithmetic. . . ." Emrich and Korson (1947), 137.

Haufrecht (1947), 61.

Ashby, *Christian Science Monitor Magazine* (April 9, 1949), 8. With "Rich man, poor man" rhyme.

Haines, *Daedalian*, 17 (1949), 28 [Texas, District of Columbia].

Harris, *Evening Bulletin* (May 30, 1949), 10 [Pennsylvania]. Ends "Mother's in the kitchen, baking meat,/Baby's in the cradle playing with her feet."

Browne, *WF*, 14 (1955), 10–11 [Colorado]. Four variants.

Evans (1955), 19 [California, with "Here comes teacher with a hickory stick" rhyme] = Evans (1961), 51.

Seeger, Folkways 7029 (1955) [Illinois].

Pope, *WF*, 15 (1956), 46 [Texas]. With "Here comes teacher with a hickory stick" rhyme.

"Children's Rhymes," *WVF*, 8 (1958), 38, 39. Two variants: one ends with "I was born in a frying pan" rhyme; the other with "I like coffee" rhyme.

Gibbs, *NYFQ*, 14 (1958), 315.

Leventhal and Cray, *WF*, 22 (1963), 237 [California, 1959].

Sutton-Smith (1959), 76, 78 [New Zealand]. Three variants, two end with "Salt, vinegar, mustard, and pepper."

Taylor, *WF*, 18 (1959), 316 [California]. Two variants: one with "Mother, mother I am ill" rhyme; one with "Here comes teacher with a hickory stick" rhyme.

Ainsworth, *WF*, 20 (1961), 180 [Maine], 181 [North Carolina], 188 [Michigan], 189 [Wisconsin].

Bluebells (1961), n.p. [Ayrshire]. With "Doctor Long is a very good man" rhyme.

Evans (1961), 19, 51. Three variants; one begins "Twinkle bells" and ends with "Mary Mack" rhyme, another ends with a "Here comes teacher" rhyme from California, 1955.

Sackett (1961), 224 [Kansas].

Worstell (1961), 19 (with "Doctor Long is a very good man" rhyme), 25 (with "My father is a butcher" rhyme).

Abrahams, *SFQ*, 27 (1963), 198 [Texas]. Seven variants; one begins "Blue bells, shotgun shells," one with "My father is a butcher" rhyme, two with "Johnny on the ocean" rhyme, one with "Johnny gave me apples" rhyme.

Butler and Haley (1963), n.p.

Ritchie (1964), 24 [Edinburgh]. "Bluebells, dummie dummie shells," ends with "Charlie Chaplin went to France" rhyme.

Ritchie (1965), 116 [Edinburgh]. With "Doctor Long is a very good
man" rhyme.
Those Dusty Bluebells (1965), 6 [Ayrshire]. With "Doctor Long is a
very good man" rhyme.
Buckley, *KFQ*, 11 (1966), 101 [Indiana]. Listed.
Hawthorne, *KFQ*, 11 (1966), 123 [Delaware].
Warner, *Yankee*, 30, No. 1 (January, 1966), 94.

(42)   **B**luebells, my cockleshells,
          Farewell, my mother.
          Bury me in the old church-yard,
          Beside by eldest brother.
          My coffin shall be white,
          Six white angels by my side,
          Two to watch and two to pray,
          And two to carry my soul away.

                    *Cf. seventeenth-century prayer. See also "I am
                    a little beggar-girl."*

Bluebells (1961), n.p. [Ayrshire]. With tune in sol-fa.

          Bobby went down to the ocean.
          See "Johnny on the ocean."

(43)   **B**ounce a ball

Buckley, *KFQ*, 11 (1966), 103 [Indiana]. Listed.

(44)   **B**ow-legged Dutchman walking down the street
          Bow-legged Dutchman have a little sweet (seat)
          Bow-legged Dutchman drink a glass of wine
          Bow-legged Dutchman close your eyes
          And count to nine:
          1-2-3-4-5-6-7-8-9.

Dodson, *Recreation* (June, 1951), 173 [North Carolina]. Ends ". . . takes
a bite of bun/. . . You'd better run."
Seeger, Folkways 7029 (1955) [Illinois].

(45)   **B**read and butter,
          For my supper.
          That is all my mother's got.

Sutton-Smith (1959), 77 [New Zealand].

(46)   Bread and butter,
          Sugar and spice,
          How many boys think I'm nice?
          One, two, three, *etc.*

Worstell (1961), 5.

(47)   Broken-hearted I wandered,
          For the loss of my true lover.
          He's a jolly, jolly horseman,
          In the battle he was slain,
          etc.

MacColl and Behan, Folkways 8501 (1958) [Glasgow].

(48)   Bronco Lane* had a pain—
          So they sent for Wagon Train*:
          Wagon Train was no good—
          So they sent for Robin Hood*:
          etc.

Ritchie (1964), 48, 49 [Edinburgh].

(49)   Bubble gum, bubble gum, chew and blow.
          Bubble gum, bubble gum, scrape your toe.
          Bubble gum, bubble gum, tastes so sweet.
          Get that bubble gum off your feet.
                    Cf. "Teddy Bear, Teddy Bear, turn around."

Time (May 29, 1950), 20.
Buckley, *KFQ*, 11 (1966), 103 [Indiana]. Listed.

(50)   Bubble gum, bubble gum in the dish,
          How many pieces do you wish?
          1-2-3-4-5-6, *etc.*

Heimbuecher, *KFQ*, 7, No. 4 (1962), 6 [Pennsylvania].

(51)   Bumblebee, bumblebee, stung Jack Fry.
           How many feet did it make him fly?
           1, 2, 3, *etc.*

Haufrecht (1947), 61.

           Buster Brown.*
           See "Teddy Bear, Teddy Bear, turn around."

           Buster, Buster, climb a tree.
           See "Teddy Bear, Teddy Bear, turn around.

(52)   The Butcher and the baker
           And the candlestick-maker,
           They all jumped over
           A rotten potato.
           I'll tell your mother
           I saw a black boy
           Kiss you in the gutter.
           How many kisses did you get?
           1, 2, 3, *etc.*
                              Cf. Gomme, 2 (1898), 202.

Sutton-Smith (1959), 80 [New Zealand].

           Butterfly, butterfly.
           See "Teddy Bear, Teddy Bear, turn around."

(53)   By the holy and religerally law
           I marry this Indian to this squaw.
           By the point of my jack-knife
           I pronounce you man and wife.

Babcock, *Lippincott's Magazine*, 38 (1886), 332 [District of Columbia].
    Two variants, one begins "By the holy evangels of the Lord."
Babcock, *AA*, o.s., 1 (1888), 267 (seven variants: two from *Lippincott's*
    above; one begins "By the old Levitical law," another "The Bible is a
    holy and visible law"; one ends "You must be kind, you must be good,/
    And split up all her oven wood," another ends "You must be kind, you
    must be true,/And kiss the bride and she'll kiss you," another, "Sober
    alive and sober proceed,/And so bring up your Indian breed")=
    Newell (1903), 253.

Clarke, *JAF*, 3 (1890), 290 [Virginia, "This Bible is a holy and visible law"] = Newell (1903), 253.

(54)   California oranges 50¢ a pack,
         Come on .... and tap me on the back.

Ainsworth, *WF*, 20 (1961), 189 [Wisconsin].
Abrahams, *SFQ*, 27 (1963), 198 [Texas].
Buckley, *KFQ*, 11 (1966), 105 [Indiana]. Listed.

(55)   Callings in, and callings out,
         I call (Rosie) in.
         Rosie's in and won't go out—
         I call (Mandie) in.

Douglas (1916), 59 [London].
Sutton-Smith (1959), 77 [New Zealand]. A shorter form.

         Can you do the sword-dance.
         See "Spanish dancers."

(56)   Caroline Pink, she fell down the sink,
         She caught the Scarlet Fever,
         Her husband had to leave her,
         She called in Doctor Blue,
         And he caught it too—
         Caroline Pink from China Town.

                    Refers to a doll.

Douglas (1916), 69 [London].

(57)   Catch a fish
         Put it in a dish,
         Catch a mucket
         Put it in a bucket,
         Catch a hen
         Put it in a pen,
         etc.

> *Related to the lullaby "Dance to
> your Daddy."*

Randolph, *MF*, 3 (1953), 83 [Arkansas].

(58)   Changing bedrooms number one,
         Changing bedrooms number two,
         Changing bedrooms number three.
         Everybody out.

Gomme, 2 (1898), 201. Related text.
Grace Partridge Smith, *HF*, 5 (1946), 59 [Illinois] = Dorson (1964), 386.
Evans (1955), 28 [California] = Evans (1961), 48.
Browne, *WF*, 14 (1955), 13 [California].
Ainsworth, *WF*, 20 (1961), 192 [Colorado].
Butler and Haley (1963), n.p.
Student oral collection (1964) [Texas]. "Changing dresses."

(59)   Charley, Charley stole some barley
         Out of the baker's shop!
         The baker came out, and gave him a clout,
         Which made poor Charley hop!

Gillington, *Old Surrey* (1909), n. p. [Surrey].
Douglas (1916), 57 [London]. "Charlie, Arlie."
Schiller, *NYFQ*, 12 (1956), 203 [New York].

(60)   Charley, Charley, wheat and rye,
         Kissed the girls and made them cry.

> *Cf. "Georgie Porgie," Opie,*
> DICTIONARY, *185–186.*

Abrahams, *SFQ*, 27 (1963), 202 [Texas].

(61)   Charlie Chaplin* came to Duluth
            To have a dentist pull his tooth.
            First he hollered, and then he screamed (yelled),
            Then he asked for a dish of ice cream (Then he
                pulled the emergency bell).

Owens, *North Star Folk News*, 4, No. 2 (1949), 2 [Minnesota].

(62)   Charlie Chaplin* has big feet,
            He thinks he owns the whole darn street.
            If the street were made of glass,
            Charlie would fall and break his _____
            Don't get excited, don't get alarmed,
            Charlie would fall and break his arm.

                            *Usually an entertainment rhyme. Cf.
                            "Three little Negroes" and "There was a
                            little fellow."*

Schiller, *NYFQ*, 12 (1956), 205 [New York].

            Charlie Chaplin* sat on a fence.
            See "Tattletale, Tattletale."

(63)   Charlie Chaplin* sat on a pin.
            How many inches did it go in?
            One, two, three, *etc.*

                    Cf. "Rin Tin Tin swallowed a pin."

Winifred Smith, *JAF*, 39 (1926), 83 [New York]. ". . . sat on a tack."
Thompson, *JAF*, 47 (1934), 386 [Pennsylvania, 1929].
Randolph, *MF*, 3 (1953), 78 [Arkansas, 1934]. "Lazy Daisy."
Mills and Bishop, *The New Yorker* (November 13, 1937), 36 [New York,
    New Jersey, California, Michigan] = Botkin (1944), 802.
Ashton, *JAF*, 52 (1939), 121 [Iowa]. "Ricky Wilson."
Brewster, *SFQ*, 3 (1939), 175.
"Stella, Stella," *Fargo Forum* (June 23, 1940), 13 [North Dakota].
Hall, *Recreation* (March, 1941), 714 [Nebraska].
Fife, *JAF*, 59 (1946), 532 [Utah].
New York Times Magazine (April 28, 1946), 8 [Pennsylvania].
Botkin (1947), 906 [Connecticut].
Emrich and Korson (1947), 132.
Musick, *HF*, 7 (1948), 10 [West Virginia]. "Rinny Tin Tin."

Withers (1948), 66. "Charlie McCarthy."
Harris, *Evening Bulletin* (May 30, 1949). 10 [Pennsylvania]. Mentions
    "Little Orphan Annie swallowed a pin."
Potter, "Charlie Chaplin," *Standard Dictionary* (1949), 213.
Browne, *WF*, 14 (1955), 9 [California].
"Children's Rhymes," *WVF*, 8 (1958), 39. "Hitler, Hitler."
Opie (1959), 108 [England].
Sutton-Smith (1959), 79 [New Zealand].
Ainsworth, *WF*, 20 (1961), 193 [Colorado].
Worstell (1961), 17.
Heimbuecher, *KFQ*, 7, No. 4 (1962), 6 [Pennsylvania]. "Tim, Tim."
Abrahams, *SFQ*, 27 (1963), 198, 211 [Texas]. Three variants, two begin
    "Rin Tin Tin."
Butler and Haley (1963), n.p.
Buckley, *KFQ*, 11 (1966), 103 [Indiana]. Listed.

> Charlie Chaplin* walks like this.
> *See "Shirley Temple walks like this."*

(64)   Charlie Chaplin* washing up
            Broke a saucer and a cup,
            How much did they cost?

Opie (1959), 108 [England].

(65)   Charlie Chaplin* went (came) to France
            To teach the ladies (elephants) how to dance;
            Heel and toe and away we go.

> *Most versions end with the "Salute to the
> captain, Bow to the Queen" lines also char-
> acteristic of "I'm a little Dutch girl" rhyme.*

Winifred Smith, *JAF*, 39 (1926), 82.
Thompson, *JAF*, 47 (1934), 386 [Pennsylvania, 1929].
Nulton, *JAF*, 61 (1948), 59 [North Carolina, 1936].
Mills and Bishop, *The New Yorker* (November 13, 1937), 36 (begins
    "One, two, three, four/Charlie Chaplin went to war") = Botkin
    (1944), 802.
Brewster, *SFQ*, 3 (1939), 175 [Indiana, two variants] = Botkin (1949),
    793.
Speroni, *CFQ*, 1 (1942), 246 [California].
Sone (1943), 199 [Texas]. "Shirley Temple."
"Jump-Rope Rhymes," *WF*, 23 (1964), 258 [California, 1944].
Fife, *JAF*, 59 (1946), 321, 322 [North Carolina], 532 [Utah].

C   27

McDowell, *New York Times Magazine* (April 14, 1946), 8.
Emrich and Korson (1947), 132.
Haufrecht (1947), 63, 64. Two variants: one "Tommy Tucker," one beginning "One, two, three, four/Superman went to war."
Withers (1948), 65.
Owens, *North Star Folk News*, 4, No. 2 (1949), 2 [Minnesota].
Potter, "Charlie Chaplin," *Standard Dictionary* (1949), 213. Two variants, one begins "One, two, three, four,/C. C. went to war."
Reck, *WF*, 8 (1949), 126 [Colorado]. With "I'm a little Dutch Girl" rhyme.
Time (May 29, 1950), 20 [Texas]. "Betty Grable."
Brewster (1952), 172 [North Carolina].
Musick, *WVF*, 2, No. 3 (1952), 5 [West Virginia].
Browne, *WF*, 14 (1955), 11 [California].
Evans (1955), 8, 13 [California, two variants] = Evans (1961), 33, 37.
Seeger, Folkways 7029 (1955) [Illinois]. "Benjamin Franklin."
Pope, *WF*, 15 (1956), 48 [Texas]. "Charlie McCarthy."
Schiller, *NYFQ*, 12 (1956), 204 [New York]. Two variants.
Holbrook (1957), 57 [England].
Leventhal and Cray, *WF*, 22 (1963), 238 [California, 1959].
Opie (1959), 110 [England and Scotland]. Six variants, one begins "One, two, three, four,/Charlie Chaplin went to war."
Scott, *Singabout*, 3, No. 3 (Winter/Spring, 1959), 5 [Australia]. "Donald Duck."
Sutton-Smith (1959), 82 [New Zealand].
Taylor, *WF*, 18 (1959), 316 [California].
Ainsworth, *WF*, 20 (1961), 194 [New Mexico, "Shirley Temple"], 198 [Utah, "Charlie Chapman"], 185 [Alabama, "Betty Grable"].
Bluebells (1961), n. p. [Ayrshire].
Worstell (1961), 2–3. Two variants.
Abrahams, *SFQ*, 27 (1963), 199 [Texas]. Five variants; "Charlie Chapman," "Marco Polo," "Shirley Temple," three with endings from "I'm a little Dutch Girl" rhymes.
Butler and Haley (1963), n.p. Ends with "Keep the kettle boiling" rhyme.
Ritchie (1964), 24 [Edinburgh]. With "Bluebells, cockleshells" rhyme.
Ritchie (1965), 129 [Edinburgh].
Those Dusty Bluebells (1965), 16 [Ayrshire].
Buckley, *KFQ*, 11 (1966), 106, 107 [Indiana]. Two variants.

(66)   Charlie Chaplin* went to war,
         When he came back his pants were tore.

"Stella, Stella," *Fargo Forum* (June 23, 1940), 13 [North Dakota].

(67)   Charlie, Charlie, Chuck, Chuck, Chuck
          Went to bed with two old ducks.
          One died, the other cried
          Charlie, Charlie, Chuck, Chuck, Chuck.

Daiken (1949), 65 [Great Britain].
Daiken (1963), 30 [Dublin].

(68)   Charlie likes whiskey,
          Charlie likes brandy,
          Charlie likes kissing girls,
          O-sugar-de-dandy!

                    *Cf. the play-party "Weevily Wheat" and
                    the Jacobite song from which it derives.*

Douglas (1916), 73 [London].

          Charlie McCarthy* went to France.
          See "Charlie Chaplin went to France."

          Chase the fox.
          See "A-hunting we will go."

(69)   Cherry, cherry, cherry wine,
          Come back here or I'll tan your 'hine.

Ritchie (1965), 130 [Edinburgh].

(70)   Chew tobacco, chew tobacco,
          Spit on the wall.
          Who do we appreciate
          Most of all?

                    A common school cheer.

Abrahams, *SFQ*, 27 (1963), 202 [Texas].

(71)   Chickety, chickety, chop;
          How many times before I stop?

C 29

LaSalle (1929), 56.
Fahey, *Journal of Health and Physical Education,* 11 (1940), 421.

Chickie, Chickie, Chinaman.
See "Tattletale, Tattletale."

(72)   Chick in the car
The car can't go.
That's the way to
Spell Chicago.

Usually a spelling riddle.

Haufrecht (1947), 63.

(73)   Chicky, cricky, cranery, crow:
I went to the well to wash my toe;
High and low, out you go,
Chicky, cricky, cranery, crow.

Comes from common game rhyme.

Abrahams, *SFQ,* 27 (1963), 202 [Texas].

Chinaman, Chinaman, over the sea.
See "I come from Chink-a-China."

(74)   Ching, chang, Chinaman,
Chop, chop, chop.
Eating candy at the candy shop.

Abrahams, *SFQ,* 27 (1963), 202 [Texas].

(75)   Ching, chang, Chinaman bought a toy doll,
Washed it, dyed it, then he caught a cold.
Send for the doctor; Doctor couldn't come
Because he had a pimple on his tum-tum-tum.

Douglas (1916), 95 [London]. ". . . penny doll, . . . and called it pretty
poll."
Sutton-Smith, *WF,* 12 (1953), 21 [New Zealand].

(76)   Ching, Ching, Chinaman
          Eats dead rats,
          Swallows them down
          Like ginger snaps!

Yoffie, *JAF*, 60 (1947), 49 [Missouri].

          Christopher Columbie-a
          Sailed across the sea.
          See "Christopher Columbus was a very brave man."

(77)   Christopher Columbus
          Sailed the ocean blue
          In fourteen hundred
          And ninety-two.

Evans (1961), 27.

(78)   Christopher Columbus was a very brave man,
          He sailed the ocean in an old tin can,
          But the waves grew higher and higher and over,
          Five, ten, fifteen, twenty, *etc.*

Scott, *Singabout*, 3, No. 3 (Winter/Spring, 1959), 4 [Australia]. ". . . in
   a frying pan."
Bluebells (1961), n. p. [Ayrshire].
Ritchie (1965), 130 [Edinburgh]. "Christopher Columbie-o/Sailed across
   the sea."
Those Dusty Bluebells (1965), 10 [Ayrshire].

(79)   Cinderella at a ball,
          Cinderella had a fall,
          When she fell she lost her shoe,
          Cinderella, Y-O-U.

Sutton-Smith (1959), 77 [New Zealand].

(80)   Cinderella, dressed in yellow,
          Went upstairs (downtown) to kiss (see) her fellow,

How many kisses did she get?
One, two, three, *etc.*

> *Often followed by "Cinderella, dressed in pink, . . . green, . . . blue," and so on.*

Winifred Smith, *JAF*, 39 (1926), 84.
Bennett, *Children*, 12 (1927), 21.
Thompson, *JAF*, 47 (1934), 385–386 [Pennsylvania, 1929].
Davis (1949), 215 [Virginia, 1932; Florida, 1938]. Two variants.
Mills and Bishop, *The New Yorker* (November 13, 1937), 34 [New Jersey, 1936; California, 1937; Michigan, 1937; New York City, 1937] = Botkin (1944), 801.
Ireland, *Recreation* (February, 1937), 564 [Indiana].
Maryott, *SFQ*, 1, No. 4 (1937), 49–50 [Nebraska].
Ashton, *JAF*, 52 (1939), 121 [Iowa].
Brewster, *SFQ*, 3 (1939), 173 (two variants) = Botkin (1944), 801.
"Stella, Stella," *Fargo Forum* (June 23, 1940), 13 [North Dakota].
Britt and Balcom, *J Gen Psy*, 58 (1941), 299 [Maryland, District of Columbia]. "Went downtown to buy an umbrella."
Hall, *Recreation* (March, 1941), 714 [Nebraska].
Park, *CFQ*, 1 (1942), 377 [California].
Sone (1943), 196 [Texas].
Eller, *North Carolina Education*, 10 (1944), 447 [North Carolina].
Mills (1944), 15 [Maryland].
Botkin (1947), 907 [Connecticut].
Emrich and Korson (1947), 133. ". . . dressed in red."
Haufrecht (1947), 62.
Musick, *HF*, 7 (1948), 12 [West Virginia]. With derivations from "Gypsy, gypsy, please tell me" rhyme.
McCaskill, *NCF*, 1 (June, 1948), 10 [North Carolina].
Withers (1948), 65. "Went downtown to buy an umbrella."
Ashby, *Christian Science Monitor Magazine* (April 9, 1949), 8.
Haines, *Daedalian*, 17 (1949), 24, 25 [Louisiana, Texas, Missouri, Arkansas, Oklahoma].
Harris, *Evening Bulletin* (May 30, 1949), 10 [Pennsylvania]. Ends "on the way her bloomers busted/How many people were disgusted."
Reck, *WF*, 8 (1949), 127 [Colorado]. With other colors.
Musick and Randolph, *JAF*, 63 (1950), 430 [Missouri]. "Ella, Ella."
Time (May 29, 1950), 20.
Brewster (1952), 171 [North Carolina].
Musick, *WVF*, 2, No. 3 (1952), 7 [West Virginia]. "Ella, Ella."
Randolph, *MF*, 3 (1953), 78 [Arkansas]. Two variants.
Browne, *WF*, 14 (1955), 6 [California]. Three variants.
Evans (1955), 13 [California] = Evans (1961), 19, 39.
Seeger, Folkways 7029 (1955) [Illinois].
Schiller, *NYFQ*, 12 (1956), 204–205 [New York]. "Polly, Polly," with

"Shirley Temple walks like this," "I had a little brother," and "Mother, mother, I am ill" rhymes.

Withers and Jablow (1956), 12 [New York City]. ". . . dressed in red."

Calitri, *Parents*, 32 (April, 1957), 53.

"Children's Rhymes," *WVF*, 8 (1958), 36, 38. Two variants, one begins ". . . white as snow/Went upstairs to kiss her beau."

Stone, *Home and Highway* (March, 1958), 23.

Leventhal and Cray, *WF*, 22 (1963), 236 [California, 1959]. Two variants.

Scott, *Singabout*, 3, No. 3 (Winter/Spring, 1959), 5 [Australia]. "On the way her 'lastic busted,/How many people were disgusted?"

Ainsworth, *WF*, 20 (1961), 182 [North Carolina], 183 [Georgia], 186 [Alabama], 186 [Michigan], 193 [Colorado], 194 [New Mexico], 195 [Utah].

Bluebells (1961), n. p. [Ayrshire].

Sackett (1961), 224 [Kansas].

Worstell (1961), 4.

Abrahams, *SFQ*, 27 (1963), 199 [Texas]. Twelve variants, one includes a number of colors.

Sandburg (1963), 123 [North Carolina]. Also ". . . dressed in lace" and ". . . dressed in green."

White, *Louisiana Miscellany*, 2, No. 2 (April, 1965), 116. "Went to the ball game . . ."

Buckley, *KFQ*, 11 (1966), 103 [Indiana]. Listed.

Hawthorne, *KFQ*, 11 (1966), 114, 121 [Delaware].

(81)   Climbing up the ladder
         In a caravan
         You only pay a sixpence
         To see a funny man;
         The funny man choked
         Tied to a rope.
         Ukelele, ukelele,
         Hop, hop, hop!

Ritchie (1965), 122 [Edinburgh].

(82)   The Clock stands still
         While the hands go around:
         One o'clock, two o'clock, three o'clock, *etc.*

Reynolds, *Christian Science Monitor* (July 11, 1941), 8 [Massachusetts].

Withers (North) (1947), 84 [New York] = Withers (1964), 97.

Withers (1948), 60.

Gullen (1950), 58. "Winding the clock."

Seeger, Folkways 7029 (1955) [Illinois].
Abrahams, *SFQ*, 27 (1963), 199 [Texas].

(83)   Cobbler, cobbler, mend my shoe,
       Have it done by half past two.
       If half past two is far too late,
       Have it done by half past eight.
       1, 2, 3, and 4,
       Back 2, 3, and 4,
       Bake it, bake it, hammer, hammer, hammer.

Those Dusty Bluebells (1965), 5 [Ayrshire].

(84)   Coffee hot, coffee cold,
       Coffee in the teapot,
       Nine days old.

> *Cf. the nursery rhyme "Pease porridge hot" (see Opie, DICTIONARY, 345).*

Ainsworth, *WF*, 20 (1961), 185 [Alabama].

(85)   Cold meat, mutton pies,
       Tell me when your mother dies.
       I'll be there to bury her—
       Cold meat, mutton pies.

Douglas (1916), 71–72 [London]. Two variants.

(86)   Come in my garden
       And give me your hand—

> *Incomplete.*

Douglas (1916), 90 [London].

(87)   Cowboy Joe
       From Mexico;
       Hands up, stick'em up—
       Cowboy Joe!

> *See also "Betty, Betty."*

Scott, *Singabout*, 3, No. 3 (Winter/Spring, 1959), 5. "Old Black Joe."
Bluebells (1961), n.p. [Ayrshire].
Ritchie (1964), 33 [Edinburgh].

(88)   Crackers, crackers,
            Penny a cracker,
            When you pull them,
            They go Bang!

Sutton-Smith (1959), 77 [New Zealand].

(89)   Crossing the bridge
            To London town
            One jumps up,
            And the other down.

Sutton-Smith (1959), 74, 77 [New Zealand]. Two variants, one "Cross
    the bridge."

(90)   Crossing the waters, one by one
            Crossing the waters, two by two.

                        Cf. "Changing bedrooms."

Douglas (1916), 92 [London].

(91)   Cross the river, cross the lake,
            I hope that Sally makes a bad mistake.

Ainsworth, *WF*, 20 (1961), 184 [Georgia].

(92)   Cups and saucers,
            Plates and dishes,
            My old man wears
            Calico britches.

                        *Gomme notes that this is a "rhyme to
                        time the jumps."*

Gomme, 2 (1898), 204 [England].
Opie (1947), 79 [England].

Holbrook (1957), 56 [England].
Sutton-Smith (1959), 80 [New Zealand].

(93)   Cups and saucers set for tea,
         How many are there? You and me.

Bluebells (1961), n. p. [Ayrshire].

(94)   Cup, saucer, plate.
         High, low, dolly pepper.
                              See "High, low, slow, dolly."

Ritchie (1965), 118, 130 [Edinburgh].

Daddy is a butcher.
         See "My father is a butcher."

Dagwood,* Blondie,* went downtown.
         See "Blondie and Dagwood went downtown."

Dagwood,* Dagwood, do you love Blondie*?
         See "Does he love me?"

(95)   Dancing Dolly had no sense:
         She bought a fiddle for eighteen pence.
         But the only tune that she could play
         Was "Sally, Get Out of the Donkey's Way!"

Gomme, 2 (1898), 203 [England].
Douglas (1916), 53 [London]. Three variants.
Daiken (1949), 63 [Great Britain].
Holbrook (1957), 56 [England].
Sutton-Smith (1959), 80 [New Zealand].

The **D**ay was dark, the night was bright.
See "One bright morning."

(96)   **D**eanna Durbin* lost her turban
            In a pool of water.

Opie (1959), 113 [England].

(97)   **D**eanna Durbin* she wore a turban
            Until she was 2, 4, 6, 8, *etc.*

Opie (1959), 113 [England].

(98)   O **D**ear me, mother caught a flea,
            Put it in the tea-pot and made a cup of tea—

                                      Incomplete.

Douglas (1916), 91 [London].

(99)   **D**ennis the Menace* had a squirt gun.
            He took it out and had some fun.
            He shot a man in the boot.
            How many squirts did he shoot?
            1, 2, 3, 4, *etc.*

Buckley, *KFQ*, 11 (1966), 107 [Indiana].

(100)   The **D**evil flew from north to south,
            With Miss Hooker in his mouth,
            And when he found she was a fool,
            He dropped her on Cherrydale School.

                                Commonly a taunt.

Butler and Haley (1963), n. p.

(101)   **D**ewey* was an admiral at Manila Bay.
            Dewey* was a candidate just the other day.
            Dewey were her eyes when she said, "I love you true."

Oh, do we love each other?
I should say we do.
Usually an autograph album rhyme.

Schiller, *NYFQ*, 12 (1956), 205 [New York].

Dictionary,
Down the ferry.
See "Ibbity, bibbity."

(102)   **D**id you ēv-a, īv-a, ōv-a
In your lēf-a, līf-a, lō
See a dēv-a, dīv-a, dōv-a
Kiss his wēf-a, wīf-a, wō?
etc.

Bennett, *Children*, 12 (1927), 20.
Britt and Balcom, *J Gen Psy*, 58 (1941), 296 [Maryland, District of Columbia].

(103)   **D**id you ever go a-fishing on a sunny day,
Sitting on a log—the log rolled away?
Put your hands in your pockets,
Your pockets in your pants,
Did you ever see a fish do the hootchy-kootchy dance?

Worstell (1961), 33.

Ding-a-ling, a-ling, Sir.
See "Hello, sir, hello, sir."

(104)   **D**-I-S-H choice
D-I-S-H choice
D-I-S-H choice
H-O-P, hop.
1, 2, 3, *etc.*

Abrahams, *KFQ*, 8 (1963), 8 [Pennsylvania].

(105)   **D**octor Brown fell in the well
And broke his collarbone.

Why don't he attend to the sick
And leave the well alone?

Buckley, *KFQ*, 11 (1966), 110 [Indiana].

Doctor! Doctor! Can you tell?
See "Mother, mother, can you tell."

Doctor, Doctor, Will I die?
See "Mother, mother, I am ill."

(106)   Doctor Foster went to Gloucester
In a shower of rain.
He stepped in a puddle
Right up to the middle
And never went there again.

A nursery rhyme (see Opie, Dictionary, *173).*

Sutton-Smith (1959), 83 [New Zealand].

(107)   Doctor Kildare* fell down the stair,
In the month of January, February, *etc.*

Those Dusty Bluebells (1965), 11 [Ayrshire].

Doctor, lawyer, merchant, chief.
See "Rich man, poor man."

(108)   Doctor Long is a very good man,
He tries to teach you all he can:
Writing, reading, 'rith-ma-tick,
But he never forgets to use the stick.

*Cf. the counting-out rhyme "Doctor Foster's
a very good man."*

Bennett, *Children*, 2 (1927), 21. "Mister Brown is a very nice man/He
teaches the best he can/What day does my birthday come?"
Daiken (1949), 70 [Great Britain] Two variants.
Bluebells (1961), n.p. [Ayrshire]. With "Bluebells, cockleshells" rhyme.
Worstell (1961), 19. With "Bluebells, cockleshells" rhyme.

Ritchie (1965), 116 [Edinburgh]. With "Bluebells, cockleshells" rhyme.
Those Dusty Bluebells (1965), 6 [Ayrshire]. With "Bluebells, cockleshells," ends "First to read and then to write/Then to smoke a licorice pipe" or "Eevory, ivory, you jump out."

(109)   Does he love me?
    Yes, no, yes, no, yes.
    Where will we get married?
    Church, synagogue, house, barn.
    How many children will we have?
    One, two, three, four, *etc.*

                See "Rich man, poor man."

Gillington, *Old Hampshire* (1909) [Hampshire].
Utley (1946), 63–64 [England]. Begins "He loves me. He don't./He'll have me. He won't/He would if he could/But he can't."
Withers (1948), 62.
Time (May 29, 1950), 20 [Texas]. "Dagwood, Dagwood, do you love Blondie?"
Frankel (1952), 63.
Opie (1959), 339 [England].
Evans (1961), 19.
Abrahams, *SFQ*, 27 (1963), 199, 203 [Texas]. Three variants, one "Dagwood, Dagwood, do you love Blondie?"
Buckley, *KFQ*, 11 (1966), 103 [Indiana]. "Dagwood, Dagwood." Listed.

(110)   Dolly dear, Dolly dear,
    Your sweetheart is dead,
                Incomplete.

Douglas (1916), 92 [London].

    Dolly Dimple can't do this (walks like this).
    See "Spanish Dancers."

(111)   Donald Duck* is a one-legged, one-legged,
        one-legged duck;
    Donald Duck is a two-legged, two-legged,
        two-legged duck;

                *Repeat for three-legged, four-legged, bow-
                legged, pigeon-toed, knock-kneed, etc. Cf.*

*"Little white rabbit" and "Little Orphan
Annie goes one foot."*

Time (May 29, 1950), 20 [Texas].
Seeger, Folkways 7029 (1955) [Illinois].
Heimbuecher, *KFQ*, 7, No. 4 (1962) [Pennsylvania]. "Donald Duck went
   to town."
Buckley, *KFQ*, 11 (1966), 103 [Indiana]. Listed.
Hawthorne, *KFQ*, 11 (1966), 124 [Delaware]. "Peter Duck."

> **D**onald Duck* went to France.
> *See "Charlie Chaplin went to France."*

(112)   **D**own at the station early in the morn
        See the little daffodils all in a row,
        See the engine master pull the little handle.
        Chug, chug, woof, woof, off we go.

> *Commonly collected as a children's song.*

Hall, *Recreation* (March, 1941), 716 [Nebraska].

(113)   **D**own by the little red schoolhouse

Buckley, *KFQ*, 11 (1966), 103 [Indiana]. Listed.

(114)   **D**own by the meadow, down by the sea,
        I kissed Johnny and he kissed me.
        1, 2, 3, *etc.*

Abrahams, *SFQ*, 27 (1963), 203 [Texas].

(115)   **D**own by the river (in the meadow, valley)
        Where the green grass grows,
        There sat (any girl's name)
        As pretty as a rose.
        She sang, she sang,
        She sang herself to sleep,
        And up came (any boy's name)
        And kissed her on the cheek.

> *Originally a singing game.*

Babcock, *AA*, o.s., 1 (1888), 268 [District of Columbia].

Gomme, 1 (1894), 99, and 2 (1898), 416 [Great Britain].

Gillington, *Old Surrey* (1909), iv.

Douglas (1916), 61, 93 [London]. Two variants.

Winifred Smith, *JAF*, 39 (1926), 83 [New York].

Heck, *JAF*, 40 (1927), 22 [Ohio]. Two variants: the first ends "O Felici, O Felici, you ought to be ashamed/To marry a boy instead of a man./ I'm a boy, I'm a boy, I'll soon be a man./I'll work for my living as hard as I can."; the second begins "Down in the middle of the dark blue sea."

Davis (1949), 216 [Florida, 1938].

Rolland, *New Masses* (May 10, 1938), 109 (with "Mother, mother I am ill" rhyme) = Botkin (1954), 565.

Ashton, *JAF*, 52 (1939), 121 [Iowa].

Brewster, *SFQ*, 3 (1939), 174 = Botkin (1944), 792.

Fahey, *Journal of Health and Physical Education*, 11 (1940), 422 [Kansas].

Britt and Balcom, *J Gen Psy*, 58 (1941), 300 [Maryland, District of Columbia].

Hall, *Recreation* (March, 1941), 716 [Nebraska].

Speroni, *CFQ*, 1 (1942), 248 [California]. With "As I went down to my grandfather's farm" rhyme.

Mensing, *HFB*, 2 (1943), 49 [Indiana].

Sone (1943), 197 [Iowa].

Mills (1944), 15 [Maryland].

Grace Partridge Smith, *HF*, 5 (1946), 59 [Illinois] = Dorson (1964), 386.

Walker, *NYFQ*, 2 (1946), 232 [New York].

Emrich and Korson (1947), 129.

Haufrecht (1947), 62.

McCaskill, *NCF*, 1 (June, 1948), 12 [North Carolina].

Musick, *HF*, 7 (1948), 9 [West Virginia].

Ashby, *Christian Science Monitor Magazine* (April 9, 1949), 8.

Harris, *Evening Bulletin* (May 30, 1949), 10 [Pennsylvania].

Haines, *Daedalian*, 17 (1949), 27.

Reck, *WF*, 8 (1949), 127 [Colorado].

Roberts, *HF*, 8 (1949), 9 [Indiana].

Musick and Randolph, *JAF*, 63 (1950), 430 [Missouri].

Time (May 29, 1950), 20 [Texas].

Musick, *WVF*, 2, No. 3 (1952), 6 [West Virginia].

Randolph, *MF*, 3 (1953), 77 [Arkansas].

Browne, *WF*, 14 (1955), 7 [Colorado]. Two variants.

Evans (1955), 11 [California] = Evans (1961), 36.

Seeger, Folkways 7029 (1955) [Illinois].

Pope, *WF*, 15 (1956), 46 [Texas].

"Children's Rhymes," *WVF*, 8 (1958), 39.

Graham, *Press and Journal* (November 30, 1959), 6 [Aberdeen].

Leventhal and Cray, *WF*, 22 (1963), 231 [California, 1959]. Two vari-

ants; one has second line "........ and .... are kissing down below."
Ainsworth, *WF*, 20 (1961), 181 [Maine], 186 [Alabama], 187 [Mich-
igan], 188 and 190 [Wisconsin], 192 [Colorado], 196 [Utah].
Worstell (1961), 1.
Heimbuecher, *KFQ*, 7, No. 4 (1962), 6 [Pennsylvania].
Abrahams, *SFQ*, 27 (1963), 199 [Texas]. Four variants.
Butler and Haley (1963), n. p.
Ritchie (1964), 31 [Edinburgh]. Ends "Pump, pump here comes the
taxi-cab/Ready for the wedding at half-past three!"
Withers (1964), 98 [New York].
Ritchie (1965), 117, 122, 123 [Edinburgh]. Four variants; one ends
with both "Sweetheart, sweetheart,/Will you marry me? . . ." and
"Pump, pump, here comes the taxi-cab"; another begins "Down in
yonder meadow," concerns "'Chrissie Fraser" bleaching clothes, and
ends "Agree, agree,/I hope we will agree/And when we are married/
I hope we will agree."; another concerns a "washing lady."
White, *Louisiana Miscellany*, 2, No. 2 (April, 1965), 115 [Louisiana].
Buckley, *KFQ*, 11 (1966), 101 [Indiana].
Hawthorne, *KFQ*, 11 (1966), 115, 122 [Delaware].
Warner, *Yankee*, 30, No. 1 (January, 1966), 81.

Down by the ocean (river) (seashore).
See "Johnny on the ocean."

Down by the station.
See "Standing on the corner."

(116)   Down in the desert
          Where the purple grass dies,
          There sat a witch with
          Yellowish-green eyes.
          Nobody came to see her
          Because she always ate them
          One by one, two by two, *etc.*

                    A parody of "Down by the river."

Abrahams, *SFQ*, 27 (1963), 203 [Texas].

(117)   Down in the dungeons seven feet deep,
          Where old Hitler lies asleep,

German boys they tickle his feet
Down in the dungeons seven feet deep.

*To the tune of "Underneath the Spreading
Chestnut Tree."*

Opie (1959), 102. Two variants, one "Underneath the water six feet
deep." [Staffordshire, Aberdeen, 1952–1954].

(118)   Down in the meadow not far off,
The bluejay sat with a whooping cough.
He whooped so hard with the whooping cough,
He whooped his head and his tail right off.

*See "Up in a loft." Usually an
entertainment rhyme.*

Douglas (1916), 53 [London]. "Up in the North a long way off."
Emrich and Korson (1947), 133.
Abrahams, *SFQ*, 27 (1963), 199 [Texas].

Down in the meadow,
Where the corn cobs grow.
See "Way down south."

Down in the valley (meadow) where the green
grass grows.
See "Down by the river."

(119)   Down in the valley where the green grass grows,
There sat little (girl's name) without any clothes.
Along came (boy's name) swinging a chain,
Down went his zipper and out it came.
Three months later she began to swell,
Six months later you could really tell.
Nine months later, out they came,
Two little (boy's name) swinging a chain.

A common bawdy rhyme.

Abrahams, *SFQ*, 27 (1963), 203 [Texas].

(120)   Down the Mississippi
         Where the boats go push.

Also a ball-bouncing rhyme.

Britt and Balcom, *J Gen Psy*, 58 (1941), 300 [Maryland, District of Columbia].
Reynolds, *Christian Science Monitor* (July 11, 1941), 8. With "Way down south where the bananas grow" rhyme.
Harris, *Evening Bulletin* (May 30, 1949), 10 [Pennsylvania]. Mentioned.
Evans (1955), 6 [California] = Evans (1961), 31.
Schiller, *NYFQ*, 12 (1956), 203 [New York].
Ford, *KFQ*, 2 (1957), 109.
Abrahams, *KFQ*, 8 (1963), 7 [Pennsylvania, 1959].
Falk, *New York Times Magazine* (July 3, 1960), 12 [New York].
Ainsworth, *WF*, 20 (1961), 192 [Wisconsin].
Butler and Haley (1963), n.p.

(121)   Down to the baker shop
         Hop, hop, hop!
         For my mother said
         Buy a loaf of bread,
         Down to the baker's shop
         Hop, hop, hop!

Ritchie (1965), 111 [Edinburgh].

(122)   Do you know where the darkies live?
         Zumba, zumba.
         Do you know where the darkies live?
         Zumba, zumba.
         Yes, I know where the darkies live,
         Zumba, zumba.
         Yes, I know where the darkies live,
         Zumba, zumba.
         The darkies live in Africa,
         etc.

Bluebells (1961), n. p. [Ayrshire].
Those Dusty Bluebells (1965), 8 [Ayrshire].

(123)   Do you like silver and gold?
         Do you like brass?

Do you like looking through
The looking glass?

Yes, I like silver and gold,
Yes, I like brass,
etc.

Douglas (1916), 53 [London] = Opie (1959), 65.

(124)   **D**ream lover, where are you?
Upstairs on the toilet stool.
Whatcha doing way up there?
Washing out my underwear.
How'd you get them so clean?
With a bottle of Listerine.
etc.

Parody of a rock-and-roll hit of 1958.

Abrahams, *KFQ*, 8 (1963), 15 [Pennsylvania, 1959].

(125)   **D**rink your whiskey,
Drink your cider,
How many legs is on a spider?
1-2-3-4-5, *etc.*

Randolph, *MF*, 3 (1953), 78 [Arkansas, 1934].

(126)   **D**rip drop, the robin's in the sea,
Please take the rope from me.
Will you come, come, unto the fair?
No, no, the fair's not there,
With you, I, must, not, miss, a, loop.

Those Dusty Bluebells (1965), 7 [Ayrshire].

(127)   **D**utch cheese and sauerkraut,
O-U-T puts you out.

Abrahams, *SFQ*, 27 (1963), 203 [Texas].

(128)   Dutch, Dutch, double Dutch,
          How much do you know?
          I know this much:
          Ten, twenty, thirty, forty, fifty, *etc.*

Bley (1957), 94.

(129)   Eachie Peachie pearie plum,
          Out goes my chum.
          My chum is no' very well
          So I must go out mysel'

Gardiner oral collection (1957–1958) [Forfar].

(130)   Eaper, Weaper, Chimbley-sweeper
          Had a wife but couldn't keep her,
          Had anovver, didn't love her,
          Up the chimbley he did shove her.

                    See Opie, Dictionary, *346–347; also*
                    commonly a counting-out rhyme.

Douglas (1916), 53 [London].
Daiken (1949), 64. Begins "Ice cream, a penny a lump."
Utley (1959), 126 [Lancashire].

(131)   Early in the morning at half-past eight
          I heard the postman knocking at the gate.
          Postman, postman, drop your letter.
          Lady, lady, pick it up.
          I spy a lark, shining in the dark,
          Echo, echo, G. O. stands for GO!

                    See "Policeman, policeman, do your duty"; "Lady,

lady, drop your handkerchief"; and, for last two lines, "Shoot! Bang!"

Gomme, 2 (1898), 202 [England]. "Every morning."
Douglas (1916), 77 [London]. ". . . eight o'clock/You may hear the postman's knock./Up jumps Mabel to open the door./Letters, one, two, three, four."
Daiken (1949), 63 [Great Britain]. Two variants.
Gullen (1950), 58. Two variants, both begin "Every morning."
Holbrook (1957), 57 [England]. "Every morning at eight o'clock/You all may hear the postman's knock. . . ."
Sutton-Smith (1959), 80 [New Zealand].

Easy, greasy, pepper, salt.
See "Salt, vinegar, mustard, and pepper."

(132) Edinburgh, Leith,
Portobello, Musselburg,
And Dalkeith;
Cockie leekie
Hennie deekie
One, two, three!

Ritchie (1965), 116 [Edinburgh].

(133) Eeny, meeny, miney, mo.
Catch Castro* by the toe.
If he hollers make him say,
"I surrender, U.S.A."

Usually a counting-out rhyme.

Abrahams, *SFQ*, 27 (1963), 203 [Texas].

(134) Eeny, meeny, miney, mo,
Catch a nigger (robber) by the toe.
If he hollers make him pay (let him go)
Fifty dollars every day (eeny, meeny, miney, mo).

Usually a counting-out rhyme.

Abrahams, *SFQ*, 27 (1963), 203 [Texas].

(135)   Eeny meeny, tipsy teeny
           Applejack and Johnny Sweeney
           Hosey-pokey, dominoky.
           Hom, pom, tusk.
           Tusk in, tusk out,
           All around the waterspout.
           Have a peach, have a plum,
           Have a stick of chewing gum.

                         Usually a counting-out rhyme.

Harris, *Evening Bulletin* (May 30, 1949) [Pennsylvania].

           Eeper weeper.
           See "Eaper, weaper."

           Eevie-ivy.
           See "Wavy wavy" and "Bluebells, cockleshells."

           Eight o'clock bells are ringing.
           See "Nine o'clock is striking."

           Ella Ella.
           See "Cinderella, dressed in yellow."

           Ena Sharples, how about a date?
           See "Hi, ho, Silver."

(136)   Engine, engine, number nine,
           Running on the Chicago (Frisco) line,
           How she's polished, how she shine,
           Engine, engine, number nine.

                         Related to the counting-out rhyme that
                         begins the same way.

Randolph, *MF*, 3 (1953), 84 [Arkansas]. Two variants, one from 1938.
Haufrecht (1947), 63.
Haines, *Daedalian*, 17 (1949), 28 [Oklahoma].
Musick and Randolph, *JAF*, 63 (1950), 429 [Missouri].
Worstell (1961), 36–37.
Heimbuecher, *KFQ*, 7, No. 4 (1962), 5 [Pennsylvania]. Two variants.
Abrahams, *SFQ*, 27 (1963), 199 [Texas]. Two variants.

(137)   English, German, Irish, French,
          Little Annie Roonie* with a ruffle in her pants.

Heck, *JAF*, 40 (1927), 41 [Ohio].

(138)   Everybody, everybody,
          Come on in.
          The first one misses
          Gonna take my end.

Evans (1955), 5 [California] = Evans (1961), 28.

          Every morning at eight o'clock.
          See "Early in the morning."

          Evie, Ivy, over.
          See "Bluebells, cockleshells" and "Keep the kettle boiling."

          Fancy dancing is a sin.
          See "A house to let."

          Fannie Stancer
          Do the split.
          See "Spanish dancers."

          Father is a butcher.
          See "My father is a butcher."

(139)   Fire, fire, fire alarm;
          John fell into Mary's arms.

First love, then came marriage;
Then John with a baby carriage.

Usually an autograph album rhyme.

Browne, *WF*, 14 (1955), 19 [California].
Gordon, *WVF*, 12 (1962), 52 [West Virginia]. "Fire, fire, false alarm";
ends "How many kisses . . ."
Buckley, *KFQ*, 11 (1966), 103 [Indiana]. "Fire, fire, false alarm."
Listed.

(140)   "Fire, fire," says Mr. McGuire,
        "Where, where?" says Mr. O'Dare,
        "At the barn," says Mr. Kern,
        And it burns hotter, hotter, *etc.*

Usually an entertainment rhyme.

Fahey, *Journal of Health and Physical Education*, 11 (1940), 422 [Kansas]. "At the fair," says Mrs. Blair."
Abrahams, *SFQ*, 27 (1963), 204 [Texas].

(141)   Fireman, Fireman going to a fire

Buckley, *KFQ*, 11 (1966), 103 [Indiana]. Listed.

(142)   Fireman, fireman number eight,
        Struck his head against a gate;
        The gate flew in, the gate flew out,
        And that's the way the fire went out.

Abrahams, *SFQ*, 27 (1963) 204 [Texas].

(143)   Fisherman, fisherman, you got me crazy
        Up the river, down the river
        One—Two—Three
        You're a bigger fool than me.

Seeger, Folkways 7029 (1955) [Illinois].

(144)   Five, ten, fifteen, twenty,
        Nobody leaves the rope empty,
        If they do, they shall suffer,
        Take an end and be a duffer.

Sutton-Smith (1959), 77 [New Zealand].

(145)   Flies in the buttermilk

        Cf. "Skip, skip/ Skip to my Lou."

Buckley, *KFQ*, 11 (1966), 103 [Indiana]. Listed.

(146)   Four little chickens all in white
        Saw some bread and began a fight.

        Incomplete.

Douglas (1916), 92 [London].

(147)   Front door, back door,
        Sally, Jim and Joe.
        On the count of sixteen
        Jump in slow.

Student oral collection (1964) [Texas].

(148)   Fudge, fudge, tell (call) the judge,
        Mother has a newborn baby.
        It isn't a girl and it isn't a boy
        It's just a newborn baby.
        It hasn't any clothes,
        So wrap it up in tissue paper.
        Put it in (Throw it down) the elevator.
        First floor miss, *etc.*

        See "Baby in the high chair."

Winifred Smith, *JAF*, 39 (1926), 83 [New York]. "Oh, Fudge."
Henry (1934), 239 [Indiana]. "Oh, Fudge."
Brewster, *SFQ*, 3 (1939), 177 = Botkin (1944), 794.

Mensing, *HFB*, 2 (1943), 48 [Indiana].

"Jump-Rope Rhymes," *WF*, 23 (1964), 258 [California, 1944]. "Mama's got a new-born baby."

Halpert, *JAF*, 58 (1945), 350 [New Hampshire].

Botkin (1947), 906 [Connecticut].

Emrich and Korson (1947), 132.

Musick, *HF*, 7 (1948), 11 [West Virginia]. Begins "Patty, Patty, had a baby."

Withers (1948), 64. "Judge, judge."

Yoder, *Saturday Evening Post* (October 30, 1948), 114.

Ashby, *Christian Science Monitor Magazine* (April 9, 1949), 8.

Harris, *Evening Bulletin* (May 30, 1949), 10 [Pennsylvania].

Reck, *WF*, 8 (1949), 28 [Colorado].

Musick and Randolph, *JAF*, 63 (1950), 429 [Missouri]. Begins "Mamma Mamma, had a baby."

Time (May 29, 1950), 29 [Georgia].

Dodson, *Recreation* (June, 1951), 173 [North Carolina].

Browne, *WF*, 14 (1955), 7 [California]. Two variants.

Evans (1955), 24 [California] = Evans (1961), 44.

Kingston (1955), 2 [Illinois].

Seeger, Folkways 7029 (1955) [Illinois].

Bley (1957), 95.

"Children's Rhymes," *WVF*, 8 (1958), 38–39. Two variants.

Stone, *Home and Highway* (March, 1958), 24.

Taylor, *WF*, 18 (1959), 316 [California]. Begins "Mama's got a new-born baby."

Ainsworth, *WF*, 20 (1961), 187 [Wisconsin, Michigan].

Bluebells (1961), n.p. [Ayrshire]. "Smudge, smudge."

Worstell (1961), 14–15.

Heimbuecher, *KFQ*, 7, No. 4 (1962), 2 [Pennsylvania]. Two variants.

Abrahams, *SFQ*, 27 (1963), 199 [Texas]. Two variants.

Butler and Haley (1963), n.p.

Leventhal and Cray, *WF*, 22 (1963), 236 [California, 1959].

Buckley, *KFQ*, 11 (1966), 103 [Indiana]. Three variants. Listed.

> Oh, **F**udge, tell the judge.
> *See "Fudge, fudge."*

(149)　　**F**uzzy Wuzzy was a Bear

Buckley, *KFQ*, 11 (1966), 101 [Indiana]. Listed.

Geneva had a baby.
See "I had a little brother/ His name was Tim."

(150)   George Washington never told a lie.
        He ran around the corner, and stole a
        cherry pie.
        Apple and cherry, apple and cherry, *etc.*

Abrahams, *KFQ*, 8 (1963), 14 [Pennsylvania, 1959]. With "Old Man
Daisy/Drives me crazy" rhyme.
Abrahams, *SFQ*, 27 (1963) 204 [Texas].
Withers (1964), 99 [Iowa]. ". . . found a cherry pie."
Hawthorne, *KFQ*, 11 (1966), 121 [Delaware].

German boys are awful hungry.
See "Turn your back on the sailor Jack."

Girl Guide.
See "I'm a little Dutch Girl."

(151)   Gladys, Gladys, come out tonight,
        The moon is shining bright.

Douglas (1916), 89 [London].

(152)   Glasgow waves go rolling over,
        Rolling over, rolling over,
        Glasgow waves go rolling over
        Earl-y in the morning.

Bluebells (1961), n. p. [Ayrshire].
Those Dusty Bluebells (1965), 12 [Ayrshire].

(153)   Glory, glory, hallelujah
          Teacher hit me with a ruler.
          I conked her on the bean
          With a rotten tangerine,
          Now teacher won't teach no more.

                              Usually a taunt.

Student oral collection (1964) [Texas].

(154)   Good bye (May), while you're away;
          Send a letter, love,
          Say you're better, love,
          Don't forget your dear old (Nell).

                         Call another girl in.

Douglas (1916), 84 [London].

(155)   "Good-by, mother"
          "Good-by, darlin' "
          "Good morning, school teacher."
          "Good morning. Where's your report card?"
          etc.

Nulton, *JAF*, 61 (1948), 56–57 [North Carolina, 1935].
Ainsworth, *WF*, 20 (1961), 183 [North Carolina].

(156)   Goody, goody, gout;
          Your shirt tail's out.
          Goody, goody, gin;
          Put it back again.

                              Usually a taunt.

Abrahams, *SFQ*, 27 (1963), 204 [Texas].

          Gooseberry, raspberry, strawberry jam.
          See "Ice cream soda."

(157) Go to town
And see the clown.

Abrahams, SFQ, 27 (1963), 204 [Texas].

(158) Grace, Grace, dressed in lace
Went upstairs to powder her face (wash her face).

Related to "Cinderella, dressed in yellow."

Randolph, *MF,* 3 (1953), 78 [Arkansas, *ca.* 1910].
Winifred Smith, *JAF,* 39 (1926), 83 [New York].
Bennett, *Children,* 12 (1927), 21.
Thompson, *JAF,* 47 (1934), 385 [Pennsylvania, 1929].
Davis (1949), 216 [Florida, 1938].
Ashton, *JAF,* 52 (1939), 122 [Iowa].
Brewster, *SFQ,* 3 (1939), 175 = Botkin (1944), 792.
"Stella, Stella," *Fargo Forum* (June 23, 1940), 13 [North Dakota].
Rae and Robb, *Christian Science Monitor Magazine* (March 21, 1942), 8.
Sone (1943), 197 [Texas].
Eller, *North Carolina Education,* 10 (1944), 464 [North Carolina]. "Lady, Lady."
Mills (1944), 15 [Maryland].
Halpert, *JAF,* 58 (1945), 350 [New Hampshire]. "Grace, Grace, monkey face."
Emrich and Korson (1947), 130. "Shirley Temple."
Haufrecht (1947), 62.
McCaskill, *NCF,* 1 (1948), 10 [North Carolina].
Musick, *HF,* 7 (1948), 13 [West Virginia].
Nulton, *JAF,* 61 (1948), 56 [North Carolina].
Withers (1948), 61.
Haines, *Daedalian,* 17 (1949), 27 [Texas].
Musick and Randolph, *JAF,* 63 (1950), 431 [Missouri].
Musick, *WVF,* 2, No. 3 (1952), 2 [West Virginia]. "Polly, Polly."
Browne, *WF,* 14 (1955), 7 [California].
Evans (1955), 20 [California].
Seeger, Folkways 7029 (1955) [Illinois].
Sutton-Smith (1959), 80 [New Zealand].
Ainsworth, *WF,* 20 (1961), 180 [Maine], 185 [Alabama, Michigan], 195 [Utah].
Worstell (1961), 17.
Heimbuecher, *KFQ,* 7, No. 4 (1962), 6 [Pennsylvania].
Abrahams, *SFQ,* 27 (1963), 199 [Texas].
Butler and Haley (1963), n. p.
Buckley, *KFQ,* 11 (1966), 103 [Indiana]. Listed.
Hawthorne, *KFQ,* 11 (1966), 115, 121 [Delaware].

Grades.
    See "Next year I will be."

Grandmother, Grandmother, (Granny, Granny)
I feel sick (I am ill).
    See "Mother, mother, I am ill."

Grannie in the kitchen.
    See "As I was in the kitchen."

(159)   Greasy rails and timber bridges
         Up the hills and down the ridges.
         Hard to stop and easy to start,
         What's the initial of my sweetheart?
         A-B-C-D, *etc.*

                        See also "Ice cream soda."

Randolph, *MF*, 3 (1953), 82 [Arkansas, late 1920's].

(160)   Green gravel, green gravel,
         Your grass is so green,
         I'll send you a letter
         To call .... in.
         I'll wash you in milk, and dress you in silk,
         And write your name with a gold pen and ink.

                        Usually a singing game.

Douglas (1916), 58 [London].

(161)   Green grows the laurel,
         And sweet falls the dew,
         Sorry was I
         When I parted from you.
         etc.

            Widely collected folk lyric.

MacColl and Behan, Folkways 8501 (1958) [Scotland, 1947].

(162)   Green is Irish
          Shamrock, too.
          I saw Irish
          How about you?

Seeger, Folkways 7029 (1955) [Illinois].

(163)   Grind the coffee
          Grind the coffee
          Choo, choo, choo.
          Grind the coffee
          Grind the coffee
          Out with you.

Mills (1944), 16 [Maryland].

(164)   Gypsy, gypsy, lived in a tent,
          Gypsy, couldn't pay rent,
          She borrowed one, she borrowed two
          And handed the rope to YOU.

                    Usually a counting-out rhyme.

Withers and Jablow (1956), 12 [New York City].
Those Dusty Bluebells (1965), 16 [Ayrshire]. Begins "Three wee gyp-
sies," ends "The rent man came and kicked them out/And now they
live in a roundabout."

(165)   Gypsy, gypsy, please tell me (do not tarry)
          What my husband's name will be (tell us
                    when we shall marry)?
          A, B, C, *etc.*

                    *See "Ice cream soda" and "Rich man, poor
                    man" for similar divination rhymes.*

Halpert, *JAF*, 58 (1945), 349 [New Hampshire].
Withers (1948), 63.
Seeger, Folkways 7029 (1955) [Illinois].
Heimbuecher, *KFQ*, 7, No. 4 (1962), 7–8 [Pennsylvania].
Abrahams, *SFQ*, 27 (1963), 199 [Texas]. "Gypsy, Gypsy, Rose-a-lee,"
    with "Rich man, poor man" rhyme.

Buckley, *KFQ*, 11 (1966), 103 [Indiana]. "Gypsy, gypsy, Rosemary."
   Listed.
Hawthorne, *KFQ*, 11 (1966), 116, 122 [Delaware]. For divining husband,
   ring, house, wedding dress.

Had a little duck,
His name was Tony Pim.
   See "I had a little brother/ His name was Tim."

Had a little girl, dressed in blue.
   See "Little Miss Pinky."

Had a little Teddy bear.
   See "I had a little brother/ His name was Tim."

(166)   .... Had a toffee shop
           And .... came a-buying.
           Susan took a whirly kick
           And sent poor Maureen flying.

Ritchie (1965), 135 [Edinburgh].

(167)   Half a pint of porter,
           Penny on the can,
           Hop there and back again,
           If you can.

Douglas (1916), 61 [London].

(168)   Half a pound of twopenny rice,
           Half a pound of treacle,

Penn' 'orth of spice
To make it nice.
Pop goes the weasel.

> *Cf. "Up and down the ladder wall."*

Gomme, 2 (1898), 202 [Sussex].
Holbrook (1957), 55 [England].

Handy—nandy,
Sugar candy.
See "Amos and Andy."

Handy Pandy.
See "Amos and Andy."

Handy Spandy, Jack a Dandy.
See "Amos and Andy."

Hanky, panky.
See "Amos and Andy."

(169)   Happy Hooligan* number nine,
Hung his britches on the line;
When the line began to swing,
Happy Hooligan began to sing.

> *As beginning for "On the mountain top stands a lady."*

Emrich and Korson (1947), 135.

(170)   Harley, Marley, pease straw;
Gin pinches is the law.
Pinch him now, pinch him then,
Pinch him till he counts to ten.

Abrahams, *SFQ*, 27 (1963), 204 [Texas].

(171)   Harry Sticks was laying bricks

Buckley, *KFQ*, 11 (1966), 103 [Indiana]. Listed.

(172)   Harvey Duff, Harvey Duff,
         Pay the rent and that's enough,
         etc.

Daiken (1949), 69 [Dublin].

(173)   Harvey, jarvey, jig, jig, jig,
         Went to buy a pig, pig, pig.
         Went to France to learn to dance,
         Harvey, jarvey, jig, jig, jig.

                 Usually a taunt; third line, see
                 "Charlie Chaplin went to France."

Haufrecht (1947), 63.

(174)   Have a cherry, have a plum,
         Have a piece of chewing gum,
         Along with RED HOT PEPPER!

Abrahams, *SFQ*, 27 (1963), 204 [Texas].

         Hello, boys, do you want to flirt?
         See "Policeman, policeman, do your duty."

(175)   Hello, sir, hello, sir.
         Meet me at the grocer's.
         No, sir. Why, sir?
         Because I have a cold, sir.
         Where'd you get the cold, sir?
         Up at the North Pole, sir.
         What were you doing up there, sir?
         Shooting polar bear, sir.
         How many did you kill, sir?
         1-sir-2-sir, *etc.*

                 Generally used as a ball-bouncing rhyme; see
                 "What are you doing here, Sir?"

Speroni, *CFQ*, 1 (1942), 252 [California]. "Ding-a-ling, a-ling, Sir."
McDowell, *New York Times Magazine* (April 14, 1946), 8.
Emrich and Korson (1947), 136.
Withers (1948), 62.
Browne, *WF*, 14 (1955), 13 [California].
Evans (1955), 17 [California, begins "May I come in, sir?"] = Evans (1961), 40.
Schiller, *NYFQ*, 12 (1956), 202 [New York, begins "May I come in, sir?"] = Botkins and Withers (1958), 81.
Stone, *Home and Highway* (March, 1958), 24.

He loves me. He don't.
See "Does he love me?"

(176) Here comes a little bird through the window,
Here comes a little bird through the door—

Incomplete.

Douglas (1916), 93 [London].

(177) Here comes Mrs. Macaroni
Riding on her snow-white pony
Through the streets of Babylonie.
This is Marion's wedding day,
etc.

Ritchie (1964), 37 [Edinburgh].
Ritchie (1965), 123 [Edinburgh].

(178) Here comes teacher a'yelling.
Wonder what I made in spelling
1, 2, 3, *etc.*

Evans (1955), 19 [California, with "Bluebells, cockleshells" and "Here comes teacher with a hickory stick" rhymes] = Evans (1961), 51.
Taylor, *WF*, 18 (1959), 316 [California]. With "Bluebells, Cockleshells" and "Here comes teacher with a hickory stick" rhymes.
Abrahams, *SFQ*, 27 (1963), 204 [Texas].
Student oral collection (1963) [Texas]. Ends with "D-O-G spells dog," etc.

(179)   Here comes teacher with a hickory (big red) stick.
          I wonder what I got in arithmetic?
          A, B, C, *etc.*

                    May come from a taunt; see Morrison below.

Musick, *HF*, 7 (1948), 9 [West Virginia].
Harris, *Evening Bulletin* (May 30, 1949), 10 [Pennsylvania]. Mentioned.
Evans (1955), 19 [California, begins with "Bluebells, cockleshells" rhyme] = Evans (1961), 51.
Morrison (1955), 3. Ends "You better get ready for arithmetic."
Seeger, Folkways 7029 (1955) [Illinois].
Pope, *WF*, 15 (1956), 46 [Texas]. With "Bluebells, cockleshells" rhyme.
Taylor, *WF*, 18 (1959), 316. With "Bluebells, cockleshells" rhyme.
Ainsworth, *WF*, 20 (1961), 190 [Alabama], 185 [Wisconsin].
Worstell (1961), 16.
Abrahams, *SFQ*, 27 (1963), 199 [Texas]. Three variants, one begins "Teacher, teacher tell me quick."

(180)   Here comes the bride
          All dressed in white.
          Here comes the fellow
          All dressed in yellow.

                    A parody of the wedding march.

Withers (1948), 63.

(181)   Here comes Uncle Jessie
          Riding through the woods
          And silver horse and buckles
          And buckles on his shoes.
          Now if he was a fella
          I tell you what to do.
          Just put some salt and pepper
          And put it on your shoe.

                    Also found as singing game.

Abrahams, *KFQ*, 8 (1963), 6–7 [Pennsylvania, 1959].

(182)   Her first name is ....
          Catch her if you can.

'Cause she's in love with ....
And that's her only man.

Abrahams, *SFQ*, 27 (1963), 204 [Texas].

(183)   He took her in the garden
         And set her on his knee,
         And said, "Baby, please,
         Won't you marry me?"
         Yes, no, maybe so.
         Yes, no, maybe so.
         etc.
              See "Does he love me?"

Abrahams, *SFQ*, 27 (1963), 205 [Texas].

(184)   Hey, everybody,
         Gather 'round Madison Town.
         Like two up.
         Two back.
         False turn.
         Birdland twice
         Kick that bird.
         Then spit that bird.

Abrahams, *KFQ*, 8 (1963), 4 [Pennsylvania, 1959]. Description of movements given.

(185)   Highest is the leader,
         Lowest must take end.

Ainsworth, *WF*, 20 (1961), 192 [Wisconsin].

(186)   High, low, slow, dolly,
         Rocky, medium, pepper.
              Descriptive of turning procedure.

Douglas (1916), 91 [London]. "Slow skip, what you like,/A dolly or a pepper."
Gardiner oral collection (1957–1958) [Forfar].

Ritchie (1965), 118 [Edinburgh]. "High low, dolly pepper."
Those Dusty Bluebells (1965), 7 [Ayrshire]. "1, 2, 3, high, low, slow, dolly, medium, rocky, pepper."
Warner, *Yankee*, 30, No. 1 (January, 1966), 93. "High, low,/Medium, wavy,/Walkie, talkie,/Salt, and/Red hot pepper."

(187)   Hi, ho, anybody home?
Meat nor drink
Nor money have I none.
Still I will be merry
Hi, ho, anybody home.

Usually a round.

Abrahams, *SFQ*, 27 (1963), 205 [Texas].

(188)   Hi, ho, Silver,* how about a date?
Meet you at the corner about half past eight.
I can rumba, I can do the splits.
I can wear my dress high above my hips.

See "Policeman, policeman, do your duty."

Time (May 29, 1950), 20 [Washington].
Opie (1959), 116 [England, 1957]. "Hi, Roy Rogers."
Abrahams, *SFQ*, 27 (1963), 205 [Texas]. "... I've got a date."
Ritchie (1964), 49 [Edinburgh]. "Ena Sharples, ..."

(189)   Hi ho! Skippety toe,
Turn the ship and away we go.
Judy and Jack dressed in black,
Silver buttons way down her back.

See "Mary Mack."

Daiken (1949), 65 [Great Britain].

(190)   Hippity hop to the baker shop,
To buy a stick of candy.

One for you and one for me,
And one for sister Annie.

Usually a nursery rhyme.

Abrahams, *SFQ*, 27 (1963), 205 [New York].

Hi, Roy Rogers.*
See "Hi, ho, Silver."

(191)   Hitler,* Hitler, I've been thinking,
What in the world have you been drinking?
Smells like beer, tastes like wine.
O, my gosh, it's turpentine.
How many bottles did you drink?
One, two, three, *etc.*

Parody of the song "Reuben and Rachel."

Evans (1955), 14 [California] = Evans (1961), 38.
Ainsworth, *WF*, 20 (1961), 182 [North Carolina], 190 [Wisconsin].
Heimbuecher, *KFQ*, 7, No. 4 (1962), 7 [Pennsylvania]. "Lincoln, Lincoln."
Butler and Haley (1963), n.p. "Reuben, Reuben."
Hawthorne, *KFQ*, 11 (1966), 115, 125 [Delaware].

(192)   Hitler,* Hitler, looks like this.
Mussolini* bows like this.
Sonja Henie* skates like this.
And Betty Grable* misses like this.

Harris, *Evening Bulletin* (May 30, 1949), 10 [Pennsylvania].

Hitler,* Hitler sat on a pin.
See "Charlie Chaplin sat on a pin."

(193)   Hoky, poky, penny a lump,
The more you eat, the more you jump.

Perhaps related to rhyme "Beans, beans,

> *the musical fruit." "Hokey pokey" is a*
> *name for ice-cream salesmen.*

Douglas (1916), 88 [London].
Ritchie (1965), 140 [Edinburgh].

(194)   Hona Mama Mona Mike
           Barcelona bona strike
           Hare ware frown venac
           Haia warrico we wo wac.

> *Usually a counting-out rhyme.*

Calitri, *Parents* (April, 1957), 86 [New York].

(195)   H-O-P!
           Try to catch me!

Musick, *WVF*, 2, No. 3 (1952), 5 [West Virginia].

(196)   Hot boiled beans and melted butter:
           Ladies and gentlemen, come to supper.

Douglas (1916), 89 [London].

           H-O-T spells red hot pepper.
           See "Red hot pepper."

(197)   A House to let (house for rent, rooms for rent)
           Inquire within;
           As I move out
           Let _____ move in (A lady got put out
               for drinking gin).

> *Also a counting-out rhyme; for an early reporting*
> *as a taunt, see Northall,* ENGLISH FOLK RHYMES,
> *306.*

Sutton-Smith (1959), 73 [New Zealand]. Two variants from 1900.
Douglas (1916), 89, 91 [London]. Two variants, one ". . . no rent to pay,/
    Knock at the door and run away."

Winifred Smith, *JAF*, 39 (1926), 83 [New York]. Two variants.
Johnson, *JAF*, 42 (1929), 305. "Tenement to let."
Rolland, *New Masses* (May 10, 1938), 109 = Botkin (1954), 566.
Brewster, *SFQ*, 3 (1939), 174–176 (two variants) = Botkin (1944), 793.
Britt and Balcom, *J Gen Psy*, 58 (1941), 300 [Maryland, District of Columbia].
Speroni, *CFQ*, 1 (1942), 251 [California].
Gibbs, *NYFQ*, 14 (1958), 312. Two variants; the second, heard in 1943, begins "Ten penny nail went to jail."
Halpert, *JAF*, 58 (1945), 350 [New Hampshire]. "A tenement, a tenement, a tenement to let."
McDowell, *New York Times Magazine* (April 14, 1946), 8.
Botkin (1947), 907 [Connecticut]. Two variants, one begins "Tenement to let."
Emrich and Korson (1947), 136.
Withers (North) (1947), 84 [New York, "Apartment to rent"] = Withers (1964), 97.
Withers (1948), 60.
Daiken (1949), 64 [Great Britain].
Reck, *WF*, 8 (1949), 129 [Colorado].
Roberts, *HF*, 8 (1949), 10 [Michigan].
Randolph, *MF*, 3 (1953), 82 [Arkansas]. Begins "Fancy dressing is a sin."
Browne, *WF*, 14 (1955), 13 [California].
Evans (1955), 5, 27 [California, two variants] = Evans (1961), 31.
Schiller, *NYFQ*, 12 (1956), 203 [New York].
Worstell (1961), 29.
Heimbuecher, *KFQ*, 7, No. 4 (1962), 5 [Pennsylvania].
Abrahams, *SFQ*, 27 (1963), 199 [Texas].
Butler and Haley (1963), n.p.
Ritchie (1964), 20 [Edinburgh]. Three variants.
Ritchie (1965), 131 [Edinburgh].
Buckley, *KFQ*, 11 (1966), 105 [Indiana]. Listed.

How many children will I have.
See "Rich man, poor man."

(198) How many messages can you carry?
One, two, three, four, *etc.*

Ritchie (1965), 112 [Edinburgh].

How many messages will I carry?
See "Rich man, poor man."

(199)   How many miles to London town?
         How many miles up and down?
         Two, four, six, eight, *etc.*

                    Cf. the game "How many miles to
                    Barley Bright."

Sutton-Smith (1959), 80 [New Zealand].

(200)   How would you like to be me?
         Up in an apple tree?
         A lump of jelly stuck in my belly.
         How would you like to be me?

MacColl and Behan, Folkways 8501 (1958) [Dublin].

              Hurry up, don't be late.
              See "Next year I will be."

(201)   I'm a bow-legged chicken, I'm a knock-
             kneed sparrow;
         I've been that way since I don't know
             when.
         You walk with a wiggle and a squiggle
             and a squawk.
         Doing the Tennessee wig-walk.
         Put your toes together and your knees
             apart;
         Bend your back and get ready to start.
         You flap your elbows just for luck,
         And you wiggle and you squaggle like
             a baby duck.

Graham, *Press and Journal* (January 25, 1960), 4 [Aberdeen].

(202)   I am a funny (pretty) Dutch girl,
           As funny (pretty) as can be;
           And all the boys around the block
           Are crazy after me.
           I have a boyfriend named Sammy.
           He comes from Alabamy
           With rings on his nose
           And pickles on his toes,
           And that's the way my story goes.

                    Usually a hand-clapping rhyme.

Musick, *HF*, 7 (1948), 11 [West Virginia].
Abrahams, *KFQ*, 8 (1963), 9 [Pennsylvania, 1959]. Two variants, one
    ends with "He gave me some peaches./He gave me some pears, etc."
Abrahams, *SFQ*, 27 (1963), 200, 208 [Texas]. Seven variants; one be-
    gins "I am a funny bunny," one "My boyfriend's name is Sammy."
Withers (1964), 100 [Iowa]. Includes "My boyfriend's name is Michael,/
    He rides on a motorcycle."

(203)   I'm a girl dressed in green.
           My mother didn't want me
           So she sent me to the Queen:
           The Queen didn't want me
           So she sent me to the King.
           The King said: "Shut your eyes
           And count sixteen."

                    Cf. the "Girl Guide" versions of
                    "I'm a little Dutch Girl."

Ritchie (1965), 132 [Edinburgh].

           I am a Girl Guide* dressed in blue.
           See "I'm a little Dutch Girl."

(204)   I am a little beggar-girl (orphan girl).
           My mother she is dead,
           My father is a drunkard
           And won't give me no bread.
           I look out the window

To hear the organ play—
God bless my dear mother,
She gone far away.
Ding-dong the castle bells
Bless my poor mother—
Her coffin shall be black,
Six white angels at her back—
Two to watch and two to pray,
And two to carry her soul away.

> *Comes from a prayer and a sentimental song.*

Douglas (1916), 71 [London].
Graham, *Press and Journal* (November 25, 1959), 2 [Aberdeen].
Ritchie (1965), 117, 124 [Edinburgh]. Two variants.

(205)   I'm a little brownie dressed in brown.
         See my stocking fallin' down.
         Pick them up, pull them down,
         I'm a little brownie dressed in brown.

> *Cf. the "Girl Guide" versions of*
> *"I'm a little Dutch Girl."*

Gardiner oral collection (1957–1958) [Forfar].
Ritchie (1965), 133 [Edinburgh].

(206)   I'm a little Dutch Girl (I'm a Girl Guide*)
         Dressed in blue.
         Here are the things
         I like to do:
         Salute to the captain,
         Bow to the queen,
         Turn my back
         On the submarine (Naughty king).

> *The last four lines are often found as an ending*
> *to "Charlie Chaplin went to France."*

Ashby, *Christian Science Monitor Magazine* (April 9, 1949), 8.
Daiken (1949), 65 [Great Britain].
Harris, *Evening Bulletin* (May 30, 1949), 10 [Pennsylvania]. Mentions
    "I am a little Girl Scout."

Reck, *WF*, 8 (1949), 126 [Colorado]. With "Charlie Chaplin went to France" rhyme.

Musick, *WVF*, 2, No. 3 (1952), 6 [West Virginia].

Schwartz, Folkways 7009 (1953) [New York]. "I'm a little sailor girl."

Browne, *WF*, 14 (1955), 13 [California].

Gardiner oral collection (1957–1958) [Forfar]. Ends "Turn your back to the sailor boy."

Holbrook (1957), 56 [England]. "I am a Girl Guide."

"Children's Rhymes," *WVF*, 8 (1958), 37. "I had a little dolly."

Abrahams, *KFQ*, 8 (1963), 7 [Pennsylvania, 1959]. Two variants, one "Little girl, little girl."

Graham, *Press and Journal* (December 7, 1959), 4 [Aberdeen].

Leventhal and Cray, *WF*, 22 (1963), 232 [California, 1959].

Sutton-Smith (1959), 81 [New Zealand].

Utley (1959), 126 [Lancashire].

Ainsworth, *WF*, 20 (1961), 182 [North Carolina], 183 [Georgia].

Worstell (1961), 35.

Abrahams oral collection (1962) [Nevis, B.W.I.]. "There's a little boy."

Heimbuecher, *KFQ*, 7 (1962), 4 [Pennsylvania].

Abrahams, *SFQ*, 27 (1963), 200 [Texas]. Five variants, one begins "Bend your elbows, bend your knees."

Ritchie (1964), 27 [Edinburgh]. Begins "Kings and Queens/And partners two," ends with "German boys/Are so funny:/This is the way/They earn their money."

Withers (1964), 99 [Iowa].

Ritchie (1965), 114–115, 132 [Edinburgh]. Three variants: one begins "Kings and Queens/And partners two," ends "Stand at ease/Bend your knees/Salute to the east/And bow to the west . . ."; the two others begin "I'm a girl guide" and end "Sailor boys are so funny/This is the way they earn their money, zoopa la la . . ." (see also "Turn your back on the sailor Jack" rhyme).

Buckley, *KFQ*, 11 (1966), 103 [Indiana]. Listed.

Fowke, *Hoot* (September, 1966), 41 [Canada]. "Girl Guide, Girl Guide . . ."

Hawthorne, *KFQ*, 11 (1966), 116, 124 [Delaware]. "I know a little . . ."

(207)   I am a little girl as tall as the table

Buckley, *KFQ*, 11 (1966), 101 [Indiana]. Listed.

(208)   I am a little girl just so high,
         I can make donuts, I can make pie;
         I broke a platter right in two,
         Mother came to whip me, Boo, Hoo, Hoo.

Buckley, *KFQ*, 11 (1966), 100 [Indiana].

I'm a little orphan girl.
See "I am a little beggar-girl."

(209)   O ...., I am ashamed of you
          For leaving .... across the ocean blue:
          Her heart is nearly broken, she's dying for a kiss—
          O ...., I am ashamed of this!

                    Also a singing game.

Ritchie (1965), 127, 142 [Edinburgh]. Two variants: one "O Wattie
Manson," the other "O Wilma Ballantyne, why did you run away?"

          I'm a Spanish dancer.
          See "Spanish dancers."

          I'm Mrs. Jones and this is Mr. Jones.
          See "My name is Alice."

(210)   I'm the monster of Loch Ness,
          My name you'll never guess,
          I can wave like a snake
          And do the hippy shake,
          I'm the monster of Loch Ness!

Ritchie (1965), 115, 125 [Edinburgh]. Two variants.

(211)   I asked my mother for fifteen cents,
          To see the elephant jump the fence,
          He jumped so high.
          He reached the sky,
          And didn't come back till the Fourth of July.

                    Rhyme of many other functions.

Sutton-Smith (1959), 74 [New Zealand, 1903]. Begins with "Pounds,
    shillings and pence" rhyme.
Brewster (1952), 172 [North Carolina]. Two variants: one, *ca.* 1923; one
    ca. 1928.
La Salle (1929), 71.
Mills and Bishop, *The New Yorker* (November 13, 1937), 39.
Fahey, *Journal of Health and Physical Education*, 11 (1940), 421 [Kan-
    sas].

Haufrecht (1947), 64.

Yoffie, *JAF*, 60 (1947), 48 [Missouri]. Two variants.

Nulton, *JAF*, 61 (1948), 55 [North Carolina]. Two variants.

Randolph, *MF*, 3 (1953), 81 [Arkansas, 1949]. With "Mary Mack" rhyme.

Abrahams, *KFQ*, 8 (1963), 6 [Pennsylvania, 1959]. Two variants, one begins with "'Mary Mack" rhyme.

Abrahams, *SFQ*, 27 (1963), 199 [Texas].

Buckley, *KFQ*, 11 (1966), 106 [Indiana].

(212)   Ibbity, bibbity, sibbity, sab;
            Ibbity, bibbity, canal boat (ranahoo);
            Dictionary goes down the ferry,
            Out goes you.

            Generally a counting-out rhyme.

Gibbs, *NYFQ*, 14 (1958), 314 [*ca.* 1900]. Begins "Dictionary/Down the ferry."

Britt and Balcom, *J Gen Psy*, 58 (1941), 293 [Maryland, District of Columbia].

Haufrecht (1947), 64. "... gibbety goat."

(213)   I call in my very best friend
            And that is Lynda Phillips:
            One, two, three, *etc.*

Ritchie (1965), 112 [Edinburgh].

            Ice cream cone.
              See "Ice cream soda."

(214)   Ice cream soda, Delaware Punch,
            Spell the initials of my (your) honey bunch.
            A, B, C, *etc.*

                This divination rhyme is related to "Rich
                man, poor man." Related initials rhymes are
                indicated below.

Gomme, 2 (1898), 202. "Ipsey, Pipsey, tell me true."

Maclagan (1901), 227 [Argyllshire]. "Gooseberry, raspberry, strawberry jam."

Douglas (1916), 51 [London]. "Black currant—red currant—raspberry tart."

Heck, *JAF*, 40 (1927), 41, 42 [Ohio]. "Apples, peach, pumpkin pie,/ How many days before I die?" and Strawberry blonde,/Cream of tartar," ending with "Rich man, poor man" rhyme.

Thompson, *JAF*, 47 (1934), 385 [Pennsylvania].

Ireland, *Recreation* (February, 1937), 564 [Michigan]. "Salt, vinegar, mustard, tart."

Davis (1949), 216 [Florida, 1938]. ". . ., gingerale , pop."

Ashton, *JAF*, 52 (1939), 121 [Iowa]. "Strawberry shortcake, huckleberry pie."

Brewster, *SFQ*, 3 (1939), 176, 177 (Four variants: "Apples, peaches, creamery butter"; "Raspberry, raspberry, raspberry jam"; "Betty, Betty, Betty Jo"; "Raspberry, strawberry, cherry pie") = Botkin (1944), 792–794.

Randolph, *MF*, 3 (1953), 82 [Arkansas, *ca*. 1940]. "Pummelty, Pommelty, apple butter."

"Stella, Stella," *Fargo Forum* (June 23, 1940), 13 [North Dakota]. "Strawberry shortcake,/Cream on tarts."

Britt and Balcom, *J Gen Psy*, 58 (1941), 294. "Ice cream, soda water, ginger ale pop."

Hall, *Recreation* (March, 1941), 715 [Nebraska]. "Raspberry, raspberry, raspberry jam."

Park, *CFQ*, 1 (1942), 377 [California]. "Mama's little dumpling."

Speroni, *CFQ*, 1 (1942), 250 [California].

Sone (1943), 197 [Texas].

Eller, *North Carolina Education*, 10 (1944), 447 [North Carolina]. "Salt, pepper, vinegar hot."

"Jump-Rope Rhymes," *WF*, 23 (1964), 258 [California, 1944]. "Rosy apples,/Mama's little tart," ends with divinations from "Rich man, poor man" rhyme.

Maloney, *HFB*, 3 (1944), 25 [Idaho]. "Strawberry shortcake, huckleberry pie."

Mills (1944), 15 [Maryland].

Fife, *JAF*, 59 (1946), 321 [North Carolina]. "Ice cream cone."

McDowell, *New York Times Magazine* (April 14, 1946). "Strawberry shortcake cream of tartar."

Walker, *NYFQ*, 2 (1946), 231 [New York]. ". . . ginger ale, pop."

Botkin (1947), 906 [Connecticut]. "Apples, peaches, pumpkin pie,/How many years before I die?"

Emrich and Korson (1947), 136. "Strawberry shortcake, huckleberry pie."

Haufrecht (1947), 61, 62, 63. Four variants: "Strawberry shortcake, shoo fly pie/Tell me the name of the apple of your eye"; ". . . lemonade pop"; "Raspberry, raspberry, raspberry jam"; and "Betty, Betty, Betty Jo."

Opie (1947), 22. "Black currant, red currant, raspberry tart."

Withers (North) (1947), 84 [New York, "Raspberry, raspberry, jam"] = Withers (1964), 100.

Withers (1948), 61. "Strawberry shortcake, cream on top."

Musick, *HF*, 7 (1948), 11 [West Virginia]. ". . . ginger ale, pop."

Ashby, *Christian Science Monitor Magazine* (April 9, 1949), 8. Two variants: "Strawberry shortcake, cream of tartar" and "Strawberry jam, cream of tartar."

Daiken (1949), 67, 70 [Great Britain]. Two variants: one beginning "A rosy apple, a lemon or a tart," the other "Strawberry, apple, my jam tart." Both have the longer divination pattern choosing the place where the couple will live, what they will be married in, etc.

Haines, *Daedalian*, 17 (1949), 29. Two variants, one "Apples, pears, peaches, plums."

Harris, *Evening Bulletin* (May 30, 1949), 10 [Pennsylvania]. Mentioned.

Reck, *WF*, 8 (1949), 128 [Colorado]. "Ice cream soda, huckleberry pie."

Musick and Randolph, *JAF*, 63 (1950), 341 [Missouri]. "Apples, peaches, creamery butter."

Dodson, *Recreation* (June, 1951), 173 [North Carolina]. "I love jelly, I like jam."

Frankel (1952), 62. "Strawberry shortcake, cream on top."

Musick, *WVF*, 2, No. 3 (1952), 5, 7 [West Virginia]. Two variants: "Ice cream soda, ginger ale pop," and "Peaches, apples, pears and plums,/ Tell me when my birthday comes."

Browne, *WF*, 14 (1955), 9 [California]. Four variants; one "Strawberry shortcake, Delaware punch," one "Ice cream soda, galaway punch," one "Strawberry shortcake, cream on top."

Seeger, Folkways 7029 (1955) [Illinois]. "Apples, peaches, creamery butter."

Schiller, *NYFQ*, 12 (1956), 202 [New York]. ". . . ginger ale pop."

Evans (1955), 8 [California, "Rosy apple, Mama's little tot"] = Evans (1961), 33.

Bley (1957), 94. "Strawberry shortcake, cream on top."

Holbrook (1957), 57 [England]. "Ipsey, Pipsey."

"Children's Rhymes," *WVF*, 8 (1958), 39. "Ice cream, soda water, ginger ale, pop."

Stone, *Home and Highway* (March, 1958), 22.

Abrahams, *KFQ*, 8 (1963), 11 [Pennsylvania, 1959]. Two variants, one "Ice cream soda, with a cherry on top."

Leventhal and Cray, *WF*, 22 (1963), 236 [California, 1959].

Opie (1959), 339 [England]. Two variants: "Black currant, red currant, gooseberry jam," and "Rosy apple, lemon tart."

Sutton-Smith (1959), 78–79 [New Zealand]. Two variants with numerous divination additions: one begins "Raspberry, strawberry, blackberry jam," the other "Apple, jelly, my jam tart."

Graham, *Press and Journal* (January 4, 1960), 4 [Aberdeen]. "Black sugar, white sugar, apple tart."

Ainsworth, *WF*, 20 (1961), 185 [Georgia, "Milk shake, milk shake"], 186 [Michigan], 186 [Wisconsin, "Light sky, dark sky"], 191 [Wisconsin, "Apples, peaches, cream on tart"], 193 [New Mexico].

Worstell (1961), 5, 17. "Sugar and cream,/Bread and butter" and "Ice cream soda, ginger ale pop."

Heimbuecher, *KFQ*, 7, No. 4 (1962), 7 [Pennsylvania]. "Ice cream soda, ginger ale pop."

Sandburg (1962), 110. ". . . lemonade punch," ends with "Mother, Mother, I am ill" rhyme.

Abrahams, *SFQ*, 27 (1963), 199 [Texas]. Seven variants.

Butler and Haley (1963), n.p. Two variants, one "Raspberry, raspberry, raspberry jam."

Sandburg (1963), 15 [District of Columbia]. ". . . lemonade punch."

Student oral collection (1964) [Texas]. "............ by the seashore, sweet as punch."

Ritchie (1965), 144 [Edinburgh]. "Raspberry, strawberry, black currant jam."

Buckley, *KFQ*, 11 (1966), 102 [Indiana]. Four variants: one "lemonade pop," one "Apples, peaches, creamery butter," one "Raspberry jam," one "Raspberry pie."

Hawthorne, *KFQ*, 11 (1966), 116, 121 [Delaware]. ". . . with a cherry on top."

(215)   Ice cream, soda water,
          Ginger ale pop.
          Cameron, Cameron,
          Always on top.
          Stand these on their heads,
          Stand these on their feet,
          Cameron, Cameron,
          Can't be beat.
                    Seems to be derived from school cheer.

Evans (1955), 18 [California].

(216)   Icklety-picklety, isia—lickerty,
          Boom ta-ra jib,
          Every man in Chinatown
          Ought to wear a wig.
          One, two, three,
          Out pops she,
          Icklety-picklety, isia—lickerty
          Boom ta-ra-ra jig.
                    Related to many counting-out rhymes.

Bluebells (1961), n.p. [Ayrshire].

(217)   I come from Chink-a-China,
My home is 'cross the sea.
I do my daily laundry
For fifty cents a week.
Oh Mary, Mary, Mary,
You ought to be ashamed.
To marry, marry, marry,
A boy without a name.

Botkin (1947), 907 [Connecticut].
Harris, *Evening Bulletin* (May 30, 1949), 10 [Pennsylvania]. Mentioned,
    "Chinaman, Chinaman, over the sea."
Browne, *WF*, 14 (1955), 19 [California]. "I went to Chinka China."
Bluebells (1961), n.p. [Ayrshire]. Two variants.
Ritchie (1964), 38 [Edinburgh]. "I live in Chinka China."
Those Dusty Bluebells (1965), 16 [Ayrshire]. Two variants.

(218)   I dreamed that my horse had wings
        and could fly,
I jumped on my horse and rode to the sky.
The man in the moon was out that night,
He laughed loud and long when I pranced
        into sight.

La Salle (1929), 56.

(219)   I go to school,
I sit upon a stool,
It is the rule,
To learn my A, B, C, *etc.*

Bluebells (1961), n.p. [Ayrshire].

(220)   I had a black man, he was double-jointed,
I kissed him, and made him disappointed.
All right, Hilda, I'll tell your mother,
Kissing the black man round the corner.
How many kisses did he give you?
One, two, three, *etc.*

Douglas (1916), 56 [London].
Opie (1947), 20 [England].

Ritchie (1965), 132 [Edinburgh]. "I know a nigger boy and he is double jointed"; many other minor variations.

(221)   I had a bloke down Hopping,
           I had a bloke down Kent,
           I had a bloke down Pimlico,
           And this is what he sent:
           O Shillali-tee-i-o.

Douglas (1916), 61–62 [London].

           I had a doll and her name was Sis.
           See "Miss, miss, little miss."

           I had a dolly dressed in blue.
           See "I'm a little Dutch Girl."

(222)   I had a dolly dressed in green,
           I didn't like her (I put her in a match-
               box)—I gave her to the Queen—
           The Queen didn't like her—she gave
               her to the cat (king)—
           The cat didn't like her because she
               wasn't fat.

Douglas (1916), 52 [London].
Utley (1959), 126 [Lancashire]. Ends "Close your eyes and count six-
teen."
Graham, *Press and Journal* (January 18, 1960), 4 [Aberdeen].

           I had a duck and his name was Dick.
           *See "I had a little brother/His name
               was Tim."*

           I had a little beer shop.
           See "Rat-a-tat-tat."

(223)   I had a little brother and his name was
           Johnny,

He played in the meadow where the frogs
croaked clear;
He ran through the meadows with a song
on his tongue
And he picked a few flowers for his mother.

How many flowers did he gather?
1-2-3-4-5, *etc.*

Butler and Haley (1963), n.p.

(224)   I had a little brother
His name was (tiny) Tim.
I put him in the bathtub
To teach him how to swim (To see
if he could swim).

He drank (up) all the water,
He ate (up) all the soap,
He died last night
With a bubble in his throat.

Nulton, *JAF*, 61 (1948), 58 [North Carolina, 1936].
Brewster, *SFQ*, 3 (1939), 177 ("Virginia had a baby") = Botkin (1944), 794.
Nulton, *Story Parade* (April, 1940), 16.
McDowell, *New York Times Magazine* (April 14, 1946), 8.
Walker, *NYFQ*, 2 (1946), 232 [New York]. "I had a brother."
Emrich and Korson (1947), 136.
Haufrecht (1947), 61. Ends "And out comes the bubbles when he jumps rope."
Reck, *WF*, 8 (1949), 128 [Colorado]. "Virginia had a baby."
Musick, *WVF*, 2, No. 3 (1952), 7 [West Virginia].
Brown, *WF*, 14 (1955), 20–21 [California]. Three variants: one beginning "I had a little teddy bear," one "Geneva had a baby," and one "I had a little monkey."
Evans (1955), 21 [California]. "Virginia had a brother."
Schiller, *NYFQ*, 12 (1956), 205 [New York]. Begins with the rhymes "Shirley Temple walks like this" and "Cinderella, dressed in yellow"; ends with ending of "Mother, mother, I am ill" rhyme.
Bley (1957), 95. "I had a duck and his name was Dick," ends with part of "Mother, mother, I am ill."
"Children's Rhymes," *WVF*, 8 (1958), 36. Ends with last lines of "Mother, Mother, I am ill."
Ainsworth, *WF*, 20 (1961), 180 [Maine, "Had a little duck,/His name was Tony Pim"], 188 [Michigan, begins "Had a little teddy bear," and

ends with a version of "Mother, mother, I am ill"], 190–191 [Wisconsin, "Minnie, Minnie, Ha Ha . . ."], 195 [Utah, ends with a version of "Mother, Mother, I am ill"].

Abrahams, *SFQ*, 27 (1963), 199 [Texas]. Two variants; both with "Mother, mother, I am ill" rhyme, one begins "Minnie-Minnie-Ha-Ha . . ."

Butler and Haley (1963), n.p. Two variants, one "Virginia had a baby."

Buckley, *KFQ*, 11 (1966), 103 [Indiana]. ". . . had a little Teddy." Listed.

Fowke, *Hoot* (September, 1966), 41 [Canada]. ". . . had a little teddy bear," ends with "In came the doctor. . . ."

Hawthorne, *KFQ*, 11 (1966), 115, 122. ". . . duck,/His name was Sunny Pin."

(225)   I had a little car, in 1958,
          Went around the cor-r-r-ner and slammed
              on the brake.

Abrahams, *SFQ*, 27 (1963), 205 [Ontario].

          I had a little dolly.
              See "Miss, miss, little miss."

          I had a little monkey.
              See "I had a little brother/His name was Tim."

(226)   I had a little monkey dressed in red,
          Along came a train and knocked him dead.

                         *Introduction for "Mother, Mother,
                         I am ill."*

Ainsworth, *WF*, 20 (1961), 184 [Georgia].

(227)   I had a little monkey.
          I sent him to the country.
          I fed him on gingerbread.
          He jumped out the winder,
          And broke his little finger.
          And now my monkey's dead.

Butler and Haley (1963), n.p.

(228)   I had a little nut tree,
           Nothing would it bear
           But a silver nutmeg
           And a golden pear.
           The King of Spain's daughter
           Came to visit me,
           And all because
           Of my little nut tree.

               Usually a nursery rhyme; see Opie,
               DICTIONARY, *330–331.*

Butler and Haley (1963), n.p. With historical explanation.
Butler, *TFSB*, 31 (1965), 6.

(229)   I had a little sausage,
           A dear little sausage:
           I put it in the oven
           For my tea-tea-tea.
           I went out to play
           And I heard the sausage say:
           "Come in little lassie
           For your tea-tea-tea."

Ritchie (1965), 141 [Edinburgh].

           I had a little sister dressed in blue.
               See "Little Miss Pinky."

(230)   I had a little sister (My little sister)
           Dressed in pink.
           She washed all the dishes
           In the sink.
           How many dishes did she break?
           One, two, three, *etc.*

Nulton, *Story Parade* (April, 1940), 14.
Musick, *HF*, 7 (1948), 8 [West Virginia].
Musick, *WVF*, 2, No. 3 (1952), 5 [West Virginia].
Sutton-Smith, *WF*, 12 (1955), 20 [New Zealand].
Sutton-Smith (1959), 79 [New Zealand].
Ainsworth, *WF*, 20 (1961), 188, 195 [Utah, Michigan]. Two variants.

I had a little teddy bear.
See "I had a little brother/His name was Tim."

(231)   I had a mule,
         His name was Jack.
         I rode his tail
         To save his back.
         His tail got loose
         And I fell back—
         Whoa, Jack!

                    One of a large family of entertainment
                    rhymes that begin "I had a mule."

Abrahams, *SFQ*, 27 (1963), 206 [Texas].

I had a teddy bear dressed in green.
See "Teddy Bear, Teddy Bear, turn around."

(232)   I have a tooth-ache,
         A gumboil, a tummy-ache,
         A pain in my left side,
         A pimple on my tongue,
         A hip, hip hurray!
         To be the queen of May
         etc.

Daiken (1949), 65 [Great Britain].

I knew a little Dutch girl.
See "I'm a little Dutch Girl."

(233)   I know a doctor, he knows me
         What do you think he brought for tea—

                              Incomplete.

Douglas (1916), 91 [London].

(234)   I know a little lady, but her name is miss,
         She went around the corner to buy some fish,
         She met a little fellow and she gave him a
           kiss.
         I know a little lady but her name is miss.

                               See "Miss, miss, little miss."

Winifred Smith, *JAF*, 39 (1926), 83. "... name is Sis."
Johnson, *JAF*, 42 (1929), 305.
Evans (1961), 24 [California].

(235)   I know a man, his name is Mister;
         He knows a lady and her name is MISS!

Withers (1948), 59.

(236)   I know a man named Michael Finnegan.
         He wears whiskers on his chinegan.
         Along came a wind and blew them in again;
         Poor old Michael Finnegan, begin again.

                               Common nursery rhyme.

Withers (1948), 68.

         I know a nigger boy and he is double-jointed.
         See "I had a black man, he was double-jointed."

(237)   I know a Scout
         Who took me out!
         He gave me chips
         To grease my lips ...

Bluebells (1961), n.p. [Ayrshire]. Begins "I love a Scout," ends "He
takes me to the P,I,C,T,U,R,E,S."
Ritchie (1964), 34 [Edinburgh].
Ritchie (1965), 141 [Edinburgh].

(238)   I know a washerwoman, she knows me,
         She invited me to tea,

> Guess what we had for supper—
> Stinking fish and bread and butter.

Douglas (1916), 60 [London].

> I know a woman
> And her name is miss.
> *See "Miss, miss, little miss."*

(239)   I know a woman, she lives in the woods,
         Weela, weela, wila,
         I know a woman, she is no good,
         Down by the River Sila.
         etc.

> *A version of Child 20, "The Cruel Mother."*

Douglas (1916), 83 [London]. "Three little children lived in the
    woods . . ."
MacColl and Behan, Folkways 8501 (1958) [Dublin].

> I like jelly, I like jam.
> *See "Ice cream soda."*

(240)   I live in an old tin can

Buckley, *KFQ*, 11 (1966), 103 [Indiana]. Listed.

> I live in Chinkie China.
> *See "I come from Chink-a-China."*

(241)   I love a girl.
         I hate a boy.
         I hate a girl.
         I love a boy.
         What's the boy's name I hate (or love)?
         A, B, C, D, *etc.*

Abrahams, *SFQ*, 27 (1963), 206 [Texas].

I love a Scout.
See "I know a Scout."

(242) I love Bill, I love Larry,
I love Tom, and Dick, and Harry.
I love boys—now, let me see
Which one will my boyfriend be?
1, 2, 3, 4, *etc.*

Mankins, *WVF*, 12 (1962), 55 [West Virginia].

(243) I love Bobby, I love Bill.
Who do I love better still?
A, B, C, *etc.*

Ainsworth, *WF*, 20 (1961), 193 [Colorado].

(244) I love (like) coffee, I love tea.
I want .... to come in with me.

Or "How many boys are stuck on me?" or
"I love the boys and the boys love me."

Randolph, *MF*, 3 (1953), 77 [Arkansas]. Two variants: one from before
1920, beginning "Some love coffee, some love tea"; one from 1947.
Winifred Smith, *JAF*, 39 (1926), 84.
Brewster, *SFQ*, 3 (1939), 174 = Botkin (1944), 791.
Rudy, Mills, and Sone, *Jack and Jill*, 4 (March, 1942), 7. With "Bluebells,
cockleshells" rhyme.
Sone (1943), 198 [Texas]. With "Bluebells, cockleshells" rhyme.
Emrich and Korson (1947), 131. With "Mother, Mother, may I go"
rhyme.
Haufrecht (1947), 62, 63. Two variants, one with "As I went down to
Grandfather's farm" rhyme.
Withers (North) (1947), 83 [New York] = Withers (1964), 97.
Haines, *Daedalian*, 17 (1949), 24. With "As I went down to Grandfather's
farm" rhyme.
Reck, *WF*, 8 (1949), 128 [Colorado].
Roberts, *HF*, 8 (1949), 10 [Indiana].
The Times (London), March 7, 1953 [England, ends "I like radio and
T.V."] = Opie (1959), 117.

Evans (1955), 14 [California] = Evans (1961), 37.

Browne, *WF*, 14 (1955), 19 [California]. Three variants.

"Children's Rhymes," *WVF*, 8 (1958), 39. Begins with "Bluebells, cockle-shells" rhyme.

Stone, *Home and Highway* (March, 1958), 22.

Leventhal and Cray, *WF*, 22 (1963), 232–233 [California, 1959]. Two variants.

Sutton-Smith (1959), 79 [New Zealand]. Two variants.

Ainsworth, *WF*, 20 (1961), 184 [Alabama], 192 [Colorado], 194 [New Mexico].

Worstell (1961), 4.

Heimbuecher, *KFQ*, 7, No. 4 (1962), 7 [Pennsylvania].

Abrahams, *KFQ*, 8 (1963), 8 [Pennsylvania,1959].

Abrahams, *SFQ*, 27 (1963), 200 [Texas]. Four variants.

Ritchie (1965), 131, 132 [Edinburgh]. Two variants, one "I hate coffee."

Buckley, *KFQ*, 11 (1966), 103 [Indiana]. Listed.

Hawthorne, *KFQ*, 11 (1966), 116, 121 [Delaware].

I love jelly, I like jam.
See "Ice cream soda."

(245)   Indian, Indian, lived in a tent.
          Indian, Indian, never paid rent.
          She borrowed one, she borrowed two.
          And passed the rope over to Y-O-U.

Withers (1948), 64.

(246)   I never went to college,
          I never went to school,
          But when it comes to boogie
          I'm an educated fool.
          Hands up, toy, toy.

Schwartz, Folkways 7009 (1953) [New York].

(247)   Inky-pinkie skinny-ma-linkie
          Andy-pandy pandy-Andy bandy-boots,

Over-dover, dover rover,
Andy-pandy pandy-Andy bandy-boots!

Sung to "K-K-K-Katie."

Ritchie (1965), 125 [Edinburgh].

(248)   Inky pinkie
Sugarallie inkie:
One two three.
Ice cream and jelly
A punch in the belly
One two three!

Cf. "Amos and Andy."

Ritchie (1965), 133 [Edinburgh].

(249)   In Leicester Square* there is a *school*
And in that school there is a *room*
And in that room there is a *desk*
And in that desk there is a *book*
And in that book there is a *picture*
And in that picture there is a *GHOST!*

Seems to come from a children's routine.

Ritchie (1964), 30 [Edinburgh].

(250)   In Liverpool,
There is a school,
And in that school,
There is a class,
And in that class,
There is a desk,
And in that desk,
There is a book,
And in that book,
There is a page,

And from that page
I learned my A, B, C, *etc.*

Bluebells (1961), n.p. [Ayrshire].

I-N spells in.
See "As I was in the kitchen."

(251)   In, spin
Let Judy come in
Out, spout
Let Judy go out.

Evans (1955), 21 [California] = Evans (1961), 42.

(252)   In the *dark dark* world
There's a *dark dark* country
In the *dark dark* country
There's a *dark dark* wood
In the *dark dark* wood
There's a *dark dark* house
And in the *dark dark* house
There is a man trying to mend
a fuse!

Ritchie (1964), 51 [Edinburgh].

(253)   Intry mintry cutry corn
Appleseed and applethorn
Wire brier limberlock,
Three geese in a flock,
One flew east and one flew west,
And one flew over the cuckoo's nest.

Usually a counting-out rhyme.

Calitri, *Parents* (April, 1957), 53. "Intry Kintry."
Butler and Haley (1963), n.p.

(254)   Inty ninty tibbety fig
          Deema dima doma nig
          Howchy powchy domi nowday
          Hom tom tout
          Olligo bolligo boo
          Out goes you.

                  Usually a counting-out rhyme.

Haufrecht (1947), 64.

          Ipsey, Pipsey, tell me true.
          See "Ice cream soda."

(255)   I saw Esau sawing wood,
          And Esau saw I saw him;
          Though Esau saw I saw him saw
          Still Esau went on sawing.

                  Usually found as a tongue-twister.

Opie (1959), 13 [New England]. With a discussion of the history of the
    piece.

(256)   I scream
          You scream
          We all scream
          For ice cream.

                  Usually a tongue-twister.

Haufrecht (1947), 64.

(257)   I see London, I see stars.
          I see someone's underdrawers.
          Are they purple, are they pink?
          Oh, my goodness, how they stink.

                          Usually a taunt.

Abrahams, *SFQ*, 27 (1963), 206 [Texas].

(258)   I see the moon, and the moon sees me,
           God bless the moon and God bless me,
           Grace in the garden, grace in the hall
           And the grace of God be on us all.

                    The last part from a common table grace;
                    for the first part see Opie, DICTIONARY, 312.

Daiken (1949), 64 [Great Britain].

           I sent a letter to my love.
           See "Itisket, itasket."

(259)   I should worry, I should care,
           I should marry a millionaire.
           He should die, I should cry,
           Then I'd marry a richer guy.

                    Usually an entertainment rhyme.

Fahey, *Journal of Health and Physical Education*, 11 (1940), 422 [Kansas].
Britt and Balcom, *J Gen Psy*, 58 (1941), 295 [Maryland, District of Columbia]. With "Mother, Mother, may I go" rhyme.
Withers (1948), 67.

           Oh, It's I have a toothache.
           See "I have a toothache."

(260)   Itisket, itasket, a green and yellow basket.
           I lost a letter to my love and on the way
           I found it, I found it, found it.
           And on the way I found it.

                    See "A tisket, a tasket." From the game
                    "Drop the Handkerchief."

La Salle (1929), 71.
MacColl and Behan, Folkways 8501 (1958) [Dublin]. "I sent a letter to my love."

           I told Ma.
           See "Johnny on the ocean."

(261)   I took a trip around the world,
And this is where I went:
From America to New Orleans;
New Orleans to Chicago,
etc.

Emrich and Korson (1947), 135. "Ann, Ann, took a trip."
Withers (1948), 70.
Frankel (1952), 63.

It was in the middle of the day.
See "One bright morning."

(262)   I ula-used to li-li-live in Yalla-larkie,
Shalla-larkie
Yalla-lankie, Shalla-lankie, low
I ula-used to li-li-live in Yalla-lankie,
Shalla-lankie
Yalla-lankie, Shalla-lankie, go.

Ritchie (1965), 124 [Edinburgh].

(263)   I want a teddy bear
With blue eyes and curly hair,
Up among the eskimoes,
Having a game of dominoes.

Sutton-Smith (1959), 77 [New Zealand].

(264)   I was born in a frying pan.
Can you guess how old I am?
1, 2, 3, *etc.*

Grace Partridge Smith, *HF*, 5 (1946), 59 [Illinois] = Dorson (1964), 386.
Ashby, *Christian Science Monitor Magazine* (April 9, 1949), 8.
Browne, *WF*, 14 (1955), 8 [California]. Two variants.
Evans (1955), 20 [California] = Evans (1961), 41.
"Children's Rhymes," *WVF*, 8 (1958), 38. Begins with "Bluebells, cockle-shells" rhyme.
Leventhal and Cray, *WF*, 22 (1963), 236 [California, 1959].

Ainsworth, *WF*, 20 (1961), 193 [Colorado].
Abrahams, *SFQ*, 27 (1963), 200 [Texas]. Two variants, one begins with "Buster Brown" version of "Teddy Bear, Teddy Bear, turn around" rhyme.
Buckley, *KFQ*, 11 (1966), 102 [Indiana].

> I was born on Grandpa's farm.
> See *"As I went down to Grandfather's farm."*

> I was in the kitchen.
> See *"As I was in the kitchen."*

> I was standing on the corner.
> See *"Standing on the corner."*

(265)   I was standing on the corner,
Not doing any harm,
Along came a policeman,
And took me by the arm.
He took me around the corner,
And he rang a little bell.
Along came a police car
And took me to my cell.

I woke up in the morning
And looked up on the wall.
The cooties and the bedbugs
Were having a game of ball.
The score was six to nothing,
The bedbugs were ahead.
The cooties hit a homerun
And knocked me out of bed.

Usually an entertainment rhyme.

Evans (1955), 4 [California] = Evans (1961), 28.
Worstell (1961), 8–9. "I woke up Monday morning."
Abrahams, *SFQ*, 27 (1963), 200 [Texas]. "I woke up one morning."

(266)   I went down the lane to buy a penny whistle,
A copper came by and pinched my penny whistle.

I ask him for it back, he said he hadn't got it . . .
Hi, Hi, Curlywig, you've got it in your pocket.

Douglas (1931), 29 [London].

I went down to Grandpa's farm.
See "As I went down to Grandfather's farm."

(267) **I** went down to the sea.
I went down to the lake.
I saw a fellow throw and break a plate,
How many whips do you think he got?

Abrahams, *SFQ*, 27 (1963), 206 [Texas].
Buckley, *KFQ*, 11 (1966), 103 [Indiana]. "I went down to the River."
Listed.

(268) **I** went down to the store

Buckley, *KFQ*, 11 (1966), 103 [Indiana]. Listed.

(269) **I** went downtown
To see Mrs. Brown;
She gave me a nickle
To buy a pickle;
The pickle was so sour,
She gave me some flour (I bought a flower)
etc.

Bennett, *Children*, 12 (1927), 21. "I went downtown—I had a nickel."
Thompson, *JAF*, 47 (1934), 384 [Pennsylvania, 1929].
Mills and Bishop, *The New Yorker* (November 13, 1937), 34 [New York, 1934; New Jersey, 1936] = Botkin (1944), 795.
Ashton, *JAF*, 52 (1939), 122 [Louisiana].
Brewster, *SFQ*, 3 (1939), 176 (with "I love coffee" rhyme) = Botkin (1944), 800.
Fahey, *Journal of Health and Physical Education*, 11 (1940), 422 [Kansas].
Nulton, *Story Parade* (April, 1940), 15. Begins "Mrs. Brown/Went up-town," ends with "Spanish dancers" rhyme.
Speroni, *CFQ*, 1 (1942), 246 [California]. With "Spanish dancers" rhyme.

Mensing, *HFB*, 2 (1943), 48 [Indiana].
Mills (1944), 15 [Maryland].
McDowell, *New York Times Magazine* (April 14, 1946), 8.
Emrich and Korson (1947), 134.
Haufrecht (1947), 62.
Yoffie, *JAF*, 60 (1947), 48–49 [Missouri].
Musick, *HF*, 7 (1948), 13 [West Virginia].
Haines, *Daedalian*, 17 (1949), 25, 26 [Texas]. Two variants.
Harris, *Evening Bulletin* (May 30, 1949), 10 [Pennsylvania]. Mentioned.
Reck, *WF*, 8 (1949), 129 [Colorado]. With "Spanish dancers" rhyme.
Musick, *WVF*, 2, No. 3 (1952), 7 [West Virginia].
Randolph, *MF*, 3 (1953), 80 [Arkansas]. With two variants, one with a variation of "Teddy Bear, Teddy Bear, turn around" rhyme.
Browne, *WF*, 14 (1955), 16–17 [California]. Three variants, two with "Spanish dancers" rhyme.
Evans (1955), 16 [California, ends with "Spanish dancers" rhyme] = Evans (1961), 38.
Gibbs, *NYFQ*, 14 (1958), 315.
Sutton-Smith (1959), 82 [New Zealand]. "Mother Brown went to town."
Ainsworth, *WF*, 20 (1961), 190 [Wisconsin, with "I am a little Dutch girl" rhyme], 192 [Colorado].
Worstell (1961), 26–27. With "Teddy Bear, Teddy Bear, turn around" rhyme.
Heimbuecher, *KFQ*, 7, No. 4 (1962), 3 [Pennsylvania]. Ends with "Teddy Bear, Teddy Bear, turn around" rhyme.
Abrahams, *SFQ*, 27 (1963), 200 [Texas]. Two variants.
Buckley, *KFQ*, 11 (1966), 108 [Indiana]. ". . . uptown."

(270)   I went down town
          To the alligator farm.
          I sat on the fence
          And the fence broke down.
          The alligator bit me
          By the seat of the pants
          And made me do the houchi-kouchi dance.

Evans (1955), 18 [California] = Evans (1961), 39.
Ainsworth, *WF*, 20 (1961), 187 [Michigan].

(271)   I went to Arkansas
          To buy myself a saw.

I never saw so many saws
As I saw in Arkansas.

Usually reported as a tongue-twister.

Ainsworth, *WF*, 20 (1961), 196 [Utah].

I went to Chinka China.
See "I come from Chink-a-China."

(272)   I went to Fulton Ferry and I couldn't get
across.
I paid a half-a-dollar for an old blind
horse.
The horse wouldn't pull, I sold it for a
bull.
The bull wouldn't holler, I sold it for a
dollar.
The dollar wouldn't pass, I stuck it in the
grass.
The grass wouldn't grow, I stuck it in the
snow.
The snow wouldn't melt, I stuck it in my belt.
The belt was too narrow, I stuck it on a
sparrow.
The sparrow wouldn't fly, I stuck it in the
sky.
And it never came down till the Fourth of
July.

Ending from "I asked my mother"; usually
an entertainment rhyme.

McDowell, *New York Times Magazine* (April 14, 1946), 8.

(273)   I went to the animal fair,
And what do you think I saw there?
The elephant sneezed

And fell on his knees,
And what became of the monkey . . .

Usually a children's song.

Douglas (1916), 77 [London].
Opie (1959), 38.

(274)   **I** went to the show;
Saw Marilyn Monroe.*
What was she wearing?

Abrahams, *SFQ*, 27 (1963), 206 [Texas].

(275)   **I** went upstairs to make my bed;
I made a mistake and bumped my head.
I went downstairs to milk my cow;
I made a mistake and milked the sow.
etc.

*The particulars of the "mistakes" differ considerably
in different versions.*

Nulton, *JAF*, 61 (1948), 58 [North Carolina, 1945].
Sutton-Smith (1959), 78 [New Zealand]. "There was an old woman and
her name was Pat."
Abrahams, *SFQ*, 27 (1963), 200 [Texas].
Buckley, *KFQ*, 11 (1966), 101 [Indiana]. Listed.

(276)   **I** went upstairs to pick up a pin.
I asked Mrs. .... if .... was in.
He may be in, he may be out,
Tomorrow the wedding bells will shout!
X, O, X, O, *etc.*

*X means "he loves me," O means "he
doesn't love me."*

Musick, *HF*, 7 (1948), 11 [West Virginia].

I went up town to see Mrs. Brown.
See "I went downtown/To see Mrs. Brown."

I will marry.
See "Rich man, poor man."

(277) I'll tell Ma when I get home
That the boys won't leave me alone.
They pull my hair and break my combs,
I'll tell Ma when I get home.

Douglas (1916), 55 [London].

(278) I wish the night was Saturday night.
Tomorrow will be Sunday:
I'll be dressed in all my best
To go out with my Johnnie.

Ritchie (1965), 113 [Edinburgh]. Two variants.

I woke up Monday morning.
*See "I was standing on the corner/Not doing
any harm."*

(279) I won't go to Macy's anymore, more, more,
There's a big fat policeman at the door,
    door, door,
He takes me by the collar, and makes me
    pay a dollar.
So I won't go to Macy's anymore, more,
    more.

Rolland, *New Masses* (May 10, 1938), 109 = Botkin (1954), 567.
McDowell, *New York Times Magazine* (April 14, 1946), 8.
Emrich and Korson (1947), 135.
Withers, *NYFQ*, 3 (1947), 214–215 [New York]. Two variants, one "I
    won't go to Germany," with lines in Yiddish.
Withers (1948), 68.
Evans (1955), 5 [California] = Evans (1961), 30.
Abrahams oral collection (1963) [Nevis, B.W.I.].

(280)   I wore rubber knickers
           Until I was
           One, two, three ...

Ritchie (1965), 141 [Edinburgh].

JJ

Jack and Jill went to town.
See "Blondie and Dagwood."

(281)   Jack and Jill went up the hill
           To fetch a pail of water
           etc.
              See Opie, Dictionary, *224, 226.*

Abrahams, *SFQ,* 27 (1963), 206 [Texas].

(282)   Jack be nimble, Jack be quick,
           Jack jump over the candlestick.
           How many times did he jump?
           1, 2, 3, *etc.*
              See Opie, Dictionary, *220, 227, for a
              history of this nursery rhyme.*

Evans (1955), 19 [California].
Abrahams, *SFQ,* 27 (1963), 200 [Texas].

           January, February, *etc.*
           See "Miss, miss, little miss" and "All in together."

(283)   Jean, Jean, made a machine.
           Joe, Joe, made it go.

Frank, Frank, turned the crank.
Out came his mother and gave him a spank;
Turned him over the river bank.

Usually a taunt.

Owens, *North Star Folk News*, 4, No. 2 (1949), 2 [Minnesota].

(284)   Jelly in the dish (bowl) (plate),
           Jelly in the dish,
           Wiggle waggle, wiggle waggle,
           Jelly in the dish.

Rudy, Mills, and Sone, *Jack and Jill*, 4 (March, 1942), 7.
Halpert, *CFQ*, 3 (1944), 154 [Alberta, Canada].
Harris, *Evening Bulletin* (May 30, 1949), 10 [Pennsylvania]. Mentions
   "Jelly bowl, jelly bowl."
Withers (1949), 59.
Evans (1955), 24 [California].
Gardiner oral collection (1957–1958) [Forfar].
MacColl and Behan, Folkways 8501 (1958) [Glasgow]. Three verses.
   Second, "Sausage in the pan"; third, "Ghostie in the house."
Graham, *Press and Journal* (December 7, 1959), 6 [Aberdeen]. Addi-
   tional verses beginning "Sausage in the pan," "Baby on the floor" and
   "Milk in the jug."
Bluebells (1961), n.p. [Ayrshire]. Additional verses beginning "Sausages
   in the pan," "Baby on the floor," "Robbers in the house."
Ritchie (1965), 133 [Edinburgh]. Additional verses beginning "Sausage
   in the pan," "Paper on the floor," "Baby in the pram," "Burglars in
   the house."

(285)   Joe, Joe, broke his toe
           Riding on a buffalo.
           When he came back, he broke his back,
           Riding on a jumping jack.

Usually a taunt.

"Stella, Stella," *Fargo Forum* (June 23, 1940), 13 [North Dakota].

(286)   John and Mary,
           Up in a tree,
           K-I-S-S-I-N-G.
           First comes love,

Then comes marriage,
Here comes Mary
With a baby carriage.

Usually an autograph album rhyme.

Ainsworth, *WF*, 20 (1961), 180 [Maine].
Abrahams, *SFQ*, 27 (1963), 200 [Texas]. Two variants.
Buckley, *KFQ*, 11 (1966), 101 [Indiana]. "Mary and Jack." Listed.

(287)   Johnnie gave me apples,
          Johnnie gave me pears.
          Johnnie gave me fifteen (fifty) cents.
          And kissed me on the stairs.

          I don't want your apples,
          etc.

          *This is found as part of many other rhymes
          performing many different functions. See "Nine
          o'clock is striking."*

Winifred Smith, *JAF*, 39 (1926), 84 [New York]. Begins "Twelve o'clock
     is striking."
Johnson, *JAF*, 42 (1929), 306. Begins with "Nine o'clock is striking"
     rhyme.
Douglas (1931), 38 [London]. Begins with "Nine o'clock is striking"
     rhyme.
Brewster, *SFQ*, 3 (1939), 174 = Botkin (1944), 792.
Britt and Balcom, *J Gen Psy*, 58 (1941), 298 [Maryland, District of Co-
     lumbia]. Begins "I don't want your apples."
Emrich and Korson (1947), 130.
Reck, *WF*, 8 (1949), 128 [Colorado].
Musick, *WVF*, 2, No. 3 (1952), 2 [West Virginia]. Ends "I'd rather wash
     the dishes,/I'd rather scrub the floor,/I'd rather kiss the iceman/
     Behind the kitchen door."
Browne, *WF*, 14 (1955), 17–18 [California]. Begins with "Nine o'clock
     is striking" rhyme.
Evans (1955), 18 [California] = Evans (1961), 40.
"Children's Rhymes," *WVF*, 8 (1958), 37.
Abrahams, *KFQ*, 8 (1963), 9–10 [Pennsylvania, 1959]. Appears as end-
     ing for "I am a funny Dutch girl" rhyme.
Abrahams, *SFQ*, 27 (1963), 200 [Texas]. Two variants: one begins "My
     boyfriend gave . . ."; the other with "Bluebells, cockleshells" rhyme.
Withers (1964), 98 [Iowa]. Begins "My mother is from England,/My

father is from France,/My boy friend came from the U.S.A.,/With a hole in the seat of his pants."
Buckley, *KFQ*, 11 (1966), 100 [Indiana].

(288)   Johnnie made a touchdown.
          Johnnie made a basketball.
          Johnnie made an OUT.

Evans (1955), 9 [California] = Evans (1961), 34.

          Johnny hops on one foot.
          See "Little Orphan Annie goes on one foot."

          Johnny, Johnny, went to France.
          See "Charlie Chaplin went to France."

(289)   Johnny, Johnny, what's the price of geese?
          Johnny, Johnny, fifty cents apiece.
          Johnny, Johnny, that's too dear.
          Johnny, Johnny, get out of here.

                   Usually a counting-out rhyme.

Thompson, *JAF*, 47 (1934), 385 [Pennsylvania, 1920].
Britt and Balcom, *J Gen Psy*, 58 (1941), 297 [Maryland, District of Columbia]. "John said to John."
Sandburg (1963), 123 [North Carolina].

(290)   Johnny Maloney
          Stick, stick, stony,
          High balla, o, Dalla,
          Johnny Maloney.

                        Usually a taunt. See "Annie cum banny."

Butler and Haley (1963), n.p.

(291)   Johnny on (over) the ocean
              (Down by the river, ocean),

Johnny on (over) the sea.
Johnny broke a milk bottle (bottle, dish,
    teacup, window, tea pot, bean pot),
And (he) blamed it on me.
I told Ma, Ma told Pa,
Johnny got a licking
And a ha, ha, ha.

See "Minny and a Minny."

Nulton, *JAF*, 61 (1948), 60 [North Carolina, 1935–1947; Tennessee, 1927]. "Down by the river."
Johnson, *JAF*, 42 (1929), 305 [Massachusetts].
Hyatt (1935), 647 [Illinois].
Davis (1949), 215 [Florida, 1938].
Ashton, *JAF*, 52 (1939), 122 [Iowa].
Brewster, *SFQ*, 3 (1939), 173, 178 (three variants) = Botkin (1944), 791, 795.
"Stella, Stella," *Fargo Forum* (June 23, 1940), 13 [North Dakota]. "Down by the ocean."
Hall, *Recreation* (March, 1941), 716 [Nebraska]. "Susie broke the milk bottle."
Rae and Robb, *Christian Science Monitor Magazine* (March 21, 1942), 8.
Speroni, *CFQ*, 1 (1942), 249 [California].
Mensing, *HFB*, 2 (1943), 49 [Indiana].
Sone (1943), 196 [Texas].
Eller, *North Carolina Education*, 10 (1944), 447 [North Carolina].
Maloney, *HFB*, 3 (1944), 24 [Idaho].
Mills (1944), 16 [Maryland].
Halpert, *JAF*, 58 (1945), 349 [New Hampshire].
Fife, *JAF*, 59 (1946), 321 [Ohio].
Grace Partridge Smith, *HF*, 5 (1946), 59 [Illinois] = Dorson (1964), 385.
Emrich and Korson (1947), 131.
Haufrecht (1947), 62.
Yoffie, *JAF*, 60 (1947), 49 [Missouri].
McCaskill, *NCF*, 1 (June, 1948), 10 [North Carolina].
Musick, *HF*, 7 (1948), 12–13 [West Virginia]. Two variants.
Withers (1948), 67. "Sally broke the milk bottle."
Ashby, *Christian Science Monitor Magazine* (April 9, 1949), 8.
Haines, *Daedalian*, 17 (1949), 27, 28. Three variants.
Harris, *Evening Bulletin* (May 30, 1949), 10 [Pennsylvania].
Reck, *WF*, 8 (1949), 178 [Colorado].
Musick and Randolph, *JAF*, 63 (1950), 430 [Missouri]. Two variants.
Dodson, *Recreation* (June, 1951), 173 [North Carolina]. "Over the mountains, over the sea."
Musick, *WVF*, 2, No. 3 (1952), 6 [West Virginia].

Randolph, *MF*, 3 (1953), 79 [Arkansas]. Three variants, one beginning
"Minnie Moocher and a ha ha ha."
Browne, *WF*, 14 (1955), 8 [California]. Four variants.
Evans (1955), 25 [California] = Evans (1961), 45.
Schiller, *NYFQ*, 12 (1956), 202 [New York]. "Down by the seashore."
Whitney, *GMW*, 9 (1956), 6 [Vermont].
Calitri, *Parents* (April, 1957), 86.
"Children's Rhymes," *WVF*, 8 (1958), 38.
Abrahams, *KFQ*, 8 (1963), 13 [Pennsylvania, 1959]. Three variants, one
ends with "Policeman, policeman, don't catch me."
Leventhal and Cray, *WF*, 22 (1963), 235 [California, 1959].
Ainsworth, *WF*, 20 (1961), 180 [Maine], 182 [North Carolina], 184
[Georgia, "Down by the Ocean"], 185 [Alabama], 186 [Michigan],
190 [Wisconsin], 192 [Colorado], 194 [New Mexico], 196 [Utah].
Sackett (1961), 224 [Kansas].
Worstell (1961), 39. "Bobby went down to the ocean."
Heimbuecher, *KFQ*, 7, No. 4 (1962), 6 [Pennsylvania].
Abrahams, *SFQ*, 27 (1963), 200 [Texas]. Two variants.
Butler and Haley (1963), n.p. Two variants, one begins "I told Ma."
Sandburg (1963), 14 [Maryland, District of Columbia].
Ritchie (1965), 136 [Edinburgh]. "Over the mountain/Over the sea."
White, *Louisiana Miscellany*, 2, No. 2 (April, 1965), 115.
Buckley, *KFQ*, 11 (1966), 101, 103 [Indiana]. Listed.
Warner, *Yankee*, 30, No. 1 (January, 1966), 80.

Johnny Red, went upstairs.
　　See "Teddy Bear, Teddy Bear, turn around."

John said to John.
　　See "Johnny, Johnny, what's the price of geese?"

Jump, jump, jump,
The bells are ringing.
　　See "Vote, vote, vote."

(292)　　Jump over the sea.
　　　　Jump under the sea.
　　　　Jump in the sea and down.
　　　　Jump over the sea.

Abrahams, *SFQ*, 27 (1963), 206–207 [Texas].

(293)   Kaiser Bill* went up the hill
         To see if the war was over;
         General French got out of his trench
         And kicked him into Dover.
         He say if the bone man come
         Stick your bayonet up his bum.

Opie (1959), 98 [Wiltshire].

(294)   Ke clop, ke clop, ke clip, ke clop
         A hundred times before we stop:
         And if we trip (as trip we may),
         We'll try again some other day.
         1-2-3-4, *etc.*

Butler and Haley (1963), n.p.

(295)   Keep the kettle boiling
         One, two, three, *etc.* (Be on time).

                        Some versions are related to the nursery
                        rhyme "Polly put the kettle on" (Opie,
                        DICTIONARY, *353).*

Douglas (1916), 53 [London]. Begins "Evie, Ivy, over."
Johnson, *JAF*, 42 (1929), 306 [Massachusetts]. Two variants.
Mills (1944), 16 [Maryland].
Utley (1946), 63. Game called "Keep the Pot-a-boiling" mentioned.
Withers (North) (1947), 83 [California; author reports that the original,
    ". . . kettle bilem," was changed for publication] = Withers (1964),
    97.
Browne, *WF*, 14 (1955), 10 [California]. Two variants.

Evans (1955), 6 [California, two variants] = Evans (1961), 32.

Abrahams, *KFQ*, 8 (1963), 9 [Pennsylvania, 1959]. Three variants: "Kittie cat a bawling"; "Tea kettle a boiling"; "Kitty kettle aboiler." Worstell (1961), 6.

Ainsworth, *WF*, 20 (1961), 181 [Maine], 196 and 197 [Utah].

Abrahams, *SFQ*, 27 (1963), 200 [Texas]. Two variants, one "Polly put the kettle on."

Student oral collection (1964) [Texas]. "Polly put the kettle on,/And (Mary) don't be late."

Ritchie (1965), 114 [Edinburgh]. "Keep the pot boiling for Mrs. Coleman's claes!/Keep the kettle boiling for Mrs. Adams' tea!"

Hawthorne, *KFQ*, 11 (1966), 122 [Delaware]. "Polly put her kettle on . . ."

Keep the pot boiling.
See "Keep the kettle boiling."

(296)   **K**ings and Queens
        And partner's two
        All dressed up in Royal blue:
        One, two,
        How do you do?
        I do very well
        With a house to masel':
        A door and a bell
        And a coconut shell:
        One, two, three, *etc.*

                See also "I'm a little Dutch girl."

Ritchie (1965), 134 [Edinburgh]. Two variants.

(297)   **K**itsy Katsy had a canoe,
        It was yellow, black and blue,
        Open the gates and let it through,
        Dance Kitsy Katsy.

                *Originally "Katie Beardie had a
                coo," an entertainment rhyme.*

Bluebells (1961), n.p. [Ayrshire].

Kittie cat a bawlin.
See "Keep the kettle boiling."

Kitty kittle a boiler.
See "Keep the kettle boiling."

(298)   Knife and fork!
         Bottle and cork!
         That's the way to
         Spell New York!
                Usually a spelling riddle.

Haufrecht (1947), 63.

(299)   Knife and fork
         Lay the cloth,
         Bring me a leg of pork,
         Don't forget the salt, mustard, vinegar, pepper!
                See "Salt, vinegar" for the last line.

Gomme, 2 (1898), 204 [England].
Gillington, *Old Hampshire* (1909), n.p. [Hampshire]. "Lay the cloth,/
    Knife and fork."
Douglas (1916), 57 [London]. Begins "Lay the cloth," ends "If it's lean,
    bring it in,/If it's fat, take it back,/Tell the old woman I don't want
    that."
Opie (1947), 23. Begins "Lay the cloth."
Holbrook (1957), 58 [England].

(300)   Ladies and Gentlemen,
         Children, too.
         There's a little white girl

Going looking for you.
Hands up, torch-a-torch.
Two years old, going on three.
Wear my dresses upon my knee.
Sister has a boyfriend,
Comes every night,
—Walks in the parlor
And turns out the lights.
Peep through the keyhole,
What did I see?
"Johnny, Johnny, Johnny,
Put your arms around me."

> See also *"My sister's got a boyfriend"*
> *for this ending.*

Abrahams, *KFQ*, 8 (1963), 14–15 [Pennsylvania, 1959].

(301) Ladies and gentlemen,
To tell you the facts,
I lost my britches
On the railroad tracks.
They flew so high
Into the sky
They didn't come back
Till the Fourth of July.

> *Cf. "My mother gave me fifty cents."*

Abrahams, *SFQ*, 27 (1963), 207 [Texas].

Ladybird, Ladybird.
> See *"Lady bug, lady bug, fly away home"* and
> *"Teddy Bear, Teddy Bear, turn around."*

(302) Lady bug, lady bug, fly away home;
Your house is on fire, your children will burn.

> *See Opie,* DICTIONARY, *263–264 ("Ladybird").*

Haufrecht (1947), 62.

Ladybug, Ladybug, turn around.
See "Teddy Bear, Teddy Bear, turn around."

(303)   A Lady in the boat
         With a red petticoat
         And her name is—MISS!

                 Resembles a riddle whose referent
                 is "the clitoris."

Britt and Balcom, *J Gen Psy*, 58 (1941), 300 [Maryland, District of Co-
lumbia].
Butler and Haley (1963), n.p.

(304)   Lady in the tight skirt
         Can't do this:
         Lady in the tight skirt
         Can't do this.
         etc.

Ritchie (1965), 141 [Edinburgh].

Lady, Lady.
   See "Teddy Bear, Teddy Bear, turn around,"
   and "Grace, Grace."

(305)   Lady, lady, at the gate
         Eating cherries from a plate.
         How many cherries did she eat?
         1, 2, 3, 4, 5, *etc.*

                 Usually a counting-out rhyme: "One, two, three,
                 four,/Mary at the cottage door." See Opie, Dic-
                 tionary, 334.

La Salle (1929), 56.
Fahey, *Journal of Health and Physical Education*, 11 (1940), 421
   [Kansas].
Gibbs, *NYFQ*, 14 (1958), 313. Begins "One, two, three, four/Johnnie's
   at the cottage door"; cherries are eaten "by the peck."
Bluebells (1961), n.p. [Ayrshire].
Abrahams, *SFQ*, 27 (1963), 207 [Texas].

(306)   **L**ady, lady, drop your handkerchief (baby, purse) ;
Lady, lady, pick it up.

> *Cf. the ring game "Drop your handkerchief." See
> "Itiskit, Itaskit" and "Teddy Bear, Teddy Bear,
> turn around."*

Gomme, 2 (1898), 204.
Maclagan, *Folk-Lore*, 17 (1906), 216 [Argyllshire].
Gillington, *Old Hampshire* (1909), n.p. [Hampshire].
Douglas (1916), 66 [London].
Bluebells (1961), n.p. [Ayrshire].
Ritchie (1965), 134 [Edinburgh].
Those Dusty Bluebells (1965), 11 [Ayrshire]. Ends "Lady, lady, spell
your name . . ."

> **L**ady, lady on the sea-shore.
> *See "Rich man, poor man."*

> **L**ady Moon, Lady Moon.
> *See "Teddy Bear, Teddy Bear, turn around."*

> **L**ady on your one foot.
> *See "Little Orphan Annie goes on one foot."*

(307)   **L**amashayda hi-a-lee-oh
Lamashayda, lee-a-low.
See the farmer swing
On the apron string.
Do, re, mi.
Fa, sol, la.
Do re, do ti, do re.

Abrahams oral collection (1962) [Nevis, B.W.I.].

(308)   **L**assie* come home
Lassie come home
Lassie come H-O-M-E.

Opie (1959), 114 [England].

(309)   Last night and the night before
         Twenty-four robbers came knocking at my door.
         I got up and let them in.
         They knocked me on the head with a rolling pin.
         And this is what they said to me:

> *Followed by a number of other rhymes. Opie*
> *(1959, p. 23) discusses the history of the rhyme.*

Thompson, *JAF*, 47 (1934), 386 [Pennsylvania, 1929].
Brewster, *SFQ*, 3 (1939), 176. With "Teddy Bear, Teddy Bear, turn
     around" rhyme.
Rae and Robb, *Christian Science Monitor Magazine* (March 21, 1942),
     9. Ends "Some went East, Some went West, *etc.*"
Speroni, *CFQ*, 1 (1942), 248 [California]. With "Teddy Bear, Teddy
     Bear, turn around" rhyme.
Sone (1943), 199 [Texas]. With "Spanish dancers" rhyme.
Maloney, *HFB*, 3 (1944), 24 [Idaho].
Halpert, *JAF*, 58 (1945), 351 [New Hampshire]. With "Peel an orange"
     and "Teddy Bear, Teddy Bear, turn around" rhymes.
Botkin (1947), 906 [Connecticut].
Emrich and Korson (1947), 133.
Haufrecht (1947), 63. Ends in "Buster, Buster" version of "Teddy Bear,
     Teddy Bear, turn around" rhyme.
Haines, *Daedalian*, 17 (1949), 25 [Texas, District of Columbia, Arizona].
     With "Teddy Bear, Teddy Bear, turn around" and "Spanish dancers"
     rhymes.
Reck, *WF*, 8 (1949), 130 [Colorado].
Brewster (1952), 171 [North Carolina]. Two variants, one with "Teddy
     Bear, Teddy Bear, turn around" and "Lady Moon" rhymes.
Browne, *WF*, 14 (1955), 14–15 [California]. Three variants; one with
     "Spanish dancers" rhyme, one with "Teddy Bear, Teddy Bear, turn
     around" rhyme.
Evans (1955), 23 [California] = Evans (1961), 43.
Seeger, Folkways 7029 (1955) [Illinois].
Pope, *WF*, 15 (1956), 47 [Texas]. With "Spanish dancers" rhyme.
Stone, *Home and Highway* (March, 1958), 24.
Abrahams, *KFQ*, 8 (1963), 14 [Pennsylvania, 1959].
Leventhal and Cray, *WF*, 22 (1963), 232–233 [California, 1959]. Three
     variants, all begin "Not last night" and end with "Spanish dancers"
     rhyme.
Opie (1959), 23 [Portsmouth, Dundee, Maryland]. Four variants, two
     begin "Not last night."
Ainsworth, *WF*, 20 (1961), 182 [North Carolina, with "Teddy Bear,
     Teddy Bear, turn around" rhyme], 184 [Georgia, with "Spanish
     dancers" rhyme], 186 [Alabama], 193 [New Mexico, with "Teddy

Bear, Teddy Bear, turn around" rhyme], 193 [Colorado, with "Span-
ish dancers" rhyme].
Abrahams, *SFQ*, 27 (1963), 200 [Texas]. Nine variants; six with
"Spanish dancers" rhyme, one with "Policeman, policeman, do your
duty" rhyme.
Butler and Haley (1963), n.p. With "Teddy Bear, Teddy Bear, turn
around" rhyme.
Buckley, *KFQ*, 11 (1966), 103 [Indiana]. Listed.
Hawthorne, *KFQ*, 11 1966), 117, 121 [Delaware]. Three variants;
two "robins," one ends "They sang and they sang so sweet,/I let them
in so they could eat" (cf. "Down by the river").
Warner, *Yankee*, 30, No. 1 (January, 1966), 80. Begins "Not last night,"
ends with "Spanish dancers" rhyme.

> **L**ay the cloth
> Knife and fork.
> *See "Knife and fork."*

> **L**azy Daisy sat on a pin.
> *See "Charlie Chaplin sat on a pin."*

(310)   **L**eave the rope,
           Stop the rope,
           Please take end.

Goddard, *Word Lore*, 2 (1927), 128 [England].

> **L**ight sky, dark sky.
> *See "Ice cream soda."*

(311)   **L**ight the fire, blacksmith, show a pretty light,
           In comes (Nellie) dressed in white,
           Pretty shoes and stocking, pretty curly hair,
           Pretty beads around her neck, but no chemise to wear.

Douglas (1916), 62 [London].

> **L**incoln, Lincoln.
> *See "Hitler, Hitler."*

(312)   Little baby blue
         Sitting on the table
         Fooling with HOT PEPPERS.

Abrahams, *SFQ*, 27 (1963), 207 [Texas].

(313)   Little Lulu*
         Dressed in bluelu,
         Down doing the hula hula.

Abrahams, *SFQ*, 27 (1963), 207 [Texas].

(314)   Little Mary Anne who lives upstairs
         With high legged boots and a feather in her hat—
         That's the way she meets her chap—

                              Incomplete.

Douglas (1916), 94 [London].

(315)   Little Miss Pinky, dressed in blue,
         Died last night at half-past two.
         Before she died she told me this,
         "Let the jump rope miss like this."

                   *See "Miss, miss." Related to "I am a little
                   Dutch girl."*

Brewster, *SFQ*, 3 (1939), 176 (begins "Had a little girl") = Botkin
    (1944), 794.
Musick, *HF*, 7 (1948), 9 [West Virginia].
Nulton, *JAF*, 61 (1948), 63 [North Carolina].
Withers (1948), 68. Begins "There was a little girl," ends "Did she go
    up?/Did she go down?"
Evans (1955), 22 [California] = Evans (1961), 41.
Whitney, *GMW*, 9 (1956), 6 [Vermont].
Leventhal and Cray, *WF*, 22 (1963), 237 [California, 1959].
Ainsworth, *WF*, 20 (1961), 193 [New Mexico].
Abrahams, *SFQ*, 27 (1963), 200 [Texas].
Butler and Haley (1963), n.p. = Butler, *TFSB*, 31 (1965), 5.
Ritchie (1965), 135 [Edinburgh]. "My little dolly," ends "I put her in
    the coffin/She fell through the bottom . . ."
Those Dusty Bluebells (1965), 5 [Ayrshire]. "Oor wee Sue," ends "They
    put her in a coffin/She fell through the bottom . . ."

Buckley, *KFQ*, 11 (1966), 103 [Indiana]. Two variants, one "Had a little girl . . ." Listed.

Hawthorne, *KFQ*, 11 (1966), 125 [Delaware].

(316)   Little Miss Pinky (or any other color the
            jumper is wearing)
        Jumps rope like a top.
        Oops, oops, she missed,
        Just like that.

Ainsworth, *WF*, 20 (1961), 187 [Michigan].

(317)   Little Orphan Annie* (Teddy Bear) goes
            one foot, one foot.
        Little Orphan Annie goes two feet, two feet.
        ("Three feet," "four feet," "O-U-T")

                    *Cf. "Little White Rabbit" and "Donald
                    Duck is a one-legged . . . duck."*

Britt and Balcom, *J Gen Psy*, 58 (1941), 301 [Maryland, District of Columbia].

Browne, *WF*, 14 (1955), 12–13 [California]. Two variants.

Evans (1955), 9 [California] = Evans (1961), 33.

"Children's Rhymes," *WVF*, 8 (1958), 36 [West Virginia].

Leventhal and Cray, *WF*, 22 (1963), 234 [California, 1959]. Three variants, one "Sailor Boy."

Ainsworth, *WF*, 20 (1961), 197 [Utah].

Abrahams, *SFQ*, 27 (1963), 200 [Texas].

Withers (1964), 98 [New York].

Buckley, *KFQ*, 11 (1966), 103 [Indiana]. Listed.

(318)   Little Orphan Annie*
        Sitting in the sun,
        Had a piece of bologny
        And wouldn't give me none.
        Take a bite, take a bite,
        It's good for your appetite.

                See "Little Sally Water."

Withers (1948), 66.

Little Orphan Annie* swallowed a pin.
See "Charlie Chaplin sat on a pin."

(319)   Little Sally Water
Sitting in a saucer.
Rise, Sally, rise.
Wipe off your eyes.
Put your hand on your hip
Don't let your backbone slip.
etc.
                    Usually a singing game.

Douglas (1916), 89–90 [London]. Two variants, one "Little Sally Sanders, sitting on the sand . . ."
Withers (1948), 66.
Abrahams, *KFQ*, 8 (1963), 12 [Pennsylvania, 1959]. Two variants, both "Little Sally Ann."

Little Spanish dancer.
See "Spanish dancers."

Little teddy bear jumps on one foot.
See "Little Orphan Annie goes one foot."

(320)   Little white rabbit, hop on one foot, one foot;
Little white rabbit, hop on two feet, two feet;
Little white rabbit, hop on three feet, three feet;
Little white rabbit, hop on no feet, no feet.

                    Cf. "Little Orphan Annie goes one foot" and "Donald Duck is a one-legged . . . duck."

Pope, *WF*, 15 (1956), 46 [Texas].

London, Liverpool, Weekly Post.
See "Manchester Guardian."

(321)   Look upon the mantle-piece,
There you'll find a ball of grease,

> Shining like a threepenny-piece—
> Out goes she!

Douglas (1916), 56 [London].

> A Lord, a laird.
> *See "Rich man, poor man."*

(322)   Mabel, Mabel,
        Set the table,
        Don't forget the Red Hot Pepper!

See also "Pepper, salt" and "Red Hot Pepper"

Douglas (1916), 91 [London].
Winifred Smith, *JAF*, 39 (1926), 84 [New York].
Thompson, *JAF*, 47 (1934), 384 [Pennsylvania].
Ireland, *Recreation* (February, 1937), 564 [Pennsylvania].
Brewster, *SFQ*, 3 (1939), 175 = Botkin (1944), 792.
Mills, *Jack and Jill*, 2 (January, 1940), 18.
Britt and Balcom, *J Gen Psy*, 58 (1941), 295 [Maryland, District of Columbia].
Hall, *Recreation* (March, 1941), 715 [Nebraska].
Speroni, *CFQ*, 1 (1942), 249 [California].
Sone (1943), 198 [Texas].
Maloney, *HFB*, 3 (1944), 24 [Idaho]. Ends "Salt, vinegar, mustard, pepper."
Mills (1944), 15 [Maryland].
Emrich and Korson (1947), 134.
Haufrecht (1947), 62.
McCaskill, *NCF*, 1 (1948), 12 [North Carolina].
Musick, *HF*, 7 (1948), 9 [West Virginia].
Withers (1948), 60.
Ashby, *Christian Science Monitor Magazine* (April 9, 1949), 8. Two variants, one ends "Salt, pepper, vinegar, hot."
Haines, *Daedalian*, 17 (1949), 28 [Texas].

Reck, *WF*, 8 (1949), 129 [Colorado].
Roberts, *HF*, 8 (1949), 10 [Massachusetts].
Frankel (1952), 62.
Musick, *WVF*, 2, No. 3 (1952), 7 [West Virginia].
Wood (1952), 99. Second line: "Just as fast as you are able."
Randolph, *MF*, 3 (1953), 79 [Arkansas]. Two variants.
Browne, *WF*, 14 (1955), 9–10 [California]. Four variants.
Evans (1955), 21 [California] = Evans (1961), 42.
Seeger, Folkways 7029 (1955) [Illinois].
Bley (1957), 94.
"Children's Rhymes," *WVF*, 8 (1958), 39 [West Virginia].
Stone, *Home and Highway* (March, 1958), 22.
Abrahams, *KFQ*, 8 (1963), 8 [Pennsylvania, 1959].
Leventhal and Cray, *WF*, 22 (1963), 236 [California, 1959]. Two variants.
Sutton-Smith (1959), 76 [New Zealand]. Ends with "Salt, vinegar, mustard, pepper."
Ainsworth, *WF*, 20 (1961), 181 [Maine], 186, 189, and 191 [Wisconsin], 195 [Utah].
Worstell (1961), 23.
Gordon, *WVF*, 12 (1962), 52.
Heimbuecher, *KFQ*, 7, No. 4 (1962), 8 [Pennsylvania].
Abrahams, *SFQ*, 27 (1963), 200 [Texas]. Three variants.
Butler and Haley (1963), n.p.
Buckley, *KFQ*, 11 (1966), 105 [Indiana].
Fowke, *Hoot* (September, 1966), 41 [Canada].
Hawthorne, *KFQ*, 11 (1966), 115, 125 [Delaware].

(323)   Mabel, Mabel, strong and able,
          Get your elbows off the table.
          We've told you once, we've told you twice,
          We'll never tell you more than thrice.

                    Usually a homiletic rhyme.

Abrahams, *SFQ*, 27 (1963), 207 [Texas].

(324)   Madame Morale, she went to the well.
          She never forgets her soap or towel.
          She washes her hands; she dries and dries.
          She combs her hair.

She jumps up high and touches the sky.
And twirls around until she drops.

Cf. "Mademoiselle/Went to the well."

Sutton-Smith, *WF*, 12 (1955), 20 [New Zealand].
Sutton-Smith (1959), 82 [New Zealand].

(325)   Mademoiselle from Armetieres, parley vous,
        She hadn't been kissed for forty years, parley vous.
        The Prince of Wales was put in jail
        For riding a horse without a tail,
        Inky pinky parley vous.

From the World War I soldier's song.

Opie (1959), 92 [England].
Ritchie (1964), 26 [Edinburgh].

(326)   Mademoiselle
        Went to the well,
        Combed her hair
        And brushed it well,
        Then picked up her basket and vanished!

Cf. "Madame Morale."

Daiken (1949), 64 [Great Britain].

Maggie* and Jiggs.*
See "Blondie and Dagwood."

(327)   Maggie,* Maggie, where is Jiggs*?
        Down in the cellar eating pigs.
        How many pigs did he eat?
        1, 2, 3, *etc.*

Heimbuecher, *KFQ*, 7, No. 4 (1962), 6 [Pennsylvania].

Mama doll, mama doll.
See "Teddy Bear, Teddy Bear, turn around."

Mama's got a new-born baby.
See "Fudge, fudge."

Mama, mama, had a baby.
See "Fudge, fudge."

Mama, mama, I am sick.
See "Mother, mother, I am ill."

Mama, mama, may I go.
See "Mother, mother, may I go."

Mama's little dumpling.
See "Ice cream soda."

(328)   Manchester Guardian, Evening News,
             I sell Evening News.

Opie (1959), 5. Five variants from as early as the 1890's; "South Wales
   Evening Post," "Wellington Journal," "London, Liverpool, Weekly
   Post," "Manchester, Bolton Evening News." Used in Great Britain
   with name of any local newspaper. Opie refers to the April 23 and 28,
   1955, issues of the *Manchester Guardian.*

(329)   Marco Polo off he ran
             To the court of Kubla Khan
             In the city of Cathay.

Those Dusty Bluebells (1965), 10 [Ayrshire].

             Marco Polo went to France.
             See "Charlie Chaplin went to France."

(330)   Mare-zlett oats
             Dozeleetoats
             Dozeleetivytoo.

                   Usually a word puzzle.

Haufrecht (1947), 63.

Marge drank some milk.
See "Sally drinks lemonade."

Margie ate some pickles (marmalade).
See "Sally drinks lemonade."

Margie drank the marbleade.
See "Sally drinks lemonade."

(331)   Marilyn Monroe*
Fell in the snow:
Her skirts blew up
And the boys cried "oh!"

Ritchie (1964), 46 [Edinburgh].

Mary ate some marmalade.
See "Sally drinks lemonade."

(332)   Mary had bread and jam,
Marmalade and treacle,
A bit for me and a bit for you,
And a bit for all the people!

Douglas (1916), 62 [London].

(333)   Mary Kelly had a lamb
Peever, peever.
Sister Kelly stole that lamb
Peever peever O.

L stands for London
T stands for town
H stands for Harry
A and B stands for Brown.

Harry Brown of London Town
Said he'd marry me.
And isn't it a blessing
To sit on Harry's knee?

Monday is my washing day
Tuesday I am done
Wednesday is my ironing day
Thursday I am done.

Friday is my shopping day
Saturday I am done
Sunday is my writing day
And Harry never come.

Singing:
One two three a-leerie
I spy Wallace Beery*
Sitting on his bumbeleerie
Kissing Shirley Temple.*

Last stanza usually a ball-bouncing rhyme.

Ritchie (1964), 36–37 [Edinburgh].

(334)   Mary Mack, dressed in black,
          Silver buttons all down her back.

          This riddle for "coffin" (Archer Taylor, *English
          Riddles from Oral Tradition*, 234 [Berkeley,
          1951]) is found as a beginning for other rhymes.

Winifred Smith, *JAF*, 39 (1926), 83.
Yoffie, *JAF*, 60 (1947), 27, 40 [Missouri]. Two variants.
Daiken (1949), 65 [Great Britain]. Begins "Hie, Ho! Skippety toe/Turn
   the ship and away we go/Judy and Jack, dressed in black . . ."
Randolph, *MF*, 3 (1953), 81 [Arkansas]. Two variants: one with "I
   asked my Mama for fifty cents" rhyme; the other ending with "Eeny-
   moe, tipsy toe,/Give her a kick and away she'll go!"
Evans (1955), 19. With "Bluebells, cockleshells" rhyme.
Abrahams, *KFQ*, 8 (1963), 6 [Pennsylvania]. Ends with "I asked my
   mother for fifteen cents" rhyme.
Abrahams, *SFQ*, 27 (1963), 200 [Texas]. With "I asked my mother for
   fifty cents" rhyme.

(335)   Mary, Mary, quite contrary
          How does your garden grow?

With silver bells and cockleshells
And the rest haven't come up yet.

See Opie, DICTIONARY, *301, for a history of this common nursery rhyme.*

Hall, *Recreation* (March, 1941), 716 [Nebraska].
Abrahams, *SFQ,* 27 (1963), 207 [Texas].

(336)   Mary, Mary, with a curl
          Will you jump as my best girl?
          Slow at first, now that's the way,
          On we go to the break of day.

Fahey, *Journal of Health and Physical Education,* 11 (1940), 422 [Kansas].

(337)   Ma said that this won't do,
          To play with the boys at half-past two—
                              Incomplete.

Douglas (1916), 94 [London].

(338)   Matthew, Mark, Luke and John,
          Hud the cuddie till I get on.
          Hud him fast, hud him steady—
          Hud him like a Finnan hoddie.

          Matthew, Mark, Luke and John,
          Hud the cuddie: I'm on,
          I'm on, the cuddie gone—
          Matthew, Mark, Luke and John.

                    Parody of a popular prayer.

Ritchie (1965), 135 [Edinburgh].

          May I come in, sir?
          See "Hello, sir, hello, sir."

(339)   Mickey Mouse* and Minnie Mouse*
         Went down to the power house.
         To see how high the water would flow.
         One foot, two feet, three feet, *etc.*

Abrahams, *SFQ*, 27 (1963), 207 [Texas].

(340)   Mickey Mouse*
         Bought a house
         Couldn't pay the rent
         And got kicked out.

Ainsworth, *WF*, 20 (1961), 181 [Maine].

(341)   Mickey Mouse* built a house
         Under an apple tree,
         Mickey Mouse called house
         Number twenty-three.

Opie (1959), 111 [London].

         Milk shake, milk shake.
         See "Ice cream soda."

(342)   Mima, Mima,
         Black Jemima,
         Lost a child
         And couldn't find her.
         Brother found her in the dell,
         Now she treats her very well.

                   *Echoes of "Peter, Peter, pumpkin eater." See
                   Opie,* DICTIONARY, *346–347.*

Ainsworth, *WF*, 20 (1961), 181 [Maine].

(343)   A Mimsies, a clapsies
         I whirl my hand, two bapsies.
         My right hand, my left hand.

Highsakey, lowsakey,
Houch my knee,
Houch my heel,
Houch my toe,
And under we go.

Harris, *Evening Bulletin* (May 30, 1949), 10 [Pennsylvania].

Minnie, Minnie, Ha Ha.
See "I had a little brother/ His name was Tim."

(344)   Minny and a Minny and a ha, ha, ha,
Kissed her fellow on a Broadway trolley car.
You tell Ma and I'll tell Pa.
Minny and a Minny and a ha, ha, ha!

Related to "Johnny on the ocean."

Mills and Bishop, *The New Yorker* (November 13, 1937), 34 [New York, 1934] = Botkin (1944), 800.
McDowell, *New York Times Magazine* (April 14, 1946), 8.
Emrich and Korson (1947), 134.
Haufrecht (1947), 62.
Musick and Randolph, *JAF*, 63 (1950), 430 [Missouri]. Begins "Minnie Moocher."
Abrahams, *SFQ*, 27 (1963), 200 [Texas].

Mississippi lived on shore.
See "Mrs. Sippy lives by the shore."

(345)   Mississippi
M-I-S-S
I-S-S-I
P-P-I

Ainsworth, *WF*, 20 (1961), 197 [Utah].
Hawthorne, *KFQ*, 11 (1966), 124 [Delaware].

(346)   Miss, miss, little miss, miss:
When she misses, she misses like this.

Brewster, *SFQ*, 3 (1939), 176 = Botkin (1944), 793.

Petersham (1945), n.p.

Emrich and Korson (1947), 132.

Haufrecht (1947), 63.

Withers (1948), 59.

Daiken (1949), 63 [Great Britain]. Begins "I know a woman,/And her name is miss."

Frankel (1952), 62.

Seeger, Folkways 7029 (1955) [Illinois].

Bley (1957), 94.

Ainsworth, *WF*, 20 (1961), 189 [Wisconsin].

Bluebells (1961), n.p. [Ayrshire]. Two variants: one begins "January, February, . . ./There was an old lady whose name was Miss"; the other begins "I had a doll and her name was Sis."

Worstell (1961), 24.

Abrahams, *SFQ*, 27 (1963), 200 [Texas].

Ritchie (1965), 115, 116, 131 [Edinburgh]. One begins "I had a little dolly/And its name was Bliss," one "Sis," one beginning "January, February, . . ."

Those Dusty Bluebells (1965), 5 [Ayrshire]. Begins "January, February, . . ./There was an old woman whose name was Sis."

Buckley, *KFQ*, 11 (1966), 105 [Indiana]. Listed.

<blockquote>
Momma, Momma, May I go.
See "Mother, Mother, may I go."
</blockquote>

(347)   Monday night, Band of Hope,
         Tuesday night, pull the rope,
         Wednesday, Pimlico,
         And out comes (Ethel Rowe).

Douglas (1916), 61 [London].

(348)   Monday night—the gramophone.
         Tuesday night we're all alone.
         Wednesday night I call the roll,
         Maureen, O Maureen,
         etc.

Daiken (1949), 63 [Great Britain].

Mother Brown went to town.
See "I went downtown/To see Mrs. Brown."

Mother's in the kitchen.
See "As I was in the kitchen."

(349)   Mother made a seedy cake,
         Give us all the bellyache—

                  See "Sally drinks lemonade."

Douglas (1916), 91 [London].

(350)   Mother, mother, can you tell
         What makes poor .... well?
         She is sick and she might die,
         And that would make poor .... cry.

                  See Newell, p. 99, for a history of this
                  rhyme.

Heck, *JAF*, 40 (1927), 19, 41. Two variants.
Maloney, *HFB*, 3 (1944), 24 [Idaho].
Roberts, *HF*, 8 (1949), 10 [Maine].
Whitney, *GMW*, 9 (1956), 6 [Vermont]. "Doctor, Doctor."

(351)   Mother, mother, have you heard?
         Papa's going to buy me a mocking bird.
         If that mocking bird don't sing,
         Papa's going to buy me a diamond ring.
         etc.

                  Usually a children's song or hand-clapping rhyme.

Nulton, *JAF*, 61 (1948), 54 [North Carolina, 1945].
Musick, *HF*, 7 (1948), 10 [West Virginia].
Abrahams, *SFQ*, 27 (1963), 200, 208 [Texas]. Three variants.

(352)   Mother, mother, I am able
         To stand on a chair and set the table;

Daughter, daughter don't forget,
Salt, vinegar, and red hot pepper.

See "Mabel, Mabel,/Set the table."

Fahey, *Journal of Health and Physical Education*, 11 (1940), 422 [Kansas].

(353)   Mother, mother, I am ill (sick).
Send for (call) the doctor from over hill (quick).
In comes the doctor, in comes the nurse,
In comes the lady with the alligator purse.
"Measles," says the doctor, "measles," says the nurse,
"Measles," says the lady with the alligator purse.
(or "I don't want the doctor," *etc.*,
"Out goes the doctor," *etc.*)

> *A common variation is "Doctor, doctor, will I die?/Yes, my darling, bye and bye" (see the English journal* NOTES & QUERIES, *3rd series, Vol. 6, 514). G. Legman here relates the "Lady with the alligator purse" to the good fairy, deus ex machina of Lucretia P. Haley's children's book,* THE PETERKIN PAPERS.

Bennett, *Children*, 12 (1927), 21. "Grandaughter."
Heck, *JAF*, 40 (1927), 41 [Ohio]. "Granny, granny."
Hudson (1928), 118 [Mississippi].
Johnson, *JAF*, 42 (1929), 305.
Thompson, *JAF*, 47 (1934), 386 [Pennsylvania, 1929].
Mills and Bishop, *The New Yorker* (November 13, 1937), 32 [New York, 1934] = Botkin (1944), 797.
Barbeau and Daviault, *JAF*, 53 (1940), 165–166. Translated into French.
Fahey, *Journal of Health and Physical Education*, 11 (1940), 422 [Kansas].
Britt and Balcom, *J Gen Psy*, 58 (1941), 296 [Maryland, District of Columbia] "Grandmother."
Speroni, *CFQ*, 1 (1942), 247 [California].
Sone (1943), 195 [Texas].
Eller, *North Carolina Education*, 10 (1944), 447 [North Carolina]. Ends "How many cars will follow me?"
Halpert, *CFQ*, 3 (1944), 154 [Alberta, Canada].
Maloney, *HFB*, 3 (1944), 24 [Idaho]. Two variants.
Petersham (1945), n.p. "Granny, Granny."
Botkin (1947), 907 [Connecticut].

Emrich and Korson (1947), 133.

Opie (1947), 22.

Withers (North) (1947), 84 [New York] = Withers (1964), 100.

Yoffie, *JAF*, 60 (1947), 49 [Missouri].

Davis (1949), 215 [Florida, 1948].

Haines, *Daedalian*, 17 (1949), 23, 24 [Texas]. Two variants.

Potter, "Skip Rope," *Standard Dictionary* (1949), 1016.

Reck, *WF*, 8 (1949), 128 [Colorado].

Musick and Randolph, *JAF*, 63 (1950), 430 [Missouri]. "Mama, mama, I am sick."

Time (May 29, 1950), 20 [Washington].

Musick, *WVF*, 2, No. 3 (1952), Spring, 2 [West Virginia].

Lloyd, A. L., *Lilliput* (September, 1952), 57. Ends "Penicillin, says the doctor . . ."

Randolph, *MF*, 3 (1953), 83 [Arkansas]. Four variants.

Browne, *WF*, 14 (1955), 15–16 [California]. Three variants.

Evans (1955), 3 [California, two variants] = Evans (1961), 26, 50.

Seeger, Folkways 7029 (1955) [Illinois].

Schiller, *NYFQ*, 12 (1956), 205 [New York]. Only the ending given, with "Shirley Temple walks like this," "I had a little brother/His name was Tim," and "Cinderella, dressed in yellow" rhymes.

Bley (1957), 95. With "I had a little brother/His name was Tim."

"Children's Rhymes," *WVF*, 8 (1958), 36, 37. Two variants, one begins with "I had a little brother/His name was Tim" rhyme.

Stone, *Home and Highway* (March, 1958), 22.

Sutton-Smith (1959), 81. Two variants, one begins "Granny, Granny."

Taylor, *WF*, 18 (1959), 316 [California]. With "Bluebells, cockleshells" rhyme.

Utley (1959), 126 [Lancashire]. Begins "Grandmother," ends "My coffin shall be black,/Six little angels at my back,/Two to watch and two to pray,/And two to carry my soul away."

Caplan, Folkways 3501 (1960) [Brooklyn].

Ainsworth, *WF*, 20 (1961), 192 [Colorado], 194 [New Mexico, two variants], 184 [Georgia, begins with "I had a little monkey dressed in red" rhyme].

Bluebells (1961), n.p. [Ayrshire]. Ends with formulaic verse "Up yon hill is too far,/You'll have to buy a motorcar./A motorcar is far too dear,/You'll have to buy a bottle of beer./A bottle of beer is far too rough,/You'll have to buy a bottle of snuff./Achoo! Achoo!" or "A pint of beer is far too strong,/You'll have to buy a treadle scone,/A treadle scone is far too tough,/You'll have to buy a box of snuff,/A box of snuff will make you sneeze,/You'll have to buy a pound of cheese./A pound of cheese costs a penny, twopence . . ."

Sackett (1961), 225 [Kansas].

Worstell (1961), 28.

Sandburg (1962), 110. With "Ice cream soda" rhyme.

Abrahams, *SFQ*, 27 (1963), 201 [Texas]. Seven variants.

Butler and Haley (1963), n.p.
Those Dusty Bluebells (1965), 15 [Ayrshire]. Same as in *Bluebells* reference above but shorter.
Buckley, *KFQ*, 11 (1966), 103 [Indiana]. Two variants listed.
Warner, *Yankee*, 30, No. 1 (January, 1966), 93.

(354)   Mother, Mother, may I go
          Down to the meadow to see my beau?
          No, my darling, you can't go
          Down to the meadow to see your beau.

          Father, Father may I go
          Down to the meadow to see my beau?
          Yes, my darling, you can go
          Down to the meadow to see your beau.

          Mother said I could not go
          Down to the meadow to see my beau.
          You tell your mother to hold her tongue.
          She had a beau when she was young.

Bennett, *Children*, 12 (1927), 21. "Mamma," ends with "I should worry, I should care" rhyme.
Britt and Balcom, *J Gen Psy*, 58 (1941), 295. "Mama, mama," ends with "I should worry, I should care" rhyme.
Rae and Robb, *Christian Science Monitor Magazine* (March 21, 1942), 8.
Emrich and Korson (1947), 131. With "I love coffee" rhyme.
Musick, *HF*, 7 (1948), 10 [West Virginia].
Withers (1948), 63. With "I love coffee" rhyme.
Evans (1961), 22. With "I love coffee" rhyme.

(355)   Mother, mother, mother, pin a rose on me.
          Two young fellows are after me.
          One is blind and the other can't see.
          Mother, mother, mother, pin a rose on me.

                                        Generally a taunt.

Withers (1948), 69.

(356)   Mother, Mother, what is that
          Hanging down that lady's back?

> Hush your mouth, you naughty thing;
> That's the lady's corset string!

Usually an entertainment rhyme.

Bennett, *Children*, 12 (1927), 21 = Britt and Balcom, *J Gen Psy*, 58 (1941), 293.
New York Times Magazine (April 28, 1946) [Pennsylvania].
Haufrecht (1947), 61. A bowdlerization; the object is on the "lady's head" and is "the lady's hat."

(357)   "Mother, mother, where's the key?"
"Go ask father."
"Father, father, where's the key?"
"Have you washed the dishes?" "Yes."
"Have you swept the floor?" "Yes."
"Turn the key in the lock and run out to play."

La Salle (1929), 71.

(358)   Mother sent me to the store.
She told me not to stay;
I fell in love with a blue-eyed boy
And I couldn't get away.
How many kisses did I receive?
Ten, twenty, *etc.*

Musick, *WVF*, 2, No. 3 (1952), 2 [West Virginia].

(359)   Mother sent me to the store
This is what she sent me for:
To get some coffee, tea and pepper.

See "Salt, vinegar, mustard, and pepper."

Seeger, Folkways 7029 (1955) [Illinois].
Evans (1961), 20 [California]. "My mother sent ..."
Student oral collection (1964) [Texas].

Mr. Brown's a very nice man.
See "Doctor Long is a very good man."

Mr. Brown went to town with his britches upside down.
See "I went downtown/To see Mrs. Brown."

(360)   Motor boat, motor boat,
         Go so slow.
         Motor boat, motor boat,
         Go so fast.
         Motor boat, motor boat,
         Step on the gas.

Abrahams, *SFQ*, 27 (1963), 208 [Texas].

Mrs. Brown lived by the shore.
See "Mrs. Sippy lives by the shore."

(361)   Mrs. Brown went to town
         Riding on a pony,
         When she came back she took off her hat
         And gave it to Mrs. Maloney.

                    Parody of "Yankee Doodle."

Douglas (1916), 62 [London].
Ritchie (1964), 13 [Edinburgh].

Mrs. Brown
Went up town.
See "I went downtown/To see Mrs. Brown."

(362)   Mrs. Day made a cake.
         The cake was soggy;
         She fed it to her doggy.
         The doggy ate the cake;
         He got the stomach-ache.
         How many days did he have it?
         1-2-3, *etc.*

Ashton, *JAF*, 52 (1939), 122 [Iowa].

Mrs. Mason.
See "Old Mother Mason."

(363)   Mrs. Red
         Went to bed.
         In the morning
         She was dead.

Ritchie (1965), 117 [Edinburgh].

(364)   Mrs. Sippy lives by the shore;
         She had children more and more;
         The oldest one was twenty-four.
         She shall marry;

              Often ends with "Rich man, poor man" rhyme.

Reynolds, *Christian Science Monitor* (July 11, 1941), 8. Two variants.
Speroni, *CFQ*, 1 (1942), 251 [California].
Halpert, *JAF*, 58 (1945), 350 [New Hampshire]. "Mississippi lives in a
   canal."
Botkin (1947), 907 [Connecticut].
Daiken (1949), 64 [Great Britain]. "Mrs. Brown," ends "she got married
   to the man next door."
Evans (1955), 24–25 [California].

(365)   Mummy, Daddy, tell me true,
         Who should I get married to?
         Paul, John, Ringo, George.*

              Cf. "Rich man, poor man."

Those Dusty Bluebells (1965), 6 [Ayrshire].

(366)   My big red ball
         Went over the wall.
         Hold my mum
         She skelpt (slapped) my bum.
         B-U-M

Ritchie (1965), 142 [Edinburgh].

My boyfriend's name is Sammy.
See "I am a funny Dutch girl."

(367)   My father has a horse to shoe.
          How many nails do you think will do?
          1, 2, 3, 4, *etc.*

               Generally a counting-out rhyme.

Botkin (1947), 906 [Connecticut].

(368)   My father is a butcher
          My mother cuts the meat,
          I'm a little hot dog
          Running down the street.
          How many hot dogs do I sell?
          One, two, three, four, *etc.*

Speroni, *CFQ*, 1 (1942), 249 [California].
Sone (1943), 197 [Texas].
Haines, *Daedalian*, 17 (1949), 27 [Texas].
Browne, *WF*, 14 (1955), 19 [California].
Evans (1955), 26 [California] = Evans (1961), 50.
Leventhal and Cray, *WF*, 22 (1963), 237 [California, 1959]. "Daddy's
     a butcher."
Sutton-Smith (1959), 79 [New Zealand]. Two variants.
Worstell (1961), 25. With "Bluebells, cockleshells" rhyme.
Abrahams, *SFQ*, 27 (1963), 201 [Texas]. "My father runs a grocery
     store."

(369)   My father went to the supermarket.

Buckley, *KFQ*, 11 (1966), 104 [Indiana]. Listed.

(370)   My girl's a corker.
          She's a New Yorker.
          I'd do most any thing
          To keep her in style:
          She's got a pair of feet
          Just like two plates of meat,
          That's where my money goes

Umpa umpa umpa papa
Umpa umpa umpa papa.
etc.

Usually a children's song; cf. "Who's got feet."

Ritchie (1965), 126 [Edinburgh].

My little dolly.
See "Little Miss Pinky, dressed in blue."

My little sister.
See "I had a little sister/Dressed in pink."

(371)   **My** love for you will never fail,
As long as a monkey has a tail,
And if that tail is cut in two,
That won't stop me loving you.

Usually an autograph album rhyme.

Student oral collection (1964) [Texas].

(372)   **My** man's a millionaire
Blue eyes and curly hair.
Works among the Eskimos
Having a game of dominoes.
My man's a millionaire!

Ritchie (1964), 33 [Edinburgh].

(373)   **My** mother and your mother were hanging out clothes.
My mother gave your mother a punch in the nose.
Did it hurt her?
Yes, no, yes, no, *etc.*

Usually a counting-out rhyme.

Mills and Bishop, *The New Yorker* (November 13, 1937), 32 [New York, 1935; Louisiana, 1936] = Botkin (1944), 797.
Britt and Balcom, *J Gen Psy*, 58 (1941), 298 [Maryland, District of Columbia].

Abrahams, *SFQ*, 27 (1963), 209 [Texas].
Hawthorne, *KFQ*, 11 (1966), 121 [Delaware].

(374)   My mother cried me up to go wi my father's dinner-o
           Champit tatties, beef and steak, three red berries and a
               hapnie cake.
           I came to the river and I couldnie get across.
           I paid ten shillings for an old blind horse:
           I jumped on its back and its bones went crack.
           We all played the fiddle the boat came back.
           The boat came back, we all jumped in.
           The boat capsized and we all fell in.

                              *"I came to the river" comes from a
                              minstrel song and is found in connec-
                              tion with many dance songs.*

Ritchie (1965), 126 [Edinburgh]. Three variants.

(375)   My mother's going to have a baby.
           It's going to be twins, triplets, boys or girls?

Abrahams, *SFQ*, 27 (1963), 209 [Texas].

           My mother is a butcher.
               See "My father is a butcher."

           My mother is from England.
               See "Johnny gave me apples."

(376)   My mother made a chocolate cake.
           How many eggs did she take?
           1, 2, 3, 4, *etc.*

Withers (1948), 70.
Seeger, Folkways 7029 (1955) [Illinois].

(377)   My mother said I never should
           Play with the gypsies in the wood.

They tugged my hair and broke my comb.
I'll tell my mother when I get home.

> *Found in many forms and in many uses, often as a
> counting-out rhyme.*

Ritchie (1965), 142 [Edinburgh]. Four variants.

(378)   My mother said
           That the rope must go
           Over my head.

Gomme, 2 (1898), 203 [England].
Holbrook (1957), 56 [England].

(379)   My mother sent me out a-fishing,
           Fishing cockles in the sea.
           My foot slipped and I tumbled in—
           Two little nigger boys laughed at me.

Douglas (1916), 72 [London].

           My mother sent me to the store.
           See "Mother sent me to the store."

(380)   My mother told me to bury him deep,
           But I didn't want to.
           I buried him deep.
           He stuck out his feet.
           The crazy man of China.

> *One verse of a recent comic version of the old
> courting-song "Old Shoes and Leggings."*

Abrahams, *SFQ*, 27 (1963), 209 [Texas].

           My mother uses salt.
           See "Salt, vinegar, mustard, and pepper."

(381)   My mother, your mother
           Live across the way (hall).

Two hundred sixty East Broadway.
Every night they have a fight
And this is what they say (call) :

> *Often followed by "Acca Bacca."*

Winifred Smith, *JAF*, 39 (1926), 84 [New York].
Johnson, *JAF*, 42 (1929), 305 [Massachusetts].
Rolland, *New Masses* (May 10, 1938), 109 = Botkin (1954), 567.
Brewster, *SFQ*, 3 (1939), 178 = Botkin (1944), 795.
Britt and Balcom, *J Gen Psy*, 58 (1941), 297. "Your mother, my mother."
Yoder, *Saturday Evening Post* (October 30, 1948), 114.
Harris, *Evening Bulletin* (May 30, 1949), 10 [Pennsylvania].
Reck, *WF*, 8 (1949), 127 [Colorado].
Schwartz, Folkways 7009 (1953) [New York].
Browne, *WF*, 14 (1955), 20 [California]. Two variants, both begin "Your
    mother, my mother."
Evans (1955), 7 [California] = Evans (1961), 31.
Seeger, Folkways 7029 (1955) [Illinois].
Schiller, *NYFQ*, 12 (1956), 206 [New York].
Ainsworth, *WF*, 20 (1961), 195 [Utah].
Worstell (1961), 22.
Heimbuecher, *KFQ*, 7, No. 4 (1962), 3 [Pennsylvania]. Two variants.
Abrahams, *SFQ*, 27 (1963), 201 [Texas]. Two variants.
Butler and Haley (1963), n.p.
Lomax (1964), 57. Ends with "Lady Moon" rhyme.
Buckley, *KFQ*, 11 (1966), 104 [Indiana].

(382)   My name is Alice, and my husband's name is Allen.
          And we come from Alabama with a carload of apples.

> *Continues with names starting with B, C,
> etc. Usually played as a ball-bouncing
> game.*

Worstell (1961), 40–41.
Student oral collection (1964) [Texas]. "My name is Mrs. Jones and this
    is Mr. Jones."

(383)   My name is Macnamara
          I'm the leader of the band
          My wife is Betty Grable,*
          She's the fairest in the land.
          Oh she can dance and she can sing,
          And she can show a leg,

The only thing she canna do,
She canna boil an egg.

Parody of the song "MacNamara's Band."

Opie (1959), 115 [Scotland].

(384)   My name is Santa Claus,
I bring you lots of toys,
For little girls and boys,
Whose name begins with A, B, C, *etc.*

Student oral collection (1964) [Texas].

(385)   My name is sweet (Jennie), my age is sixteen,
My father's a Father (farmer) and I am a Queen.
Got plenty of money to dress me in silk
But nobody loves me but (Gladys dear).

Douglas (1916), 72 [London].

(386)   My old man number one (two, *etc.*).
He plays nick knock on the sun (shoe, *etc.*).
Nick knack, pollwag, zinga-zore,
My old man will play no more.

Usually a children's song.

Withers (1948), 72–73.

(387)   My sister's got a boyfriend
Who comes every night.
They go into a corner
And turn out the light.
I peek through the keyhole
And this is what I hear:
"Johnny, Johnny,
Take your arms away."

A corruption of the popular song "I Won-

der *Why,*" ca. *1925. Cf.* "*Ladies and gentlemen,/Children, too.*"

Britt and Balcom, *J Gen Psy,* 58 (1941), 299 [Maryland, District of Columbia].

(388)   My teacher is *balmy*
         She wear a *taumy*
         She joined the *army*
         At the age of one, two, three, *etc.*

Ritchie (1964), 42 [Edinburgh].
Those Dusty Bluebells (1965), 11 [Ayrshire]. Ends "My teacher's crazy,/
She joined the navy,/When she was 1, 2, 3, . . ."

(389)   Nebuchadnezzar, King of the Jews,
         Sold his wife for a pair of shoes.
         When the shoes began to wear
         Nebuchadnezzar began to swear,
         When the swearing began to stop
         Nebuchadnezzar bought a shop.
         etc.

              Usually an entertainment rhyme.

Ritchie (1965), 135, 139 [Edinburgh]. Two variants, one "Archee-ball-
ball-ball-ball."

(390)   Nelly the elephant packed her trunk
         And said goodbye to the circus.
         Off she went with a trumpety-trump
         Trump, trump, trump.

Ritchie (1965), 142 [Edinburgh].

(391)   Never leave the rope empty
        Go to church on Ash Wednesday.

Goddard, *Word Lore*, 2 (1927), 128.

(392)   News time
        One cent
        Help your mother pay the rent.
        Your father's in jail
        For stealing a pail.
        News time
        One cent.
                Seems to come from a taunt.

Schiller, *NYFQ*, 12 (1956), 206 [New York].

(393)   Next year I will be in the
        First, Second, Third, Fourth, *etc.*
        My teacher is
        H-O-T.

Seeger, Folkways 7029 (1955) [Illinois].
Leventhal and Cray, *WF*, 22 (1963), 233 [California, 1959]. Three vari-
    ants: one begins "Hurry up, don't be late," the other two "Running to
    school."
Abrahams, *SFQ*, 27 (1963), 211 [Texas]. Begins "Running through
    school."
Hawthorne, *KFQ*, 11 (1966), 120 [Delaware].

        Night after night and the night before.
        See "Last night and the night before."

(394)   The Night was dark, the war was over,
        The battlefield lay soaked in blood;
        And there I spied a wounded soldier
        A lying dying as he said:
        God bless my home and dear old Scotland,
        God bless my wife and only child;
        God bless the men that fought for freedom,

A-holding up the Union Jack.
Quack, Quack.

Graham, *Press and Journal* (January 13, 1960), 6 [Aberdeen].

(395)   Nine o'clock is striking,
          Mother may I go out?
          All the boys are waiting
          For to take me out.
          One has an apple,
          One has a pear,
          etc.

> *See "Johnny gave me apples." The beginning of this rhyme stems from a group of rhymes, one of which begins the game "Old Mommy Witch," another of which ends "Don't go near the water."*

Douglas (1916), 69 [London]. "Eight o'clock," ends "Then he tears the leg of my drawers,/And that's the last of all."
Winifred Smith, *JAF*, 39 (1926), 84 [New York]. "Twelve o'clock."
Bennett, *Children*, 12 (1927), 21.
Johnson, *JAF*, 42 (1929), 306 [Massachusetts].
Davis (1949), 216 [Florida, 1938].
Britt and Balcom, *J Gen Psy*, 58 (1941), 299 [Maryland, District of Columbia].
"Jump-Rope Rhymes," *WF*, 23 (1964), 258 [California, 1944]. Begins "Tik-tok, tik-tok."
Walker, *NYFQ*, 2 (1946), 232 [New York].
Yoffie, *JAF*, 60 (1947), 33 [Missouri].
Browne, *WF*, 14 (1955), 17–18 [California].
"Children's Rhymes," *WVF*, 8 (1958), 37. "Twelve o'clock."

(396)   Nineteen hundred forty-two
          Truman* lost a shoe;
          Went to France,
          Lost his pants,
          Now he's in a zoo.

Musick, *WVF*, 2, No. 2 (1952), 2 [West Virginia].
"Children's Rhymes," *WVF*, 8 (1958), 37 [West Virginia].

(397)   North, South, East, West,

Buckley, *KFQ*, 11 (1966), 104 [Indiana]. Listed.

Not last night and the night before.
See "Last night and the night before."

(398)   Now you're married
And you must be good;
Make your husband
Chop the wood;
Count your children
One by one;
1, 2, 3, 4, *etc.*

Derived from the many similar autograph album rhymes.

Thompson, *JAF*, 47 (1934), 385 [Pennsylvania, 1929].
Nulton, *JAF*, 61 (1948), 62 [North Carolina, 1943–1946].
Sandburg (1963), 15 [District of Columbia].

Obadiah.
See "Anthy Maria."

(399)   Old Black Joe from Mexico,
Hands up, stick 'em up,
Don't forget to pick 'em up,
Old Black Joe.

Scott, *Singabout*, 3, No. 3 (Winter/Spring, 1959), 5 [Australia].

(400)   **O**ld Dan Tucker

Buckley, *KFQ*, 11 (1966), 101 [Indiana]. Listed.

(401)   **O**ld King Cole was a merry old soul
         And a merry old soul was he.
         etc.

                  Common nursery rhyme; see Opie, DICTIONARY, *134.*

McCaskill, *NCF*, 1 (June, 1948), 12 [North Carolina].

(402)   **O**ld lady, old lady,
         Lived in a shoe.
         Old lady, old lady
         What to do?
         Old lady, old lady
         Stubbed her toe;
         Old lady, old lady,
         Out you go!

                       See "Teddy Bear, Teddy Bear, turn around."
                       Cf. the nursery rhyme (Opie, DICTIONARY,
                       435).

New York Times Magazine (April 28, 1946) [New York].
Haufrecht (1947), 62.

(403)   **O**ld Man Daisy (Lazy),
         He went crazy (drives me crazy),
         Up the ladder,
         Down the ladder.

Heck, *JAF*, 40 (1927), 41.
Johnson, *JAF*, 42 (1929), 305.
LaSalle (1929), 71.
Thompson, *JAF*, 47 (1934), 384 [Pennsylvania, 1929].
Brewster, *SFQ*, 3 (1939), 176 [Indiana, 1934] = Botkin (1944), 793.
Fahey, *Journal of Health and Physical Education*, 11 (1940), 421 [Kansas].
Eller, *North Carolina Education*, 10 (1944), 464 [North Carolina].
Grace Partridge Smith, *HF*, 5 (1946), 58 [Illinois] = Dorson (1964), 386.

O

Withers (North) (1947), 83 [New York, "Why are you so lazy?"] =
Withers (1964), 97.

Withers (1948), 61.

Haines, *Daedalian*, 17 (1949), 26 [District of Columbia].

Reck, *WF*, 8 (1949), 129 [Colorado].

Evans (1955), 15 [California] = Evans (1961), 37.

Pope, *WF*, 15 (1956), 46 [Texas]. Begins "Up the ladder."

"Children's Rhymes," *WVF*, 8 (1958), 36. Begins "Up the ladder."

Abrahams, *KFQ*, 8 (1963), 14 [Pennsylvania, 1959]. Two variants, one
begins "George Washington never told a lie."

Leventhal and Cray, *WF*, 22 (1963), 233 [California, 1959]. "Old Man
Moses."

Ainsworth, *WF*, 20 (1961), 182 [North Carolina], 186 [Alabama], 193
[New Mexico].

Worstell (1961), 7.

Butler and Haley (1963), n.p.

Buckley, *KFQ*, 11 (1966), 105 [Indiana]. Listed.

> Old Man Daisy
> What do you think I did?
> *See "Oh, say, kid."*

(404)   Old Mother Mason
Broke her basin
Traveling down to the railway station.
How much do you think it cost?
Penny, two pence, *etc.*

Also found as a counting-out rhyme.

Douglas (1916), 93 [London].

Scott, *Singabout*, 3, No. 3 (Winter/Spring, 1959), 5 [Australia]. "Old
Miss Mason . . ./Right in the middle of Woy Woy Station."

Sutton-Smith (1959), 74 [New Zealand].

Utley (1959), 125.

(405)   Old Mother Rich
Fell in a ditch,
Picked up a rotten apple,
And thought she was rich.

*Connected usually with the dialogue
game "Old Mommy Witch."*

Heck, *JAF*, 40 (1927), 41 [Ohio].
Evans (1955), 23 [California] = Evans (1961), 43.

(406)   **O**ld Mother Whittlehouse
          Had a big fit,
          First she did the merry-go-round,
          And then she did the split.

Park, *CFQ*, 1 (1942), 377 [California].
Emrich and Korson (1947), 133.
Evans (1961), 27.

(407)   **O**ld Mr. Kelly had a pimple on his belly.
          His wife cut it off and made it into jelly.

Evans (1961), 28.

(408)   **O**ldsmobile, Chevrolet, Studebaker, Ford—
          Now I jump my shining cord.

                    "Cord" is obviously the prototype of the mod-
                    ern sports car and should have been capital-
                    ized.

Botkin (1947), 907 [Connecticut].

(409)   **O**le King Cole
          Was a merry old soul.
          He tried to get to heaven
          On a telephone pole.
                         See the nursery rhyme, Opie, DICTION-
                         ARY, *134.*

Ainsworth, *WF*, 20 (1961), 196 [Utah].

(410)   **O**liver Jump
          Oliver Jump
          Oliver Jump Jump Jump

> Oliver kick
> Oliver Kick
> Oliver Kick Kick Kick
>
> Oliver Twist
> Oliver Twist
> Oliver Twist Twist Twist
>
> Oliver Jump Jump Jump
> Oliver Kick Kick Kick
> Oliver Twist Twist Twist.

Ritchie (1965), 142 [Edinburgh].

(411)   Oliver Twist, he can't do this
So what's the use of trying?

> No. 1, touch your tongue;
> No. 2, touch your shoe;
> No. 3, bend your knee;
> No. 4, touch the floor;
> No. 5, wave good-bye;
> No. 6, do the splits;
> Good-bye Oliver Twist.

Bluebells (1961), n.p. [Ayrshire].
Those Dusty Bluebells (1965), 7 [Ayrshire].

On a hillside stands a lady.
See "On the mountain top stands a lady."

(412)   Once upon a time
A goose drank wine.
The monkey chewed tobacco on the trolley car line.
The trolley car broke,
The monkey choked,
They all went to heaven on a billy goat.

> *Derives from a formula opening of English tales.*

Heimbuecher, *KFQ*, 7, No. 4 (1962), 6 [Pennsylvania].

(413)   One and two and how are you?
         I do very well;
         And I live by myself
         And my name is Mrs. Bell.

Gardiner oral collection (1957–1958) [Forfar].

(414)   One 'brella, two 'brellas, three 'brellas, *etc.*

Daiken (1949), 64 [Great Britain].

(415)   One bright morning in the middle of the night.
         Two dead boys got up to fight.
         Back to back they faced each other.
         Drew their swords and shot each other.
         Two deaf policemen heard the noise,
         Came and shot those two dead boys.
         If you don't believe this is true,
         Ask the blindman, he saw it too.

                    Generally collected as a nonsense rhyme.

Herriman, *WVF*, 3 (1953), 52 [West Virginia]. "It was in the middle of
    the day."
Leventhal and Cray, *WF*, 22 (1963), 237 [California, 1959]. Two vari-
    ants: "One dark morning" and "The day was dark, the night was light."
Ainsworth, *WF*, 20 (1961), 184 [Georgia].

(416)   One day A-E and Jimmy were going to a movie,
         Jimmy found that he had no money.
         A-E said, "I will let you borrow twenty-five cents."
         When the movie was over,
         Jimmy said, "A-E, I-O-U twenty-five cents."

Abrahams, *SFQ*, 27 (1963), 209 [Texas].

(417)   One-ery two-ery ickery Ann
         Fillicy fallacy Nicholas Den

Queever quaver Long Island Duck
Stinchim, Stanchem, Buck.

Usually a counting-out rhyme.

Haufrecht (1947), 64.

(418)   One evening,
When I was playing the piano
And ma was sewing a green strip
And pa was reading the paper
etc.

Seems to be an improvisation.

Nulton, *JAF*, 61 (1948), 60–61 [North Carolina, from child who said her
mother had used it as a child, *ca.* 1909.]

(419)   One for the money,
Two for the show,
Three to make ready,
And count as you go.
One, two, three, *etc.*

Usually used to start a race.

Botkin (1944), 778.
Roberts, *HF*, 8 (1949), 11 [Illinois, Indiana].
Sutton-Smith (1959), 75 [New Zealand]. The British equivalent race-
starting rhyme, "One to make ready"; ends with "Salt, vinegar, mus-
tard, pepper."
Ainsworth, *WF*, 20 (1961), 183 [North Carolina].

(420)   One I love, two I love,
Three I love I say,
Four I love with all my heart,
Five I cast away;
Six he loves, seven she loves,
Eight both love.

> Nine he comes, ten he tarries,
> Eleven he courts, twelve he marries.
>
> *Usually a divination rhyme.*

Opie, *Dictionary*, 331–332.

(421)   One I see,
        Two I see,
        Three I see,
        Four I see,
        Five I see,
        Six I see,
        Seven I see,
        Eight I see,
        Nine I see,
        Tennessee.

> *Usually a catch.*

Abrahams, *SFQ*, 27 (1963), 209 [Texas].

(422)   One little, two little, three little Indians.
        Four little, five little, six little Indians.
        etc.

> *Usually a children's song.*

Hall, *Recreation* (March, 1941), 716 [Nebraska].

(423)   One o'clock the gun went off.
        I dare not stay no longer.
        If I do my mother will say
        Playing with the boys up yonder.

        Stockings red, garters blue,
        Trimmed all round with silver:
        A red, red rose upon my head
        And a gold ring on my finger.

        Heigh-ho, my Johnnie-O,
        My bonny, bonny Johnnie-O:

The only one I love best
Is my bonny, bonny Johnnie-O.

Ritchie (1964) [Edinburgh].

(424)   One potato, two potato,
          Three potato, four.
          Five potato, six potato,
          Seven potato, more.
          1-2-3, out goes she
          In the middle of the deep blue sea.

                    Usually a counting-out rhyme.

Abrahams, *SFQ*, 27 (1963), 209 [Texas].

          Onery, twoery, threery, same.
              See "Salt, vinegar, mustard, and pepper."

          One to make ready.
              See "One for the money."

(425)   One, two, buckle your (my) shoe,
          Three, four, shut the door,
          Five, six, pick up sticks,
          Seven, eight, lay them straight (shut the gate),
          Nine, ten, a big fat hen (begin again).

                    Often a counting-out rhyme; see Opie, DICTION-
                    ARY, *333.*

Babcock, *AA*, o.s., 1 (1888), 266 [District of Columbia].
Chamberlain, *JAF*, 8 (1895), 253.
Douglas (1916), 63 [London].
Winifred Smith, *JAF*, 39 (1926), 84 [New York].
Brewster, *SFQ*, 3 (1939), 178 = Botkin (1944), 795.
Hall, *Recreation* (March, 1941), 715 [Nebraska].
Reynolds, *Christian Science Monitor* (July 11, 1941), 8.
Rudy, Mills, and Sone, *Jack and Jill*, 4 (March, 1942), 7. "*Un*buckle
    your shoe . . ." (the text smacks of conscious rehandling).
Maloney, *HFB*, 3 (1944), 24 [Idaho].
Emrich and Korson (1947), 137.
Haufrecht (1947), 63.

Withers (North) (1947), 83 [New York] = Withers (1964), 97.

Withers (1948), 59.

Haines, *Daedalian*, 17 (1949), 24 [Texas].

Roberts, *HF*, 8 (1949), 11 [Maine].

Frankel (1952), 63. "... tie your shoe."

Randolph, *MF*, 3 (1953), 81 [Arkansas].

Browne, *WF*, 14 (1955), 18 [California].

Sutton-Smith (1959), 82 [New Zealand]. Begins "One, two, touch my shoe" and ends "Salt, mustard, pepper, vinegar."

Sackett (1961), 224 [Kansas].

Abrahams, *SFQ*, 27 (1963), 201 [Texas].

Buckley, *KFQ*, 11 (1966), 101 [Indiana]. Listed.

(426)   One, two, three,
          Bumble, bumble bee.
          Four, five, six,
          Bumble, bumble bee.

Abrahams, *SFQ*, 27 (1963), 209 [Texas].

(427)   One, two, three
          Cats in the well.
          Four, five, six,
          Pick up sticks.
          Seven, eight, nine,
          Cut the clothesline.
          Nine, ten, eleven,
          Cat's gone to heaven.

> *Cf. the nursery rhymes "Ding, dong, bell" and "One, two, button my shoe."*

Butler and Haley (1963), n.p.

          One, two, three, four,
          Charlie Chaplin* went to war.
              See "Charlie Chaplin went to France."

(428)   One, two, three, four, five,
          I caught a fish (hare) alive.

Why did you let him go?
Because he hurt my finger so.

> *Usually a counting-out rhyme; see Opie,* DICTION-
> ARY, *334–335.*

Douglas (1916), 63 [London].
Abrahams, *SFQ*, 27 (1963), 210 [Texas].

(429)   One, two, three, four, five, six, seven,
          All good children go to heaven.
          All the rest go down below (some go up and some go
              down),
          To eat supper with Old Black Joe.
          How many bad ones go below?
          One, two, three, four, five, *etc.*

> *This rhyme and the following five are related
> to a common counting-out rhyme.*

Sone (1943), 195 [Texas].
Petersham (1945), n.p. First two lines only.
Haines, *Daedalian*, 17 (1949), 28 [Texas].
Abrahams, *SFQ*, 27 (1963), 210 [Texas].

(430)   One, two, three, four, five, six, seven,
          All good children go to heaven,
          No, yes, no, yes, no, yes, no,
          If you are bad you cannot go.

Randolph, *MF*, 3 (1953), 79 [Arkansas, *ca.* 1930].

(431)   One, two, three, four, five, six, seven,
          All good children go to heaven,
          Seven, six, five, four, three, two, one,
          All bad children suck their thumbs.

Randolph, *MF*, 3 (1953), 79 [Arkansas, *ca.* 1930].
Musick and Randolph, *JAF*, 63 (1950), 431 [Missouri].
Seeger, Folkways 7029 (1955) [Illinois]. Ends ". . . jumping rope is
    fun."

(432)   One, two, three, four, five, six, seven,
          All good children go to heaven:
          When they die their sin's forgiven,
          One, two, three, four, five, six, seven.

Ritchie (1965), 136 [Edinburgh].

(433)   One, two, three, four, five, six, seven,
          All good people go to heaven.
          When they get there God will say
          "Where's the book you stole away?"
          If you say, "I do not know,"
          He will send you down below
          Where everything is RED HOT PEPPERS!

Student oral collection (1964) [Texas].
White, *Louisiana Miscellany*, 2, No. 2 (April, 1965), 116. Ends "Where
   it is *H O T* hot."

(434)   One, two, three, four, five, six, seven,
          All good children go to heaven.
          When they get there, the angels will say
          (Name of school) children, right this way.

Fahey, *Journal of Health and Physical Education*, 11 (1940), 421 [Kan-
   sas].

(435)   One, two, three, four
          I spy Pearl White
          Sitting on a black horse
          Knitting for the Red Cross.

                    Related to the game "I spy."

Gibbs, *NYFQ*, 14 (1958), 314.

          One, two, three, four,
          Jennie at the cottage door.
             See "Lady, lady at the gate."

(436)   **O**ne, two, three, four,
Jump the circle, shut the door.
One, two, three, four,
Eat the apple, drop the core.

Abrahams, *SFQ*, 27 (1963), 210 [Texas].

(437)   **O**ne, two, three, four,
Mother washed the floor;
Floor dried, mother cried.
One, two, three, four.

> *Usually a counting-out rhyme.*

Ainsworth, *WF*, 20 (1961), 180 [Maine].

(438)   **O**ne, two, three, four,
Skip and skip till you can't no more.
Five, six, seven, eight,
Skip, skip, or you'll be late.
Nine, ten, start again.

Abrahams, *SFQ*, 27 (1963), 210 [Texas].

One, two, three, four
Superman* went to war.
> *See "Charlie Chaplin went to France."*

One, two, three, high, low.
> *See "High, low, slow, dolly."*

(439)   **O**ne, two, three,
Momma caught a flea;
Flea died, Momma cried,
One, two, three.

> *Usually a counting-out rhyme; see also "O dear me."*

Abrahams, *SFQ*, 27 (1963), 210 [Texas].

(440)   One, two, three, my ankle (toe, knee, chest, nut),
         Four, five, six, my ankle.

Yoffie, *JAF*, 60 (1947), 48 [Missouri].

(441)   One, two, three, o'lary (O'Leary)
         My first name is Mary,
         Don't you think that I look cute,
         In my papa's bathing suit?

> *Rhymes with this beginning are commonly
> used for ball-bouncing.*

Park, *CFQ*, 1 (1942), 377 [California].
Yoffie, *JAF*, 60 (1947), 48 [Missouri].
Browne, *WF*, 14 (1955), 21 [California].
Evans (1955), 22 [California] = Evans (1961), 46.
Worstell (1961), 32.

(442)   One, two, three, one, two, three.
         If you are able to jump,
         You can jump.
         Bet this is the number you have to jump.
         1-2-3, 4-5-6, *etc.*

Abrahams, *SFQ*, 27 (1963), 210 [Texas].

(443)   One, two, three, ·
         Red, white, and blue,
         Ten, twenty, thirty, *etc.*

Sutton-Smith (1959), 76 [New Zealand].

(444)   One, two, three,
         Tommy hurt his knee.
         He couldn't slide, and so he cried,
         Out goes he.

> *Cf. "One, two, three,/Momma
> caught a flea."*

Abrahams, *SFQ*, 27 (1963), 210 [Texas].

One, two, tie your shoe.
See "One, two, buckle your shoe."

(445)   On the carpet she shall kneel,
          Stand up-right upon your heel—

                                        Incomplete.

Douglas (1916), 94 [London].

(446)   On the mountain top (hillside) stands
              a lady (woman),
          Who she is I do not know.
          All she has is gold and silver,
          All she wants is a brand new beau.
          O, come in, my Sally dear,
          And out I shall go.

              Usually a singing game.

Mills and Bishop, *The New Yorker* (November 13, 1937), 36 [New York,
    1934; begins "Happy Hooligan, number nine"] = Botkin (1944), 801.
Butler, *TFSB*, 31 (1965), 6 [Virginia, 1945].
Emrich and Korson (1947), 135.
Musick, *HF*, 7 (1948), 11 [West Virginia].
Musick, *WVF*, 2, No. 3 (1952), 6 [West Virginia]. "On the hill."
Schwartz, Folkways 7009 (1953) [New York].
Browne, *WF*, 14 (1955), 14 [California].
Evans (1955), 11 [California] = Evans (1961), 34.
Bley (1957), 94.
Graham, *Press and Journal* (November 26, 1959), 3 [Aberdeen].
Ainsworth, *WF*, 20 (1961), 196 [Utah].
Bluebells (1961), n.p. [Ayrshire].
MacColl and Seeger, Folkways 3565 (1962) [Durham, England].
Abrahams, *SFQ*, 27 (1963), 210 [Texas].
Butler and Haley (1963), n.p.

Oor wee Sue.
See "Little Miss Pinky, dressed in blue."

(447)   Order in the court,
          The judge is eating beans,

His wife is in the bathtub
Counting submarines.

> *Related to the children's rhyme-game "Order in the Court."*

Evans (1955), 16 [California] = Evans (1961), 36.
Student oral collection (1964) [Texas].

(448) Our boots are made of Spanish (of leather),
Our stockings are made of silk,
Our pinafores are made of cotton
As white as white as milk,
Here we go around, around
And we all must touch the ground.

> *Cf. the game "Three Dukes A-Riding."*

Douglas (1916), 64 [London].

(449) O-U-T spells out goes you.
You old dirty dishrag you.

> *Usually an ending for a counting-out rhyme.*

Abrahams, *SFQ*, 27 (1963), 210 [Texas].

Over in the meadow where the green grass grows.
See "Down by the river."

(450) Over the garden wall
I let the baby fall,
My mother came out,
And gave me a clout,
Over the garden wall.

Scott, *Singabout*, 3, No. 3 (Winter/Spring, 1959), 4 [Australia].
Sutton-Smith (1959), 78 [New Zealand].
Butler, *TFSB*, 31 (1965), 5 [New Zealand].

Over the mountain, over the sea.
See "Johnny on the ocean."

(451)   **O**xford boys are very nice
Cambridge boys are better.

Incomplete, probably obscene.

Douglas (1916), 88 [London].

Paddy on the railway.
See "Piggy on the railway."

Panda Bear.
See "Teddy Bear, Teddy Bear, turn around."

(452)   The **P**arson in the pulpit
Couldn't say his prayers,
He gabbled and he gabbled
Till he tumbled down the stairs.
The stairs gave a crack,
And he broke his old back,
And all the congregation
Gave a quack, quack, quack.

Originally a taunt.

Opie (1947), 23.

(453)   **P**assing the Doctor, one, two, three
Passing the Doctor, out goes she.

Bluebells (1961), n.p. [Ayrshire].

Those Dusty Bluebells (1965), 15 [Ayrshire]. "Pass the Doctor," ends "So early in the morning."

(454)   **P**atacake, patacake, baker's man
          So I will master, as fast as I can.
          Roll it, roll it, roll it.
          Knead it, knead it, knead it.
          Toss it up in the oven and bake it.

                         Cf. the hand-clapping rhyme; see
                         Opie, DICTIONARY, *341–342.*

Haufrecht (1947), 62. Two variants.

Buckley, *KFQ*, 11 (1966), 104 [Indiana]. Listed.

          Patty, Patty had a baby.
          See "Fudge, fudge."

          Peaches, apples, pears and plums.
          See "Ice cream soda."

(455)   **P**eaches in the parlor,
          Apples on the shelf.
          ....'s getting tired
          Of sleeping by herself.
          How many nights did she sleep by herself?

                                        Usually a taunt.

McCaskill, *NCF*, 1 (June, 1948), 11 [North Carolina].

(456)   **P**eaches, plums, pumpkin butter,
          Little Johnny Green is my true lover,
          Little Johnny Green give me a kiss,
          When I miss, I miss like this.

                         "Johnny Green" also appears in the nursery
                         rhyme "Ding, Dong Bell"; see Opie,
                         DICTIONARY, *149.*

Randolph, *MF*, 3 (1953), 84 [Arkansas, 1926].

(457)   Peel an orange
        Round and round.
        Peel a banana
        Upside down.
        If you can count to 24,
        You may have an extra turn.

Halpert, *JAF*, 58 (1945), 351 [New Hampshire]. With "Last night and
the night before" and "Teddy Bear, Teddy Bear, turn around" rhymes.
Seeger, Folkways 7029 (1955) [Illinois].
Ainsworth, *WF*, 20 (1961), 180 [Maine].

(458)   Penny on the water, twopence on the sea,
        Threepence on the railway—out goes she.

                        *Usually a counting-out or race-
                        starting rhyme.*

Douglas (1916), 93 [London].
Scott, *Singabout*, 3, No. 3 (Winter/Spring, 1959), 4 [Australia].

(459)   Pepsi Cola hits the spot
        Turn the rope and give her hot.
        H-O-T spells hot.

                        *Parody of a Pepsi Cola radio and
                        television commercial.*

Ainsworth, *WF*, 20 (1961), 182 [North Carolina].

        Peter Duck.
        See "Donald Duck is a one-legged . . . duck."

        Phyllis Hay on the shore.
        See "Rich man, poor man."

(460)   Piggy on the railway, picking up the stones
        Up came an engine, and broke Piggy's bones.
        "Oh" said Piggy, "that's not fair"—
        "Oh," said the driver, "I don't care."

                        Also used as a counting-out rhyme.

Douglas (1916), 56 [London].
Bennett, *Children,* 12 (1927), 20. "Teddy."
Holbrook (1957), 56 [England].
Gardiner oral collection (1957–1958) [Forfar]. "Teddie," ends " 'Well,' said the driver, 'you shouldna be there'."
Sutton-Smith (1959), 80 [New Zealand]. "Polly."
Those Dusty Bluebells (1965), 7 [Ayrshire]. "Paddy," ends " 'Aha,' says the engine-man, 'ye shouldnae've been there'."

(461)   **P**itch, patch, patch my britches,
          How many stitches?

MacColl and Seeger, Folkways 3565 (1962) [Durham, England].

(462)   **P**.K. chewing gum, penny a packet (racket).
          First you chew it, then you crack it.
          Then you stick it in your jacket
          P.K. chewing gum, penny a packet.

Gardiner oral collection (1957–1958) [Forfar].
Ritchie (1965), 143 [Edinburgh]. "Then your mother kickaupa racket."

(463)   **P**laying cowboys can be fun

Buckley, *KFQ*, 11 (1966), 101 [Indiana]. Listed.

          O **P**leeceman, pleeceman.
          See "Policeman, policeman, don't whip me."

(464)   **P**lee, Plee Blackie went to his garden.
          When he went to his garden the robber
          Was hiding behind the garage.
          Their mother came got Plee, Plee Blackie.
          He found Plee, Plee Blackies was gone.
          The robber and Plee, Plee Blackie went
              to jail.
                    Seems to be an improvisation.

Fife, *JAF*, 59 (1946), 332 [North Carolina].

(465) Policeman, policeman, don't whip (blame) me;
       Whip that nigger behind that tree;
       He stole peaches, I stole none;
       Put him in the calaboose just for fun.

Usually collected as a taunt.

Douglas (1916), 54 [London]. "Policeman, don't touch me,/I have a
   wife and family."
Heck, *JAF*, 40 (1927), 42 [Ohio].
Daiken (1963), 27 [Dublin, 1929]. "O Pleeceman, pleeceman, don't
   take me,/I've gotta wife and famil-ee."
Brewster, *SFQ*, 3 (1939), 178 ("Teacher, teacher") = Botkin (1944),
   795.
Daiken (1949), 69.
Graham, *Press and Journal* (November 30, 1959), 6 [Aberdeen].
Ritchie (1965), 143 [Edinburgh]. "He stole sugar/He stole tea."
Buckley, *KFQ*, 11 (1966), 101 [Indiana]. Listed. "Teacher, teacher."

(466) Policeman (postman), policeman, do your duty,
       Here comes ...., the American beauty.
       She can wiggle, she can woggle,
       She can do the splits.
       She can wear (pull) her skirts (dress) up
         to her hips.

*Also commonly ends "She can dance, She
can sing/She can do most anything."
Cf. "Hi, ho, Silver"; Opie (1959), 236,
relates this rhyme to a Valentine verse.*

Haufrecht (1947), 61.
Randolph, *MF*, 3 (1953), 82 [Arkansas].
Schwartz, Folkways 7009 (1953) [New York]. With "Teddy Bear, Teddy
   Bear, turn around" rhyme.
Evans (1955), 12 [California] = Evans (1961), 34.
Abrahams, *KFQ*, 8 (1963), 10 [Pennsylvania, 1959]. Two variants.
Leventhal and Cray, *WF*, 22 (1963), 238 [California, 1959].
Ainsworth, *WF*, 20 (1961), 181 [Maine], 184 [California], 186 [Michi-
   gan], 187 [Michigan, "Send this letter to my cutie"], 190 [Wisconsin],
   196 [Utah].
Heimbuecher, *KFQ*, 7, No. 4 (1962), 4 [Pennsylvania].
Abrahams, *SFQ*, 27 (1963), 201 [Texas].
Withers (1964), 99 [Iowa and New York]. Begins "Hello, boys, do you
   want to flirt?/Here comes *Betty* in a gingham skirt."

Polly in the kitchen.
See "As I was in the kitchen."

Polly on the railway.
See "Piggy on the railway."

Polly, Polly, dressed in lace.
See "Grace, Grace."

Polly, Polly, walks like this.
See "Shirley Temple walks like this."

Polly put the kettle on.
See "Keep the ketle boiling."

Pom Pom Pomyadown Jeanie (Pom Pom Pompadour).
See "Vote, vote, vote."

(467)   Pom, Pom, the pipes are calling

Buckley, *KFQ*, 11 (1966), 105 [Indiana]. Listed.

(468)   A Poor little boy without any shoe,
         1-2-3 and out goes you.

Abrahams, *SFQ*, 27 (1963), 210 [Texas].

(469)   Poor old lady,
         She swallowed a fly.
         Poor old lady,
         She's going to die.
         etc.
                    Usually a children's song.

Evans (1955), 10 [California] = Evans (1961), 35.

(470)   Popeye* went down in the cellar
         To drink some spinach juice.

> How many gallons did he drink?
> One, two, three, *etc.*

Halpert, *JAF*, 58 (1945), 349 [New Hampshire].
Withers (1948), 67.

> **P**op, Pop, Pop.
> *See "Vote, vote, vote."*

> **P**orridge hot, porridge cold.
> *See "Bean porridge hot."*

(471)   The **P**ostman's bell goes ting-a-ling-a-ling . . .
The milkman's horse goes clippety clop . . .
The horses' shoes go klack klock.

Those Dusty Bluebells (1965), 12 [Ayrshire].

(472)   **P**ounds, shillings, and pence
The monkey jumped the fence.
The fence gave way, and the man had to
    pay
Pounds, shillings, and pence.

        Cf. "I asked my mother for fifteen cents."

Douglas (1916), 54–55 [London].
Sutton-Smith (1959), 74 [New Zealand].

(473)   **P**owder box, powder box, powder your nose,
How many petals are in a rose?

Haines, *Daedalian*, 17 (1949), 26 [Texas].

(474)   **P**ummelty, pommelty, apple butter,
What is the name of my true lover?
Riddledy, riddlety, riddlety rin.

How does my true lover's name begin?
A-B-C-D, *etc.*

Cf. "Ice cream soda."

Randolph, *MF*, 3 (1953), 82 [Arkansas, *ca.* 1940].

Pump, pump, the gasoline.
See "Vote, vote, vote."

(475)   **Q**ueen bee, chasing me,
         I call in ....

Student oral collection (1964) [Texas].

(476)   **Q**ueen Elizabeth lost her shoe
         At the Battle of Waterloo
         It happened on Monday, Tuesday, . . .

Ritchie (1965), 143 [Edinburgh].

The **Q**ueen of Hearts.
See "Ice cream soda."

(477)   **Q**ueen, Queen,
         Where did you get your chicken?
         Queen, Queen,
         Where did you get your duck?
         Queen, Queen,
         Where did you get your goat?
         I got my chicken out of the yard.

I got my duck out of the pool.
I got my goat out of the garden.

Nulton, *JAF*, 61 (1948), 55.

(478)   Rabbie Burns was born in Ayr.
          Now he's in Trafalgar Square.
          If you want tae see him there
          Jump on a bus and skip the fare.

Ritchie (1965), 143 [Edinburgh].

          Rah, Rah, Rah.
          See "Vote, vote, vote."

          Rainy, rainy weather.
          See "All in together."

          Raspberry, Raspberry, Raspberry Jam.
          See "Ice cream soda."

          Raspberry, strawberry, blackberry (black currant) jam.
          See "Ice cream soda."

          Raspberry, strawberry, cherry pie.
          See "Ice cream soda."

(479)   Rat-a-tat-tat, who is that?
          Only Grandma's pussy cat.
          What do you want?
          A pint of milk.

Where's your money?
In my pocket.
Where's your pocket?
I forgot it!
O you silly pussy-cat.

Douglas (1916), 64 [London].
Opie (1959), 10–11 [Durham, Yorkshire]. Three variants; one from
  Douglas with a discussion of antecedents from nursery rhyme books,
  one begins "I had a little beer shop/A man walked in./I asked him
  what he wanted./A bottle of gin."

(480)   **R**ed-headed sapsucker,
         Sitting on a vine,
         Wants a chew of 'bacca
         But he won't get mine.

                    Usually a taunt.

Nulton, *JAF*, 61 (1948), 64. Two variants: one from 1945, the other,
  1946. The second is a version of the taunt ".......... sitting on a fence."

(481)   **R**ed hot bricks.
         Gotta get over what the leader's is,
         Or else you're out.

Ainsworth, *WF*, 20 (1961) 191 [Wisconsin].

(482)   **R**ed-hot in the pot:
         Twice as much as the leader's got.

Speroni, *CFQ*, 1 (1942), 249 [California].

(483)   **R**ed hot pepper
         With an H-O-T:
         10, 20, 30, 40, *etc.*
                    See Mabel, Mabel,/Set the table."

Fahey, *Journal of Health and Physical Education*, 11 (1940), 421 [Kan-
  sas].

Gibbs, *NYFQ*, 14 (1958), 316.
Abrahams, *SFQ*, 27 (1963), 201 [Texas]. Two variants: one begins
"H-O-T spells"; the other, "Give me H-O-T P-E-P-P-E-R!"

(484)   **R**ed roses, blue roses, yellow roses too.
        Have some jumps for Mrs. Blue.
        1-2-3-4-5, *etc.*

Leventhal and Cray, *WF*, 22 (1963), 235 [California, 1959].

(485)   **R**ed, white and blue:
        I don't speak to you.

                        Incomplete.

Douglas (1916), 91 [London].

(486)   **R**ed, white, and blue
        My mother caught the flu:
        My father lost his walking stick—
        And I blame you!

Ritchie (1965), 136 [Edinburgh].

(487)   **R**ed, white, and blue;
        Stars shine over you.

                *Often collected as "Red, white, and
                yellow" or ". . . and green."*

Winifred Smith, *JAF*, 39 (1926), 84.
Ireland, *Recreation* (February, 1937), 564 [Kentucky].
Ashton, *JAF*, 52 (1939), 120 [Iowa].
Brewster, *SFQ*, 3 (1939), 175 (three variants) = Botkin (1944), 792.
Mills (1944), 16 [Maryland].
Musick, *WVF*, 2, No. 3 (1952), 3, 5 [West Virginia]. Ends "Sky's over
    you," with explanation that at that point the jumper stoops while rope
    is twirled over head.
Browne, *WF*, 14 (1955), 11 [California].
Ainsworth, *WF*, 20 (1961), 183 [Georgia], 196 [Utah].
Butler and Haley (1963), n.p.

(488)   Red, white and blue,
         Your father is a Jew,
         Your mother is a Japanese (Chinaman),
         And so are you!

                    Usually a taunt.

Britt and Balcom, *J Gen Psy*, 58 (1941), 294 [Maryland, District of Columbia].
Hurvitz, *Jewish Social Studies*, 16 (1954), 142–143 [Ohio]. Four variants.

         Reuben, Reuben.
         See "Hitler, Hitler."

(489)   Rich man, poor man, beggarman, thief,
         Doctor, lawyer, Indian chief.

                    *A divination rhyme, used also to count
                    buttons, and so on. It often follows the
                    question "Who shall I marry?" or "What
                    shall I be when I grow up?" and is fre-
                    quently followed by other divination ques-
                    tions. See also "Does he love me?"*

Babcock, *AA*, o.s., 1 (1888), 267 [District of Columbia]. "Silk, satin, velvet, calico, rags."
Douglas (1916), 67 [London]. "Lady, lady on the sea-shore,/She has children one to four,/The eldest one is twenty-four,/Then she shall marry a tinker, tailor, *etc.*"
Heck, *JAF*, 40 (1927), 42 [Ohio]. With "Ice cream soda" rhyme.
Thompson, *JAF*, 47 (1934), 385 [Pennsylvania, 1929].
Ashton, *JAF*, 52 (1939), 121 [Iowa].
"Stella, Stella," *Fargo Forum* (June 23, 1940), 13 [North Dakota]. Two variants, one "Silk, satin, calico, rags."
Hall, *Recreation* (March, 1941), 716 [Nebraska]. Gives rhyme plus other divination combinations.
Speroni, *CFQ*, 1 (1942), 251 [California]. Begins with "Mrs. Sippy lives by the shore" rhyme.
Sone (1943), 196 [Texas].
Halpert, *CFQ*, 3 (1944), 154 [Alberta, Canada]. "Tinker, tailor, soldier, sailor."
"Jump-Rope Rhymes," *WF*, 23 (1964), 258 [California, 1944]. At the end of "Ice cream soda" rhyme.
Maloney, *HFB*, 3 (1944), 25 [Idaho].

Halpert, *JAF*, 58 (1945), 350 [New Hampshire].

Fife, *JAF*, 59 (1946), 321–322 [North Carolina]. "What kind of house do you have?"

Botkin (1947), 907 [Connecticut]. Begins with "Mrs. Sippy lives by the shore" rhyme.

Emrich and Korson (1947), 134.

Nulton, *JAF*, 61 (1948), 64.

McCaskill, *NCF*, 1 (June, 1948), 11 [North Carolina]. Two variants, one "You will marry."

Ashby, *Christian Science Monitor Magazine* (April 9, 1949), 8. As ending to "Bluebells, cockleshells" rhyme.

Daiken (1949), 63 [Great Britain], 68 [Dublin]. A topical Irish Civil War rhyme.

Randolph, *MF*, 3 (1953), 84 [Arkansas].

Evans (1955), 24–26 [California]. As ending to "Mississippi lives by the shore" rhyme.

Graham, *Press and Journal* (November 26, 1959), 3 [Aberdeen]. "A lord, a laird, a lily, a leaf;/A piper, a drummer, a hummer, a thief."

Ainsworth, *WF*, 20 (1961), 182 [North Carolina].

Worstell (1961), 18. With other divination patterns.

Butler and Haley (1963), n.p. Begins "I love my Papa, that I do/And Mama says she loves him too,/But Papa says he fears someday/With some bad man I'll run away."

Abrahams, *SFQ*, 27 (1963), 201 [Texas]. Four variants; one beginning "I will marry," one starting "What you gonna drive?" and one, distantly related, beginning "How many children will I have?"

Daiken (1963), 26 [Dublin]. "A tinker an'/A tailor an'/An I.R.A.*/An auxie man,/A Black-and-tan/A thief . . ."

Ritchie (1965), 112, 127, 131 [Edinburgh]. Three variants: one begins "Phyllis Hay on the shore/She has children three and four./The eldest one is twenty-four/And married to a:/Tinker, tailor/Soldier, sailor . . ."; also a divination, "How many messages can I carry"; one "This year,/Next year/Sometime/Never."

Buckley, *KFQ*, 11 (1966), 102 [Indiana]. "At what age shall I marry?"; "Who shall I marry?"; "How many children shall I have?"; "What kind of children shall I have?"; "How many years will I live?"

      Ricky Wilson sat on a pin.
      See "Charlie Chaplin sat on a pin."

      Rin Tin Tin* sat on a pin.
      See "Charlie Chaplin sat on a pin."

(490)   **R**in Tin Tin*
       Swallowed a pin;

He went to the doctor,
The doctor wasn't in.
He opened the door
And fell on the floor,
And that was the end of Rin Tin Tin.

Cf. "Charlie Chaplin sat on a pin."

Opie (1959), 113–114 [England, 1952–1954; Maryland, 1947; New York, 1936; New Jersey, 1934].

(491)   **R**obin Hood* and his merry men
Went to school at half past ten.
The teacher said "Late again!"
Robin Hood and his merry men.

Cf. "Ali Baba."

Ritchie (1965), 139, 144 [Edinburgh]. Two variants, one "Ali Baba and his forty Men."

(492)   **R**ock-a-bye Baby, in the tree top.
When the wind blows, the cradle will rock.
When the bough breaks, the cradle will fall,
And down will come Baby, cradle and all.

Usually collected as a lullaby.

Seeger, Folkways 7029 (1955) [Illinois].

(493)   **R**ock-and-roll is here to stay,
Here to stay, here to stay;
Rock-and-roll is here to stay.
Now work out ....

Abrahams, *KFQ*, 8 (1963), 15 [Pennsylvania, 1959].

Rooms for rent.
See "A house to let."

(494)　　Roses are red, violets are blue
　　　　Honeysuckles are sweet and so are you.

Usually an autograph album rhyme.

Those Dusty Bluebells (1965), 11 [Ayrshire].

(495)　　Roses are red; violets are blue.
　　　　I love _____ to jump in with me.

Cf. "I love coffee."

Leventhal and Cray, *WF*, 22 (1963), 235 [California, 1959]. Three
　　variants.

(496)　　Roses red, roses white,
　　　　Roses in my garden;
　　　　I would not part
　　　　With my sweetheart
　　　　For twopence, ha'penny farthing.

Gomme, 2 (1898), 204. May begin "B-L-E-S-S-I-N-G."

(497)　　Rosy apples, lemon and a pear,
　　　　A bunch of roses she shall wear.
　　　　Gold and silver by her side,
　　　　I shall make her my bride,
　　　　Take her by the hand,
　　　　Lead her across the water,
　　　　Give her kisses one, two, three
　　　　And call her a lady's daughter.

See also "Ice cream soda."

Douglas (1931), 35 [London].

　　　　Rosy apples,
　　　　Mama's little tart.
　　　　See "Ice cream soda."

(498)   Round and round the butcher shop.
          Can't stay any longer.
          If I do my mother said
          I'm the butcher's daughter.

Student oral collection (1964) [New Jersey].

(499)   Round apple, round apple,
          As round as can be.
          She's dying to see
          John Murphey, John Murphey,
          He's dying to see.
          Annie Askins, Annie Askins go 'round:
          Up comes her dear father
          With knife in her hand,
          Sez, Give me your daughter
          Or your life I shall have.
          Who cares not, who cares not,
          For Annie loves me
          And I love her.

Daiken (1949), 64 [Great Britain].

(500)   Roy Rogers*
          Betty Grable*
          Rita Hayworth*
          Clark Gable*

                    *A game called "stars," which can include names of
                    any motion picture personality.*

Ritchie (1965), 136 [Edinburgh].

(501)   Run in.
          Run in again.
          Run out.
          Then call another one to come in.

Abrahams, *SFQ*, 27 (1963), 211 [Texas].

Running to school.
See "Next year I will be."

Running through school.
See "Next year I will be."

Sailor boy, sailor boy.
See "Little Orphan Annie goes on one foot."

(502)   S, A, I, L, O, R, Sailor,
          1, 2, 3, Sailor
          1, 2, Sailor
          Sailor, sailor, sailor.

Bluebells (1961), n.p. [Ayrshire].
Those Dusty Bluebells (1965), 13 [Ayrshire].

(503)   The Sailor went to sea
          To see what he could see:
          And all that he could see
          Was the sea, the sea, the sea.

                    Collected in many functions.

Browne, *WF*, 14 (1955), 12 [California].
Abrahams, *SFQ*, 27 (1963), 201 [Texas].

(504)   Sally drinks lemonade (ate a pickle),
          Sally drinks beer (ate some pie).
          Sally drinks other things (ate some sauerkraut)

That makes her feel so queer (thought she
  might die).
Oops, says the lemonade,
Oops, says the beer,
Oops, says the other things
That make her feel so queer.

Britt and Balcom, *J Gen Psy*, 58 (1941), 295 [Maryland, District of Columbia]. "Mary ate some marmalade."
Nulton, *JAF*, 61 (1948), 58 [North Carolina, 1945].
Grace Partridge Smith, *HF*, 5 (1946), 60 [Illinois, "Sally drank marmalade"] = Dorson (1964), 386–387.
Musick, *HF*, 7 (1948), 12 [West Virginia]. "Marge drank the marmalade."
Haines, *Daedalian*, 17 (1949), 23 [Texas]. "Margie had some marmalade."
Musick and Randolph, *JAF*, 63 (1950), 432 [Missouri]. "Margie ate some pickles."
Morrison (1955), 69. "Sally drank."
Seeger, Folkways 7029 (1955) [Illinois].
Ainsworth, *WF*, 20 (1961), 184 [Georgia].
Worstell (1961), 31. "Margie drank some marmalade."
Butler and Haley (1963), n.p. "Marge drank the marmalade"; ". . . some milk."
Warner, *Yankee*, 30, No. 1 (January, 1966), 94.

(505)   Sally go round the moon, Sally.
         Sally go round the sun.
         Sally go round the ominlebus (*sic*)
         On a Sunday afternoon.

                   Commonly a singing game.

Douglas (1916), 52 [London].

(506)   Sally Rand* has lost her fan;
         Give it back, you naughty man.

Evans (1961), 27.
Worstell (1961), 13.

(507)   Salome was a dancer.
         She danced before the king,

And every time she danced,
She wiggled everything.

Evans (1955), 30 [California] = Evans (1961), 51.
Opie (1959), 38. Ends " 'Stop!' said King Herod, 'You can't do that 'ere.'/
Salome said, 'Baloney!'/And kicked the chandelier."

(508)   Salt makes you thirsty,
         Pepper makes you sneeze.
         We'll make someone
         Wobble at the knees.

Ainsworth, *WF*, 20 (1961), 181 [Maine].

         Salt, pepper, vinegar hot.
         See "Ice cream soda."

(509)   Salt, vinegar, mustard, and pepper.
         *See "Mabel, Mabel,/Set the table" and "Mother sent
         me to the store."*

Gomme, 2 (1898), 204 [England]. Ends "Knife and fork,/Lay the
     cloth" rhyme.
Gibbs, *NYFQ*, 14 (1958), 314 [popular between 1900 and 1930]. "Pep-
     per, salt, mustard, cider vinegar!"
Heck, *JAF*, 40 (1927), 41 [Ohio]. Begins "Easy, greasy, take it easy
     (jump like a weasel)."
Wood and Goddard (1938), 814.
Hall, *Recreation* (March, 1941), 715 [Nebraska].
Ó Súilleabháin (1942), 668 [Ireland]. "Salt, mustard, ginger, pepper."
Rae and Robb, *Christian Science Monitor Magazine* (March 21, 1942), 9.
Maloney, *HFB*, 3 (1944), 24 [Idaho]. With "Mabel, Mabel/Set the
     table" rhyme.
Daiken (1949), 63 [Great Britain].
Reck, *WF*, 8 (1949), 129 [Colorado].
Potter, "Skip-Rope," *Standard Dictionary* (1950), 1016. "My mother
     uses salt, ginger, mustard, pepper."
Brewster (1952), 172 [North Carolina].
Browne, *WF*, 14 (1955), 10 [California].
Evans (1955), 20 [California]. Begins "My mother sent me to the store."
Withers and Jablow (1956), 13. "Salt, pepper, sugar, spider,/How many
     legs has a bowlegged spider?"
Ford, *KFQ*, 2 (1957), 109.
Holbrook (1957), 57 [England]. Ends "Up in a loft" rhyme.

Sutton-Smith (1959), 76, 82 [New Zealand]. Eight variants: one beginning "Baker, baker"/Bake your bread"; one beginning "Onery, twoery, threery, same"; six with other rhymes—"One for the money," "Mabel, Mabel,/Set the table," "Bluebells, cockleshells" (2), "Turn your back on the sailor Jack," and "One, two, buckle my shoe."
Worstell (1961), 49.
Abrahams, *SFQ*, 27 (1963), 201 [Texas]. Ends "Cedar, cedar, red hot pepper."
Buckley, *KFQ*, 11 (1966), 105 [Indiana]. Begins "Easy, greasy, take it easy."

>   Salt, vinegar, mustard, tart.
>   *See "Ice cream soda."*

(510)   Oh, Say kid,
           What do you think I did?
           I upset the cradle
           And out fell the kid.
           The kid began to holler;
           I took him by the collar;
           Collar broke loose
           And I got the deuce.

Winifred Smith, *JAF*, 39 (1926), 82.
Bennett, *Children*, 12 (1927), 21. Begins "Old Man Daisy."
Britt and Balcom, *J Gen Psy*, 58 (1941), 297 [Maryland, District of Columbia]. "Old Man Daisy."
Roberts, *HF*, 8 (1949), 12 [Massachusetts]. Begins "Virginia, Virginia, what do you think I did."
Evans (1961), 21.

(511)   S-C-H-double O-L
           Spells school for you and me.

Abrahams, *SFQ*, 27 (1963), 211 [Texas].

(512)   School starts at what time?
           I don't know—it may be at one o'clock,
           Two o'clock, . . .

Hawthorne, *KFQ*, 11 (1966), 120 [Delaware].

(513)   Send a letter, send a letter,
         Be content in the weather.

Douglas 1916, 92 [London].

         Settin' on the doorstep.
         See "Standing on the corner."

(514)   Sheep in the meadow
         Cows in the corn
         Jump in on the month you were born.
                  See "Little Boy Blue" in Opie, DICTIONARY, *98–99.*

Emrich and Korson (1947), 136.
Abrahams, *SFQ*, 27 (1963), 201 [Texas].

         Shirley Temple* dressed in lace.
         See "Grace, Grace."

(515)   Shirley Temple* takes a bow
         John Boles* shows her how.

Britt and Balcom, *J Gen Psy*, 58 (1941), 294 [Maryland, District of Columbia].

(516)   Shirley Temple* walks like this;
         Shirley Temple talks like this;
         Shirley Temple smiles like this;
         Shirley Temple throws a kiss.

Botkin (1947), 907 [Connecticut].
Owens, *North Star Folk News*, 4, No. 2 (1949), 2 [Minnesota].
Schiller, *NYFQ*, 12 (1956), 204. "Polly, Polly," with elements from "Cinderella, dressed in yellow," "Mother, mother I am ill," and "I had a little brother/His name was Tim" rhymes.
Opie (1959), 113 [Swansea]. Ends ". . . says her prayers, . . . falls downstairs."
Sutton-Smith (1959), 82 [New Zealand]. "Charlie Chaplin."

Shirley Temple* went to France.
See "Charlie Chaplin went to France."

(517)   Shoot! Bang! A house on fire:
         I spy a lark shining in the dark.
         Echo, echo,
         G, O, stands for GO!

                    *Cf. "Early in the morning" for
                    the last lines.*

Daiken (1949), 71 [Great Britain].

(518)   Silent minister, one, two, three . . .
         (Elephant feet, fairy feet . . .)

Bluebells (1961), n.p. [Ayrshire].

         Silk, satin, calico, rags.
         See "Rich man, poor man."

(519)   Sister had a date last night,
         Boy friend held her very tight.
         Brothers made a friendly bet.
         How many kisses did she get?

Student oral collection (1964) [Texas].

         Sitting on the front porch (doorstep).
         See "Standing on the corner."

(520)   Skinamalinky long legs,
         Umbrella feet,
         Went to the cinema
         And fell through the seat.

Cameron, *Folk-Lore*, 67 (1956), 176 [Aberdeen].

(521)   Skip, hop, hep, hep!
         This will give you lots of pep.
         If you do this twice a day
         You'll be able to swim across the bay.

Owens, *North Star Folk News*, 4, No. 2 (1949), 2 [Minnesota].

(522)   Skip, skip,
         Skip to my Lou,
         Skip, skip,
         Skip to my Lou,
         Skip to my Lou, my darling,
         etc.

                 *Usually collected as a singing or
                 play-party game.*

Seegar, Folkways 7029 (1955) [Illinois].

         Slow skip, what you like.
         See "High, low, slow, dolly."

         Smudge, smudge, tell the judge.
         See "Fudge, fudge."

(523)   Soldier, soldier, you may be
         Just come home from Germany.

Douglas (1916), 89 [London].

(524)   Solomon Grundy
         Born on Monday
         Christened on Tuesday
         Married on Wednesday
         Sick on Thursday
         Worse on Friday
         Died on Saturday
         Buried on Sunday

And that was the end of
Solomon Grundy.

> *Common nursery rhyme; see*
> *Opie,* DICTIONARY, *392.*

Abrahams, *SFQ*, 27 (1963), 211 [Texas].

(525)   Somebody, nobody.
> *See "I love coffee."*

Goddard, *Word Lore*, 2 (1927), 128 [Bournemouth].

Some love coffee, some love tea.
See "I love coffee."

South Wales Evening Post.
See "Manchester Guardian."

(526)   Spanish dancers do the splits;
Spanish dancers do the kicks.
Spanish dancers do the rounds;
Spanish dancers touch the ground.
Spanish dancers, get out of town.

> *Often found in conjunction with*
> *other rhymes.*

Ashton, *JAF*, 52 (1939), 120 [Iowa]. "Dolly Dimple."
Brewster, *SFQ*, 3 (1939), 178 = Botkin (1944), 795.
Fahey, *Journal of Health and Physical Education*, 11 (1940), 422 [Kansas]. "Fannie Stancer."
Nulton, *Story Parade* (April, 1940), 15. With "I went downtown/To see Mrs. Brown" rhyme.
Speroni, *CFQ*, 1 (1942), 251 [California]. "Dolly Dimple."
Mensing, *HFB*, 2 (1943), 49 [Indiana].
Sone (1943), 199 [Texas]. With "Last night and the night before" rhyme.
Halpert, *CFQ*, 3 (1944), 154. Two variants, one begins "Dolly Dimple."
Bryant, *NYFQ*, 2 (1946), 294 [New York]. "Dolly Dimple."
Emrich and Korson (1947), 131.
Haufrecht (1947), 63.

Withers (1948), 69. "Dolly Dimple."

Haines, *Daedalian*, 17 (1949), 25 [Texas]. With "Last night and the night before" rhyme.

Reck, *WF*, 8 (1949), 129 [Colorado]. With "I went downtown/To see Mrs. Brown" rhyme.

Musick, *WVF*, 2, No. 3 (1952), 6 [West Virginia]. "Little Spanish dancer."

Browne, *WF*, 14 (1955), 14, 16–17 [California]. Four variants; one with "Last night and the night before" rhyme, two with "I went downtown/To see Mrs. Brown" rhyme.

Evans (1955), 16 [California; two variants, one begins with "I went downtown/To see Mrs. Brown" rhyme] = Evans (1961), 38, 49.

Pope, *WF*, 15 (1956), 47 [Texas]. Two variants, one with "Last night and the night before" rhyme.

"Star Rating," *Manchester Guardian Weekly* (April 10, 1958), 13 [England]. Begins "Beryl Grey is a star, S-T-A-R."

Stone, *Home and Highway* (March, 1958), 27.

Leventhal and Cray, *WF*, 22 (1963), 232–233 [California, 1959]. With "Last night and the night before" rhyme.

Ainsworth, *WF*, 20 (1961), 184 [Georgia, with "Last night and the night before" rhyme], 189 [Wisconsin, two variants], 195 [Utah, with "Last night and the night before" rhyme].

Bluebells (1961), n.p. [Ayrshire]. "Can you do the sword-dance?/Can you do the kicks?/Can you do the birlie-round?/Can you do the splits?"

Worstell (1961), 20.

Heimbuecher, *KFQ*, 7, No. 4 (1962), 4 [Pennsylvania]. "I'm a Spanish dancer."

Abrahams, *SFQ*, 27 (1963), 201 [Texas]. With "Last night and the night before" rhyme.

Hawthorne, *KFQ*, 11 (1966), 117–118, 123 [Delaware]. Three variants; one "Dancer, dancer," one begins "Mexico, Mexico,/Over the hills of Texaco."

Warner, *Yankee*, 30, No. 1 (January, 1966), 80. With "Not last night" rhyme.

(527)   Stand at the bar
          Smoking a cigar
          Laughing at (Riding on) the donkey
          Ha-ha-har!

Daiken (1949), 63 [Great Britain].

Ritchie (1965), 137 [Edinburgh]. Ends "Take my arm/I do no harm/I only smoke a cigar."

(528)   Standing on the corner
          Chewing bubble gum,
          Along came a beggar (little boy)
          And asked me for some.
          O you dirty beggar!
          O you dirty bum!
          Ain't you ashamed
          To ask for gum?

                              *A common children's song about being
                              picked up by the police begins the same
                              way.*

Brewster, *SFQ*, 3 (1939), 173 = Botkin (1944), 791.
Musick, *HF*, 7 (1948), 9 [West Virginia]. "Setting on the doorstep."
Harris, *Evening Bulletin* (May 30, 1949), 10 [Pennsylvania]. "Down by
    the station/Sat a little bum/All day sittin' there,/Chewin' chewin'
    gum./'Ah' said the policeman,/'Can't you give me some?'/'Plenty
    at the drugstore,'/Said the little bum."
Owens, *North Star Folk News*, 4, No. 2 (1949), 1, 2 [Minnesota]. Two
    variants.
Musick and Randolph, *JAF*, 63 (1950), 431 [Missouri]. "Settin' on the
    doorstep."
Musick, *WVF*, 2, No. 3 (1952), 6 [West Virginia]. "Sitting on the door-
    step."
Evans (1955), 20 [California, "I was standing on the corner"] = Evans
    (1961), 40.
Seeger, Folkways 7029 (1955) [Illinois].
"Children's Rhymes," *WVF*, 8 (1958), 38. "Sitting on the front porch."
Ainsworth, *WF*, 20 (1961), 192 [Colorado], 196 [Utah].
Worstell (1961), 12.
Abrahams, *SFQ*, 27 (1963), 201 [Texas].
Buckley, *KFQ*, 11 (1966), 101 [Indiana]. Listed.

(529)   Star bright

Buckley, *KFQ*, 11 (1966), 104 [Indiana]. Listed.

          Stars.
              See "Roy Rogers."

(530)   Stella, Stella dressed in black
          Set down on a carpet tack.

Jumped right up and hollered Hell!
How many times did Stella yell?
1-2-3-4, *etc.*
> *Cf. "Cinderella, dressed in yellow."*

Randolph, *MF*, 3 (1953), 78 [Arkansas, *ca.* 1933].

(531)   Stockings red and garters blue,
          Shoes laced up with silver—
> *Incomplete.*

Douglas (1916), 93 [London].

Strawberry, apple, my jam tart.
See "Ice cream soda."

Strawberry blonde,
Cream of tartar.
See "Ice cream soda."

Strawberry shortcake,
Cream of tartar (huckleberry pie, shoo fly pie,
lemonade pop).
See "Ice cream soda."

Sugar and cream,
Bread and Butter.
See "Ice cream soda."

(532)   Sugar, salt, pepper, cider
          How many legs has a bowlegged spider?

Potter, "Skip-Rope," *Standard Dictionary* (1950), 1016.

Sunny, sunny weather.
See "All in together."

(533)   Susan, Susan, thought she was losin',
          So she gave the whole thing up.

Martin, Martin, was only startin',
But he finished and won the cup.

Sounds like an adult-made homiletic.

Botkin (1947), 906 [Connecticut].

Susie broke the milk bottle.
See "Johnny on the ocean."

(534)   Susie went into a house,
Susie moved out,
And Jack moved in.

Abrahams, *SFQ*, 27 (1963), 211 [Texas].

Suzie Doozy.
See "Teddy Bear, Teddy Bear, turn around."

(535)   Sweet, sweet Caroline,
Dipt her face in Terpentine,
Terpentine, made it shine.
Sweet, sweet Caroline.

Also a counting-out rhyme.

Douglas (1916), 61 [London].

(536)   Swing your right foot,
Turn around;
Suzy Q
And truck on down.

Britt and Balcom, *J Gen Psy*, 58 (1941), 293 [Maryland, District of Columbia]. Notes connection with "Big Apple," popular dance of 1937–1938).

(537)   Take a little bird and hop in the corner,
         Take a little bird and hop away—
                                        Incomplete.
Douglas (1916), 94 [London].

(538)   Tattletale, Tattletale, settin' on a fence
         Trying to make a dollar out of fifteen cents.
                                   Usually a taunt.
Brewster, *SFQ*, 3 (1939), 175 ("Charlie Chaplin") = Botkin (1944),
   793.
Haufrecht (1947), 63. "Tommy Tucker."
Yoffie, *JAF*, 60 (1947), 49 [Missouri]. "Ching, ching, Chinaman."
Ainsworth, *WF*, 20 (1961), 187 [Michigan]. "Chickie Chinaman."
Abrahams, *SFQ*, 27 (1963), 201 [Texas].
Buckley, *KFQ*, 11 (1966), 101 [Indiana]. Listed.

(539)   Teacher, teacher, call the roll.
         Now call in somebody that you know:
Abrahams, *SFQ*, 27 (1963), 212 [Texas]. Two variants, one ends "Who
   is absent? I don't know."

         Teacher, Teacher don't whip me.
         See "Policeman, Policeman, don't whip me."

(540)   Teacher, teacher, here comes teacher
Buckley, *KFQ*, 11 (1966), 104 [Indiana]. Listed.

(541)   Teacher, Teacher, I declare,
           I see someone's underwear.
           N-A-N-C-Y.

                    Usually a taunt.

Abrahams, *SFQ,* 27 (1963), 212 [Texas].

(542)   Teacher, teacher, oh so tired,
           How many times were you fired?
           One, two, three, *etc.*

Ainsworth, *WF,* 20 (1961), 194 [New Mexico].

(543)   Teacher, teacher with the ruler

Buckley, *KFQ,* 11 (1966), 104 [Indiana]. Listed.

           Tea kettle a 'boilin'.
             See "Keep the kettle boiling."

(544)   The Team was in a huddle,
           The captain raised his head;
           All was silent
           And this is what he said:
           You've gotta F-I-G-H-T,
           You've gotta F-I-G-H-T.

                    Obviously comes from a school cheer.

Abrahams, *SFQ,* 27 (1963), 211 [Texas].

           Teddy bear, teddy bear, hop on one foot, one foot.
             See "Little Orphan Annie goes one foot."

(545)   Teddy Bear, Teddy Bear, turn around.
           Teddy Bear, Teddy Bear, touch the ground.
           Teddy Bear, Teddy Bear, tie your shoes.
           etc.

                    Teddy and his associates, "Lady," "Ladybird," "Lady-

bug," "Betty," "Buster," "Butterfly," are asked to do numerous tasks, usually ending with "turn out the light," and "say goodnight."

Winifred Smith, *JAF*, 39 (1926), 84. Two variants, one, "Mama doll, Mama doll."

Bennett, *Children*, 2 (1927), 21. Two variants: "Old Lady" and "Johnny Red."

La Salle (1929), 71. "Buster Brown."

Thompson, *JAF*, 47 (1934), 384–385 [Pennsylvania]. Four variants; "Lady, Lady," "Buster, Buster," "Butterfly, Butterfly."

Ireland, *Recreation* (February, 1937), 564 [Texas].

Ashton, *JAF*, 52 (1939), 120 [Iowa]. Two variants.

Brewster, *SFQ*, 3 (1939), 174, 176–177 (5 variants; one beginning "Old lady," one with "Last night and the night before" rhyme) = Botkin (1944), 791.

Fahey, *Journal of Health and Physical Education*, 11 (1940), 422 [Kansas].

Nulton, *Story Parade* (April, 1940), 15, 16. Two variants, one "Lady Moon."

"Stella, Stella," *Fargo Forum* (June 23, 1940), 13 [North Dakota]. "Butterfly, butterfly."

Britt and Balcom, *J Gen Psy*, 58 (1941), 294 [Maryland, District of Columbia]. "Shirley Temple."

Hall, *Recreation* (March, 1941), 716 [Nebraska].

Speroni, *CFQ*, 1 (1942), 248, 250 [California]. Two variants, one with "Last night and the night before" rhyme.

Mensing, *HFB*, 2 (1943), 49 [Indiana].

Sone (1943), 199 [Texas].

Eller, *North Carolina Education*, 10 (1944), 464 [North Carolina]. Two variants, one "Butterfly."

Halpert, *CFQ*, 3 (1944), 155 [Alberta, Canada].

Maloney, *HFB*, 3 (1944), 24 [Idaho].

Mills (1944), 15 [Maryland]. Two variants, one, "Butterfly, Butterfly."

Halpert, *JAF*, 58 (1945), 351 [New Hampshire]. With "Peel an orange" and "Last night and the night before" rhymes.

Petersham (1945), n.p.

New York Times Magazine (April 28, 1946). "Old lady, Old lady,/Lived in a shoe" rhyme.

Bryant, *NYFQ*, 2 (November, 1946), 293–294 [New York].

Walker, *NYFQ*, 2 (1946), 231–232 [New York].

Botkin (1947), 407 [Connecticut]. Two variants: one, "Butterfly," the other, "Lady, lady."

Emrich and Korson (1947), 130–131.

Haufrecht (1947), 62, 63. Three variants; one "Old lady," one "Buster, Buster" with "Last night and the night before" rhyme.

Yoffie, *JAF*, 60 (1947), 50 [Missouri]. "Old lady, Old lady."

Withers (North) (1947), 84 [New York, "Butterfly, butterfly] = Withers (1964), 98.

McCaskill, *NCF*, 1 (June, 1948), 10–11 [North Carolina].

Musick, *HF*, 7 (1948), 8 [West Virginia].

Withers (1948), 69. "Lady bird."

Davis (1949), 215 [Florida, 1938].

Ashby, *Christian Science Monitor Magazine* (April 9, 1949), 8.

Daiken (1949), 64 [Great Britain].

Haines, *Daedalian*, 17 (1949), 24, 25, 27 [Texas and District of Columbia]. Three variants, one with "Last night and the night before" rhyme.

Harris, *Evening Bulletin* (May 30, 1949), 10 [Pennsylvania]. Mentioned.

Reck, *WF*, 8 (1949), 127 [Colorado].

Roberts, *HF*, 8 (1949), 10, 11 [Mississippi and Indiana]. Two variants, one begins "Lady, Lady."

Phillips, *The Dalhousie Review*, 29 (April, 1950), 62 [Canada].

Musick and Randolph, *JAF*, 63 (1950), 431 [Missouri]. "Butterfly, Butterfly."

Potter, "Skip-Rope," *Standard Dictionary* (1950), 1016.

Dodson, *Recreation* (June, 1951), 172 [North Carolina].

Frankel (1952), 64. "Buster Brown."

Musick, *WVF*, 2, No. 3 (1952), 5, 7 [West Virginia]. Two variants, one "Lady Moon."

Randolph, *MF*, 3 (1953), 80, 83 [Arkansas]. Two variants; one, "Betty, Betty," ends with "Spanish dancers" rhyme.

Browne, *WF*, 14 (1955), 12, 15 [California]. Six variants, one with "Last night and the night before" rhyme.

Evans (1955), 17 [California] = Evans (1961), 22–23.

Seeger, Folkways 7029 (1955) [Illinois].

Withers and Jablow (1956), 12 [New York City].

Bley (1957), 95. "Buster Brown."

Calitri, *Parents*, 32 (April, 1957), 53.

Abrahams, *KFQ*, 8 (1963), 12 [Pennsylvania, 1959]. Two variants.

Graham, *Press and Journal* (December 22, 1959), 4 [Aberdeen]. Two variants.

Leventhal and Cray, *WF*, 22 (1963), 233–234 [California, 1959]. Two variants.

Scott, *Singabout*, 3, No. 3 (Winter/Spring, 1959), 4 [Australia].

Sutton-Smith (1959), 81, 82. Two variants: one begins "I had a teddy dressed in green"; the other, "Lady bird."

Ainsworth, *WF*, 20 (1961), 181 [Maine], 182 [North Carolina], 185 [Alabama], 187 [Michigan], 191 [Wisconsin], 193 [New Mexico, with "Last night and the night before" rhyme], 194 [New Mexico], 197 [Utah].

Evans (1961), 39.

Sackett (1961), 225 [Kansas].

T   189

Worstell (1961), 21, 27, 42. Two variants: one "Buster, Buster," the
other with "I went downtown/To see Mrs. Brown" rhyme.
Heimbuecher, *KFQ*, 7, No. 4 (1962), 3 [Pennsylvania]. With "I went
donwtown/To see Mrs. Brown" rhyme.
Abrahams, *SFQ*, 27 (1963), 201 [Texas]. Eight variants; one "Buster,
climb the tree" and "Anda Panda," one "Panda Bear."
Butler and Haley (1963), n.p. Two variants, one with "Last night and
the night before" rhyme.
Sandburg (1963), 123 [North Carolina]. Three variants; one "Butterfly,
Butterfly," one "Buster, buster."
Mulac (1964), 285. "Suzie Doozie."
Withers (1964), 97, 98. Two variants: one from Withers (North), the
other from Iowa.
Butler, *TFSB*, 31 (1965), 7. With notes on foreign parallels.
Ritchie (1965), 114 [Edinburgh]. Two variants.
Buckley, *KFQ*, 11 (1966), 105 [Indiana].
Hawthorne, *KFQ*, 11 (1966), 115, 118, 123 [Delaware].
Warner, *Yankee*, 30, No. 1 (January, 1966), 80, 93.

Teddy on the railroad.
See "Piggy on the railway."

(546)   **T**en black bottles
         Sitting on a fence.
         One fell down
         And then there were nine.
         Nine . . . *etc.*

                        Usually a formulaic song.

Abrahams, *SFQ*, 27 (1963), 212 [Texas].

         Tenement to let.
         See "A House to let."

(547)   **T**en little cowboys looking very fine

Buckley, *KFQ*, 11 (1966), 101 [Indiana]. Listed.

         Ten penny nail, went to jail.
         See "A house to let."

(548)   Texaco, Texaco
           Over the hills to Mexico
           Where the red-hot peppers grow.

Abrahams, *SFQ*, 27 (1963), 212 [Texas].
Hawthorne, *KFQ*, 11 (1966), 116, 123 [Delaware]. "Mexico,/Over the
   hills of Texaco," ends with "Spanish dancers" rhyme.

(549)   There came a girl from France,
           There came a girl from Spain,
           There came a girl from the U.S.A.,
           And this is how she came.
           Hopping on one foot . . .

                    Continues with other motions.

Bluebells (1961), n.p. [Ayrshire].
Those Dusty Bluebells (1965), 14 [Ayrshire].

(550)   There came two Spaniards just from Spain
           Talking about your daughter Jane.
           My daughter Jane is yet too young
           To be controlled by anyone.
           Be she young or be she old
           For all the money she must be sold.
           Then don't let her gallop
           Don't let her trot
           Don't let her play
           In a mustard pot.

                    Commonly a singing game.

Douglas (1916), 67 [London]. "There came six Jews from Juda Spain."
Evans (1961), 22 [California].

(551)   There's somebody under the bed.
           Whoever can it be?
           I feel so very ill,
           I call Bonny in.
           Bonny lit the candle—
           Nobody there!

Hi, hi, diddly-i-e
And out goes she!

Daiken (1949), 63 [Great Britain].

(552)   There she goes, there she goes,
Peerie heels, and pointed toes.
Look at her feet, she thinks she's neat,
Black stockings and dirty feet.
There's a rat, there's a rat,
There's a rat in Janie's hat.
There's a mouse in Janie's house.

Usually a taunt.

Bluebells (1961), n.p. [Ayrshire].
Ritchie (1965), 138 [Edinburgh]. "Like an elephant on her toes."
Those Dusty Bluebells (1965), 6 [Ayrshire].

(553)   There was a farmer, had a dog
His name was Bobby Bingo
B-I-N-G-O, B-I-N-G-O, B-I-N-G-O
His name was Bobby Bingo.

Usually a singing game.

Bluebells (1961), n.p. [Ayrshire]. With tune in sol-fa.

(554)   There was a little fellow; his name was Jack.
He wanted to go to Heaven in a Cadillac,
The carburetor broke and down he fell.
Instead of going to Heaven, he went to ....
Now don't get excited, don't lose your head.
Instead of going to Heaven, he went to bed.

*Usually an autograph album rhyme. See "Three
Little Negroes" and "Charlie Chaplin has big
feet."*

Browne, *WF*, 14 (1955), 19 [California].

There was a little girl.
See "Little Miss Pinky, dressed in blue."

(555)   There was a little nigger—
         Put him in a trigger,
         Sent him to the ten cent store.
         Fell out the window,
         Broke his little finger,
         And then he went home.

Britt and Balcom, *J Gen Psy*, 58 (1941), 298 [Maryland, District of Columbia].

(556)   There was a man, a man indeed
         Sowed a garden full of seed;
         When the seed began to grow,
         'Twas like a garden full of snow;
         When the snow began to melt,
         'Twas like a ship without a belt.
         etc.
              Cf. Opie, DICTIONARY, *286.*

Graham, *Press and Journal* (December 29, 1959), 4 [Aberdeen].

(557)   There was an old lady from Botany Bay;
         What have you got to sell today?

Douglas (1916), 88 [London].

(558)   There was an old woman
         And her name was Pat.
         And when she died
         She died like *that.*
         They put her in a coffin
         And she fell to the bottom,
         Just like *that.*
         They put her in bed,

> And she bumped her head,
> Just like *that*.
>
>> *Related to the nursery rhyme "I had*
>> *an old dog, and his name was Rover."*

Sutton-Smith (1959), 77, 78 [New Zealand]. Two variants, one related
to "I went upstairs to make my bed" rhyme.
Butler, *TFSB*, 31 (1965), 5 [New Zealand].

(559)   There was an old woman
        Who lived in a shack,
        She had so many children
        That she lost track.
        1-2-3, *etc.*

>> *See Opie,* DICTIONARY, *434–435.*

Mankins, *WVF*, 12 (1962), 56 [West Virginia].

(560)   This house to let, no rent to pay
        Knock at the door and run away.

>> *Cf. "A house to let."*

Douglas (1916), 52 [London].

        This year, next year.
          See "Rich man, poor man."

        Three little children.
          See "I know a woman."

(561)   Three little Negroes dressed in white
        Wanted to go to Harvard on the tail of a kite.
        The kite string broke and down they fell.
        They didn't go to Harvard; they went to ....
        Now don't get excited, and don't turn pale.
        They didn't go to Harvard; they went to Yale!

>> *Common folk rhyme; see also the*
>> *jump-rope rhymes "There was a little*

> fellow" and "Charlie Chaplin has big
> feet."

Ainsworth, *WF*, 20 (1961), 188 [Michigan].

> Three wee gypsies lived in a tent.
> *See "Gypsy, gypsy, lived in a tent."*

(562)   Three wee tatties in a pot
          Lift the lid an' see if they're hot.
          If they're hot, cut their throat,
          Three wee tatties in a pot.

Bluebells (1961), n.p. [Ayrshire].

> Tik-tok, tik-tok.
> *See "Nine o'clock is striking."*

(563)   Tillie the Toiler,* never late,
          She's always at the office at half-past eight.

Fowke, *Hoot* (September, 1966), 41 [Canada].

(564)   Tillie the Toiler* sat on a boiler.
          The boiler got hot.
          Tillie got shot.
          How many times did Tillie get shot?
          One, two, three, *etc.*

Worstell (1961), 21.

> Tim, Tim, sat on a pin.
> *See "Charlie Chaplin sat on a pin."*
>
> Tinker, tailor, soldier, sailor.
> *See "Rich man, poor man."*
>
> Tinkle bells and cockle shells.
> *See "Bluebells, cockleshells."*

(565)   Tommy, Tommy, in the tub
          Mother forgot to put in the plug,
          One heart, one soul,
          There goes Tommy down the hole.

            Cf. song "Alice, Where Are You Going?"

Emrich and Korson (1947), 137.
Abrahams, *SFQ*, 27 (1963), 201 [Texas]. Two variants: one begins
    "Albert, Albert"; one "Two, four, six, eight/Meet me at the garden
    gate."

            Tommy Tucker sat on a fence.
              See "Tattletale, Tattletale."

            Tommy Tucker went to France.
              See "Charlie Chaplin went to France."

(566)   Tomorrow, tomorrow, tomorrow,
          Never comes.
          Tomorrow, tomorrow, tomorrow,
          Always runs.

Abrahams, *SFQ*, 27 (1963) [Texas].

(567)   O Tonight is Saturday night,
          Tomorrow will be Sunday.

Douglas (1916), 89 [London].

            Toots and Casper* went downtown.
              See "Blondie and Dagwood."

(568)   Tough luck:
          You may miss,
          You may not,
          You may fall down
          And go bawl.
          You have fallen down.

You have missed.
Tough luck.

Abrahams, *SFQ*, 27 (1963), 212 [Texas].

(569)   **T**ruman's* in the White House
Waiting to be elect (*sic*) ;
Dewey's* in the garbage
Waiting to be collect (*sic*).

> *A political rhyme from the 1948 U. S.
> presidential campaign.*

Owens, *North Star Folk News*, 4, No. 2 (1949), 2 [Minnesota].

(570)   **T**urn your back on the sailor Jack.
Sailor Jack is very funny.
That's the way he makes his money,
Salt, mustard, ginger, pepper.

> *See "Salt, vinegar, mustard, and pepper."*

Sutton-Smith (1959), 82 [New Zealand].
Bluebells (1961), n.p. [Ayrshire]. "German boys are awful funny."
Ritchie (1964), 27 [Edinburgh]. "German boys/Are so funny . . ."
  Begins with a version of "I'm a little Dutch girl" rhyme.
Ritchie (1965), 132 [Edinburgh]. "Sailor boys are so funny," as ending
  for a version of "I'm a little Dutch girl" rhyme.

(571)   **T**urn your back, you saucy cat,
And say no more to me.

Douglas (1916), 92 [London].

Twasn't last night, but the night before.
> *See "Last night and the night before."*

Twelve o'clock is striking.
> *See "Nine o'clock is striking."*

(572)   Two, four, six, eight,
          Don't make love at the garden gate.
          'Cause love is blind,
          But the neighbors ain't.

                    Usually an autograph album rhyme.

Abrahams, *KFQ*, 8 (1963), 12 [Pennsylvania, 1959].

(573)   Two, four, six, eight.
          Meet me at the garden gate.
          If I'm late, do not wait.
          Two, four, six, eight.

Emrich and Korson (1947), 135.
Withers (1948), 61.
Abrahams, *SFQ*, 27 (1963), 201. With "Tommy, Tommy" rhyme.

(574)   Two, four, six, eight,
          Papa caught a rattlesnake.
          The snake it died,
          And Papa cried.
          Two, four, six, eight.

                    *Related to the counting-out rhyme "One,
                    two, three,/Mother caught a flea."*

Schiller, *NYFQ*, 12 (1956), 206.

          Two in together.
            See "All in together."

(575)   Two in the middle and two at the end,
          Each is a sister and each is a friend.
          A shilling to save and a penny to spend,
          Two in the middle and two at the end.

Douglas (1916), 58 [London]. "Two in the rope and two take end."
Daiken (1949), 65 [Great Britain].

(576)   Two little dickie-birds
         Sitting on a wall.
         One named Peter,
         The other named Paul.
         Fly away Peter,
         Fly away Paul.
         Come back Peter,
         Come back Paul.

                   Usually a finger game.

Scott, *Singabout*, 3, No. 3 (Winter/Spring, 1959), 5 [Australia].
Graham, *Press and Journal* (December 22, 1959), 4 [Aberdeen].

(577)   Two little monkeys
         Jumping on the bed,
         One fell off
         And broke his head,
         Took him to the doctor,
         And the doctor said:
         That's what you get
         For jumping on the bed.

                   Usually an entertainment rhyme.

Student oral collection (1964) [Texas].

(578)   Two years old,
         Goin' on three—
         I wear my dress
         Above the knee.
         I walk in the rain,
         I walk in the snow,
         And it's nobody business
         If I do have a beau.

Britt and Balcom, *J Gen Psy*, 58 (1941), 299 [Maryland, District of
    Columbia].

Underneath the water.
See "Down in the dungeons."

(579)   Up and down Jamaica Street
        Riding on an Eagle;
        That's the way the money goes,
        Pop goes the weasel!

                Cf. "Up and down the ladder wall."

MacColl and Behan, Folkways 8501 (1958) [Glasgow].

(580)   Up and down Jamaica Town,
        A house made out of glass.
        I stepped into a lady's house
        And there she made me laugh.

Abrahams, *SFQ*, 27 (1963), 212 [Texas].

(581)   Up and down the ladder wall,
        A half-penny loaf will do us all.
        A bit for you, a bit for me,
        And a bit for all the familee.

                Cf. "Half a pound of twopenny rice."

Gomme, 2 (1898), 202–203. Four variants: two "city wall," one a parody
    of "Pop Goes the Weasel"; one ends "I buy milk, you buy flour,/You
    shall have *pepper* in half an hour."
Douglas (1916), 57 [London]. "Up the ladder, down the wall," ends "I'll
    buy milk and you buy flour,/There'll be pepper in half an hour."

Daiken (1949), 64 [Great Britain].
Holbrook (1957), 56 [England].

(582)   Up and down, up and down,
           All the way to London Town:
           Swish swosh, swish swosh
           All the way to King's Cross:
           Legs swing, legs swing,
           All the way to Berlin:
           Heel toe, heel toe
           All the way to Jer-i-cho!
           etc.

Ritchie (1964), 37 [Edinburgh].
Ritchie (1965), 119 [Edinburgh].

(583)   Up in a loft
           A long way off
           The donkey's got the whopping cough.
           The doctor said
           That he must take
           Salt, vinegar, mustard, pepper.

                      *See "Salt, vinegar, mustard, and pepper"
                      for final line; see "Down in the meadow
                      not far off."*

Douglas (1916), 92 [London].
Holbrook (1957), 57 [England].
Ritchie (1965), 138 [Edinburgh]. "Up in the North," "What shall we
give him to make him better?"

           Up the ladder, down the ladder.
           See "Old Man Daisy,/He went crazy."

           Up the ladder, down the wall.
           See "Up and down the ladder wall."

(584)   Up to Fargo with your cargo
           Down to Hibbing, stop you fibbing;

Up to Duluth, tell the truth
Down the creek to catch some trout;
One, two, three, you'd better look out.

*Refers to towns in North Dakota
and Minnesota.*

Owens, *North Star Folk News*, 4, No. 2 (1949), 1 [Minnesota].

Virginia had a baby.
See "I had a little brother/His name was Tim."

Virginia had a brother.
See "I had a little brother/His name was Tim."

Virginia, Virginia, what do you think I did?
See "Oh, say kid."

(585)   **V**ote, vote, vote for .... :
She'll call (Here come) ....
     to her door,
.... is a lady
She isn't any baby
So we don't need .... any more.

*Many variants in third and fourth lines;
found also as a taunting song.*

Douglas (1916), 60 [London].
Halpert, *JAF*, 58 (1945), 350 [New Hampshire]. "Jump, jump, jump,/
The bells are ringing."
Musick, *HF*, 7 (1948), 8 [West Virginia].
Daiken (1949), 69 [Ringsend, England]. Sung to the tune of "Tramp,
Tramp, Tramp, the Boys are Marching."

Browne, *WF*, 14 (1955), 11 [California].

Evans (1955), 29 [California] = Evans (1961), 47.

Schiller, *NYFQ*, 12 (1956), 203 [New York]. Middle lines: "Take a piece of pie/And throw it in her eye."

Ainsworth, *WF*, 20 (1961), 190 and 191 [Wisconsin], 194 [New Mexico], 195 [Utah].

Heimbuecher, *KFQ*, 7, No. 4 (1962), 5 [Pennsylvania]. Two variants, both begin "Pom, Pom, Pompadour."

Abrahams, *SFQ*, 27 (1963), 201 [Texas].

Butler and Haley (1963), n.p. "Pop, pop, pop."

Student oral collection (1964) [Texas]. Two variants: one "Pom Pom Pompadour," one "Pump, pump, the gasoline."

Ritchie (1965), 128 [Edinburgh]. "She's the one/Who gives us all the fun."

Buckley, *KFQ*, 11 (1966), 104 [Indiana]. ". . . calls .... into the rope/........ is the one that will have jolly fun/And she won't see .... anymore."

(586)   Wash the dishes,
          Dry the dishes,
          Turn the dishes over,
          A rick tick one, a rick two . . . ten.

Bluebells (1961), n.p. [Ayrshire].
Those Dusty Bluebells (1965), 11 [Ayrshire].

          Wasn't last night but the night before.
          See "Last night and the night before."

(587)   Water, water, wallflower
          Growing up so high,
          We are all children
          And we must all die:
          Except Mary Jones, the fairest of them all,
          She can dance and she can sing

And she can do the Highland fling.
Fly, fly, fly, away, turn your back
  to the wall again.

> *Commonly a singing game.*

Bluebells (1961), n.p. [Ayrshire].

O, Wattie Manson.
  See "O ...., I am ashamed of you."

(588)   Wavy, wavy, turn the rope over,
         Mother's at the butcher's buyin' fresh meat;
         Baby's in the cradle, playin' wi'
           a radle (rattle).
         One, two, three, and a porridgee.

> *Cf. "Bluebells, cockleshells."*

Kerr, *Miscellanea of Rymour Club*, 2 (1914), 146 [Scotland, 1913].
Graham, *Press and Journal* (December 22, 1959), 4 [Aberdeen]. "Eevie-
  ivy," ends "Sister's at the table/Eating all she's able."
Ritchie (1965), 129, 139 [Edinburgh]. Two variants; one begins "Baby
  in the cradle," the other "Yankie pankie sugarallie ankie."

(589)   Way down south where bananas grow,
         The ant stepped on an elephant's toe.
         Then the elephant cried with tears in his eyes,
         Why don't you pick on somebody your size?

> *This is a common comic verse. Cf. "Down*
> *in the valley where the green grass grows."*

Reynolds, *Christian Science Monitor* (July 11, 1941), 8. Two variants,
  one "Down the Mississippi where the steamboats putt."
Speroni, *CFQ*, 1 (1942), 251 [California].
Nulton, *JAF*, 61 (1948), 58 [North Carolina, 1946]. "Down in the
  meadow/Where the corn cobs grow."
Roberts, HF, 8 (1949), 12 [Illinois].
Evans (1955), 20 [California].

(590)   Way down south where the sharecroppers grow,
         I saw some croppers croppin' to and fro;

They cropped some peas, they cropped some beans,
They cropped right up to the top of the trees.
etc.

> *This seems to be a recent composition based on a folk
> formula; currency is doubtful.*

Butler and Haley (1963), n.p.

(591)   We are three spivs of Trafalgar Square*
          Flogging nylons tuppence a pair,
          All fully fashioned, all off the ration,
          Sold in Trafalgar Square.

Opie (1959), 195 [London, 1952].

(592)   Weedy, weedy, weedy, wop.
          Sour sop ripe and drop.
          Drop on .... head
          .... say "What dat?"
          Oh, weedy, weedy, weedy wop.

Abrahams oral collection (1962) [Nevis, B.W.I.].

          Wellington Journal, Evening News.
          See "Manchester Guardian."

(593)   .... Went for a ride.
          .... fell out and .... cried.
          Oh my darling, oh, my dear,
          Let's get married in half-a-year.

Student oral collection (1964) [New Jersey]. Two variants, one "went to
    town, ... ripped a hole in her evening gown" (cf. "Blondie and
    Dagwood").

(594)   "We'll walk this lady"
          So they say,
          "A smooth foot lady"
          So they say,

Come rolling under
Just a little bit faster . . .

May be a ring game.

Holzknecht, *JAF*, 41 (1928), 577 [Kentucky] = Botkin and Withers
(1958), 37.

(595)   What are you doing here, Sir?
Drinking up the beer, Sir.
Where did you get the beer, Sir?
It wasn't far or near, Sir.
Yea, Sir, no, Sir,
I must be on my way, Sir.

Cf. "Hello, sir, hello, sir."

Butler and Haley (1963), n.p.

(596)   What's your name?
Puddin' Tame.
Ask me again
And I'll tell you the same.
Where do you live?
In a sieve.
What's your number?
Cucumber.

Usually a formulaic dialogue.

Abrahams, *SFQ*, 27 (1963), 213 [Texas].

What kind of house do you have?
See "Rich man, poor man."

(597)   What O she jumps,
She skips and jumps,
If she don't jump.
I'll make her bump.

Douglas (1916), 73 [London].

What shall I be when I grow up?
See "Rich man, poor man."

What you gonna drive?
See "Rich man, poor man."

(598)   When Buster Brown* was one (two, *etc.*)
         He used to suck his thumb (buckle his shoe, *etc.*)
         Thumb me over, thumb me over,
         A, B, C, *etc.*
                    Usually a formulaic song.

Withers (1948), 70–71.

(599)   When it rains the Mississippi River
         Gets higher, higher, and higher.

Ainsworth, *WF*, 20 (1961), 185 [Georgia].

(600)   When I was single I used a powder puff.
         Now I am married I cannie get the stuff.
         Oh, it's a life, a weary, weary, life,
         It's better to be single than be a married wife.
         One shouts "Mammy, give me a piece of jam!"
         The other shouts, "Daddy, put me in the pram!"
         When I was single I used to go and dance,
         Now I am married I cannie get the chance.
         One shouts "Mammy, put me to bed!"
         The other shouts "Daddy, scratch my wooden
            leg!"
                    Usually an adult complaint-song.

Ritchie (1964), 33 [Edinburgh].

(601)   When I was young and able
         I sat upon the table;
         The table broke

> And gave me a poke,
> When I was young and able.

Gomme, 2 (1898), 202 [England].
Holbrook (1957), 56 [England].

> **W**hen I went down to grandfather's farm.
> *See "As I went down to grandfather's farm."*

(602)   **W**here are you going, Bill?
          Downtown, Bill?
          What for, Bill?
          To pay my gas bill.
          How much, Bill?
          Ten-dollar bill.

Botkin (1947), 906 [Iowa].

(603)   **W**here did you get your cold?

Buckley, *KFQ*, 11 (1966), 104 [Indiana]. Listed.

(604)   **W**here was Moses when the light went out?

Buckley, *KFQ*, 11 (1966), 104 [Indiana]. Listed.

(605)   **W**histle while you work!
          Jenny made a shirt:
          Jessie wore it, Benny tore it,
          Mary made it worse!

                    Cf. popular song of late 1930's.

Ritchie (1965), 112 [Edinburgh].

(606)   **W**ho's got feet
          Like Arthur's seat?
          Who's got a bunion
          Like a pickled onion?

Who's got legs
Like ham and eggs?
etc.

> *Cf. "My girl's a corker."*

Ritchie (1965), 144 [Edinburgh].

(607)   Who's in the well?
Only the pussy cat.
Who pulled him out?
Little Tommy Stout.
Oh, you naughty pussy cat.

> *See Opie,* DICTIONARY, *149.*

Douglas (1916), 70 [London].

(608)   Who is knocking at my door?
"It is I," said the fly,
"1, 2, 3, 4."

> *Perhaps derived from the nursery rhyme
> "Who killed Cock Robin" or the obscene
> song "Bollicky Bill the Sailor."*

Abrahams, *SFQ*, 27 (1963), 213 [Texas].

Who shall I marry?
> *See "Rich man, poor man."*

.... Why did you run away?
> *See "O ...., I am ashamed of you."*

(609)   Willie, Willie, I am waiting,
I can't wait no longer for you,
Three times the whistle blows,
Are you coming yes or no?—

> *Incomplete.*

Douglas (1916), 94 [London].

O, **W**ilma Ballantine.
See "O ...., *I am ashamed of you."*

(610) The **W**ind and the rain and the wind blew high.
The rain comes blattering from the sky.
.... says she'll die,
If she doesn't get a fellow with a rolling eye.
etc.

Daiken (1949), 61 [Belfast and Cork].
Scott, *Singabout*, 3, No. 3 (Winter/Spring, 1959), 4 [Australia]. Second
line: "Snowflakes falling from the sky"; other minor variations.
Evans (1961), 27.

(611) The **W**oods are dark, the grass is green,
All the girls I love to see
Excepting (Rose Taylor), she's so pretty,
She belongs to London City.

Douglas (1916), 58–59 [London].

(612) **W-P-A.***
W-P-A.
You're let out;
Go get your pay.

Nulton, *JAF*, 61 (1948), 59.

Wrap her up in tissue paper
Throw (send) her down the elevator.
See "Baby in the high chair" and "Fudge, fudge."

Yankie, pankie.
See "Wavy, wavy."

(613)   Yellow, yellow,
          Who's your fellow?
          A, B, C, *etc.*
                    Cf. taunts that play on colors.

Ainsworth, *WF*, 20 (1961), 196 [Utah].

(614)   You can fall from a steeple
          You can fall from above:
          But for heaven's sake,
          Don't fall in love.
                    Usually an autograph album rhyme.

Ritchie (1965), 145 [Edinburgh].

(615)   Oh You dirty beggar, oh you dirty bum

Buckley, *KFQ*, 11 (1966), 101 [Indiana]. Listed.

(616)   You naughty boy,
          You stole my toy,
          You named him Roy,
          You naughty B-O-Y
          You stole my T-O-Y
          You named him R-O-Y.

Bluebells (1961), n.p. [Ayrshire].
Ritchie (1965), 119 [Edinburgh].

(617) **Y**ou naughty flea,
       You bit my knee.

Douglas (1916), 90 [London].

(618) **Y**ou naughty girl
       You stole my curl:
       You named it Twirl—
       You naughty GIRL!

Cf. "You naughty boy."

Ritchie (1965), 145 [Edinburgh].

(619) **Y**ou naughty lady
       You stole my baby:
       You named it Sadie,
       You naughty LADY!

Cf. "You naughty boy."

Ritchie (1965), 145 [Edinburgh].

       Your mother, my mother.
         See "My mother, your mother."

       You will marry.
         See "Rich man, poor man."

APPENDIX A

Jump-Rope Games—Names and Terms

Included here are (1) all jump-rope games noted in the articles cited that have no specific rhymes connected with them; and (2) all terms for motions used when jumping, for ways of turning the rope, and for description of the roles of players. No attempt is made to define or to cross-reference terms for the same thing. This Appendix is supplied to assist those who wish to study the games of jump-rope, rather than the rhymes. Names of games are in italics.

American ropes: Ritchie (1965), 121.
baby in the cradle: Ritchie (1965), 116.
baby's cradle: Hall, 714.
back door: Sone, 198; Eller, 447; Ainsworth, 180.
baking bread: Babcock (1888), 266; Sutton-Smith (1959), 74; Holbrook, 55.
ball bouncing: Hall, 714.
ball tap: Hall, 714.
beat skipping: Ritchie (1965), 115–116.
begging: Holbrook, 55.
birls: Ritchie (1965), 112.
birthday party: Pope, 47.
black sheep: Ritchie (1965), 113.
blindsies: Allen, 42.
bluebells: Sutton-Smith (1959), 83.
building house: Hall, 714.
building-up the castle: Ritchie (1965), 120.
bumps: Ritchie (1965), 118.
ca'ed (cawed): Maclagan (1901), 227; Maclagan (1906), 216; McCormick, 91; Watson, 42; Sutton-Smith (1959), 74; Ritchie (1965), 113.
chase the fox: Sutton-Smith (1959), 74; Holbrook, 57.
Chinese jump-rope: Abrahams, *KFQ*, 13; Hawthorne, 125; Ritchie (1965), 121.
chorers: Sutton-Smith (1959), 20.
clean the windows: Maclagan (1901), 228.
climb the stair: Maclagan (1901), 228.

combing the hair: Maclagan (1901), 228.
continues: Ritchie (1965), 139.
cops and robbers: Pope, 48.
crossed elbows: Hall, 713.
cut the cheese: Hall, 713.
dance: Hall, 714.
dolly: *Bluebells,* n.p.; Ritchie (1965), 118.
double-Dutch: Yoffie, 31; Magill, 8; Gibbs, 313; Nulton (1948), 65;
    Holbrook, 55; Sutton-Smith (1959), 74, 83; Abrahams, *KFQ,* 4; Haw-
    thorne (1966), 126.
double-French: Nulton (1948), 65.
double-Irish: Yoffie, 31; Abrahams, *KFQ,* 4.
double-rope: Sone, 198; Ainsworth, 180.
duck skipping: Sutton-Smith (1959), 83.
elastications: Ritchie (1965), 121.
ender: Nulton (1948), 65; Abrahams, *KFQ,* 41.
exams: Sutton-Smith (1959), 83.
feet together and apart: Hall, 714.
fireys: Ritchie (1965), 118.
follow-my-leader: Ritchie (1965), 114.
four no miss: Ritchie (1965), 115.
fox and goose: Babcock (1886), 332; Babcock (1888), 266; Hawthorne
    (1966), 120.
French Dutch: Holbrook, 55.
French rope: Maclagan (1906), 216; Sutton-Smith (1959), 83; Ritchie
    (1965), 117; Hawthorne (1966), 126.
front door: Sone, 198; Eller, 447; Ainsworth, 180.
German rope: Maclagan (1906), 216; Ritchie (1965), 117.
grinding coffee: Eller, 447.
heel, heel: Hall, 714.
high: *Bluebells,* n.p.; Ritchie (1965), 118.
high waters: Maclagan (1906), 217; Nulton (1948), 57; Sone, 198; Pope,
    47; Ainsworth, 180; Sutton-Smith (1959), 83; Hawthorne (1966), 125.
hop: Maclagan (1901), 228.
hopsies: Allen, 42.
hot peas: Nulton (1948), 65; Eller, 447; Ainsworth, 180.
hot peppers: Sone, 198; Nulton (1948), 65; Ainsworth, 180.
Indian jumping: Abrahams, KFQ, 5.
Irish: Abrahams, *KFQ,* 4.
jump turn: Hall, 714.
ladder: Holbrook, 55; Ritchie (1965), 122.
legs crossed: Hall, 714.
leg swing: Hall, 714; Ritchie (1965), 119.
lift and lay: Maclagan (1901), 228.

loops: Sutton-Smith (1959), 83.

low: *Bluebells,* n.p.; Ritchie (1965), 118.

low water: Maclagan (1906), 216.

lucky number: Pope, 48.

medium: *Bluebells,* n.p.

months of the year: Pope, 47.

mustard: Ritchie (1965).

mustard hot: Randolph, 79.

Old King Cole: McCaskill, 12.

one no miss: Ritchie (1965), 115.

out my window: Eller, 447; Ainsworth, 180.

over: Sone, 198; *Bluebells,* n.p.

over and under the water: Sutton-Smith (1959), 83.

over the moon: Sutton-Smith (1959), 83.

pepper: Maclagan (1901), 228; Maclagan (1906), 216; Speroni, 245;
   Nulton (1948), 65; Randolph, 78; Magill, 8; Sutton-Smith (1959), 74;
   Bluebells, n.p.; Ritchie (1965), 117.

pile of bricks: Babcock (1886), 332; Babcock (1888), 267.

plainie-dykie: Ritchie (1965), 117.

plain ropes: Ritchie (1965), 113ff.

plain skipping: Ritchie (1965), 113ff.

porridgee: Ritchie (1965), 118.

red hot pepper: Yoffie, 31.

rocking the cradle: Babcock (1888), 266; Emrich and Korson, 137; Sone,
   197–198; Holbrook, 54.

rock: Hall, 714.

rocky: *Bluebells,* n.p.

Rosie: Maclagan (1901), 228.

round rope heights: Ritchie (1965), 121.

running through school: Hall, 714.

running through the moon: Ritchie (1965), 120.

salt: Maclagan (1901), 228; Maclagan (1906), 216; Ritchie (1965), 137.

school: Pope, 46–47; Hawthorne (1966), 120.

scissors: Richtie (1965), 124.

single hop: Hall, 714.

singles: Abrahams, *KFQ,* 5.

skip: Hall, 714.

slow: *Bluebells,* n.p.

snake: Hall, 714; Pope, 47; Ritchie (1965), 120.

snakes and ladders: Sutton-Smith (1959), 83.

split the pie: Emrich and Korson, 133.

steady ender: Nulton (1948), 65.

stepsixes: Allen, 42.

sugar: Maclagan (1906), 216.
sweep the floor: Maclagan (1906), 216.
swing: Nulton (1948), 65.
swish swosh: Ritchie (1965), 119.
tea: Maclagan (1906), 216.
ten and a journey: Ritchie (1965), 115.
throw: Nulton (1948), 65.
tidal waves: Ritchie (1965), 120.
toe tap on back: Hall, 714.
trilling: Nulton (1948), 66.
tumbleerie: *Bluebells,* n.p.
turn: Nulton (1948), 65.
turners: Eller, 447; Ainsworth, 179.
two feet: Hall, 714.
two no miss: Ritchie (1965), 115.
under the moon: Sutton-Smith (1959), 83.
up and down: Ritchie (1965), 119.
up the ladder: Eller, 447; Ainsworth, 180.
vinegar: Ritchie (1965).
visiting: Holbrook, 54.
washing the face: Maclagan (1901), 228.
wavy: *Bluebells,* n.p.; Ritchie (1965), 116 ("wavie").
white sheep: Ritchie, 113.
winding the clock: Holbrook, 55.
wolf over the river: Pope, 47.
yokey: Allen, 18.
zoop: Ritchie (1965), 116.

APPENDIX B

Names Mentioned in the Rhymes

Actual persons whose last names are given in the rhymes are entered by last name. Other names are entered as they appear in the rhymes.

Ali Baba. Hero of *The Arabian Nights* story "Ali Baba and the Forty Thieves."

Amos and Andy. Title characters in a radio and television comedy series depicting urban Negro life.

Andy Gump. Character in the comic strip "The Gumps," created by J. M. Patterson in 1917.

Beery, Wallace (1886–1949). American motion picture character actor.

Betty Boop. Character in early animated motion picture cartoons and a comic strip originated by Max Fleischer; supposed to have been a parody of singer Helen Kane.

Blondie. Central character in the comic strip "Blondie," created in 1930 by Murat Bernard (Chic) Young.

Boles, John (1900–1969). American actor during the late twenties and and thirties.

Bronco Lane. Central character in "Bronco," a television series about the American West.

Buster Brown. Title character in a comic strip created in 1897 by Richard Outcault.

Castro, Fidel (1927–   ). Cuban revolutionary who became Prime Minister of Cuba in 1959.

Chaplin, Charlie (1889–   ). Charles Spencer Chaplin, English-born motion picture comedian, famous for his good-natured tramp role.

Charlie McCarthy. Dummy created by ventriloquist Edgar Bergen (1903–   ).

Cookie. Daughter of Blondie and Dagwood Bumstead in the comic strip "Blondie," created in 1930 by Murat Bernard (Chic) Young.

Dagwood. Central character in the comic strip "Blondie," created in 1930 by Murat Bernard (Chic) Young.

Dennis the Menace. Title character in the comic strip created by Hank Ketcham in 1951.

Dewey, George (1837–1917). American admiral; commander of the Asiatic Squadron that destroyed the Spanish fleet during the Spanish-American War.

Dewey, Thomas (1902–   ). American politician and Republican presidential candidate in 1944 and 1948.

Dr. Kildare. Central character in a series of novels written by Frederick Faust under the psuedonym Max Brand; later serialized in motion pictures and television.

Donald Duck. Animated cartoon and comic strip character created by Walt Disney in 1938.

Durbin, Deanna (1922–   ). American motion picture actress noted for adolescent and ingénue roles.

Fred and Wilma. Central characters of "The Flintstones," a comic strip and animated television series created by Hanna and Barbera.

Franklin, Benjamin (1706–1790). American statesman and philosopher who played a leading role in the formation of the United States.

Gable, Clark (1901–1960). American motion picture actor.

Girl Guide. A member of a British organization for girls founded by Robert S. S. Baden-Powell and his sister Lady Agnes.

Grable, Betty (1916–   ). American motion picture actress.

Grey, Beryl (1927–   ). English dancer.

Happy Hooligan. Title character in a cartoon strip created by Frederick Burr Opper around 1900.

Hayworth, Rita (1918–   ). American motion picture actress.

Henie, Sonja (1913–   ). Norwegian-born ice-skating champion and actress in American motion pictures.

Hitler, Adolph (1889–1945). Fascist chancellor and Führer of Germany from 1933 to 1945.

I.R.A. Irish Republican Army, secret nationalist organization working for independence from Great Britain.

Jiggs. See *Maggie and Jiggs.*

Johnson, Amy (1903–1941). Pioneer British aviatrix who set many long-distance flight records before her death as a World War II transport pilot.

Kaiser Bill. William II, emperor of Germany and king of Prussia, 1888–1918.

Lassie. Dog portrayed in the book *Lassie Come Home* (1940) by Eric Knight; later featured in motion pictures and television.

Leicester Square. An area in London.

Little Annie Rooney. Comic strip originated in 1927, written by Brandon Walsh and drawn by Darrel McClure.

Little Lulu. Title character in a comic strip written by Marge.

Little Orphan Annie. Title character in a comic strip created by Harold Gray in 1924.

Lone Ranger. Title character in comic strips, motion pictures, and radio and television series set in the American West.

Maggie and Jiggs. Cartoon characters in the comic strip "Bringing Up

Father," created by George McManus in 1911.

Mickey Mouse. Animated character in the first sound cartoon by Walt Disney (1928); became the title character of a cartoon strip in 1930.

Minnie Mouse. Girl friend of Mickey Mouse (see above).

Monroe, Marilyn (1926–1962). American motion picture actress.

Mussolini, Benito (1883–1945). Fascist dictator and Premier of Italy from 1922 to 1945.

Paul, John, Ringo, George. Paul McCartney, John Lennon, George Harrison, and Ringo Starr, members of the Beatles, a popular English singing group.

Popeye. Title character in a cartoon strip created by E. C. Segar in 1929; also featured in animated cartoons.

Rand, Sally (1913–   ). Exotic dancer noted for her fan dance performance.

Rin Tin Tin. Trained dog performing in motion pictures and television.

Robin Hood. Legendary English outlaw, supposedly residing in Sherwood Forest, noted for his skill in archery and his practice of robbing from the rich and giving to the poor.

Rogers, Roy (1912–   ). American motion picture actor and singer in films about the American West.

Silver. The horse belonging to the Lone Ranger.

Superman. Possessor of superhuman powers and central character in the comic strip created by Jerry Siegel and Joe Shuster in 1938.

Temple, Shirley (1928–   ). American child actress in motion pictures.

Tillie the Toiler. Scatter-brained secretary in a comic strip of the same name created in 1921 by Russell Channing Westover.

Toots and Casper. Title characters in a comic strip created by James E. Murphey in 1918.

Trafalgar Square. A square in London named in memory of Admiral Horatio Nelson's victory at Trafalgar, Spain.

Truman, Harry (1884–   ). President of the United States from 1945 to 1953.

Wagon Train. Television series depicting the adventures of a party of settlers crossing the American West in the latter part of the nineteenth century.

W.P.A. Work Projects Administration, a United States federal agency (1935–1943) charged with creating public works in order to alleviate unemployment.

WORKS CITED

UNPUBLISHED ORAL COLLECTIONS

Abrahams, Roger. Collected in Nevis, British West Indies, 1963.

Gardiner, C. A., Esq., M.A. Collected in Arbroath, Angus, and Forfar, Scotland, 1957–1958.

Student collection. Collected in Texas, 1963–1964, and New Jersey, 1964. The Folklore Archives of The University of Texas at Austin.

RECORDINGS

Caplan, Israel. *When I Was a Boy in Brooklyn.* Folkways Record 3501. New York, 1960.

MacColl, Ewan, and Dominick Behan. *The Singing Streets.* Folkways Record 8501. New York, 1958.

MacColl, Ewan, and Peggy Seeger. *The Elliots of Birtley.* Folkways Record 3565. New York, 1962.

Seeger, Pete. *Jump Rope.* Folkways Record 7029. New York, 1955.

Schwartz, Tony. *1, 2, 3, and a Zing-Zing-Zing.* Folkways Record 7009. New York, 1953.

PUBLISHED MATERIAL

Asterisks indicate works providing explanation
of the games that accompany the rhymes.

Abrahams, Roger D. "Jump-Rope Rimes from Texas," *Southern Folklore Quarterly*, 27 (1963), 196–213.

*———. "Some Jump-Rope Rhymes from South Philadelphia," *Keystone Folklore Quarterly*, 8 (1963), 3–15.

*Ainsworth, Catherine Harris. "Jump Rope Verses Around the United States," *Western Folklore*, 20 (1961), 179–199. *See also* Eller, Catherine [Ainsworth].

*Allen, Robert Thomas. "The Tribal Customs of Space-Age Children," *Macleans*, July 6, 1963, pp. 18–19, 42–45.

Ashby, Phyllis. "Jump-Rope Jingles," *The Christian Science Monitor Magazine*, April 9, 1949, p. 8.

*Ashton, John W. "Some Jump Rope Rhymes from Iowa," *Journal of American Folklore*, 52 (1939), 119–123.

*Babcock, W. H. "Carols and Child-Lore at the Capital," *Lippincott's Magazine*, 38 (1886), 332.

*————. "Games of Washington Children," *American Anthropologist*, o.s., 1 (1888), 266–268.

Bennett, H. C. "Lyrics of the Pavements," *Children: The Magazine for Parents*, 12 (1927), 20–21.

Bley, Edgar S. *The Best Singing Games.* New York: Sterling Publishing Co., 1957.

Bluebells My Cockle Shells. Collected by the pupils of Cumnock Academy. Kilmarnock, Scotland: Cumnock Academy, 1961.

Botkin, B. A. (ed.). *A Treasury of American Folklore.* New York: Crown Publishers, Inc., 1944. Pp. 791–803; from Brewster (1939) and Mills and Bishop (1937).

———— (ed.). *A Treasury of New England Folklore.* New York: Crown Publishers, Inc., 1947.

———— (ed.). *Sidewalks of America.* New York & Indianapolis: Bobbs-Merrill Co., 1954. Pp. 565–567; from Rolland (1938).

————, and Carl Withers (eds.). *The Illustrated Book of American Folklore.* New York: Grosset & Dunlap, 1958. Pp. 37, 49, 81; from Musick (1951).

Brewster, Paul G. "Rope Skipping, Counting-Out and Other Rhymes of Children," *Southern Folklore Quarterly*, 3 (1939), 173–185.

———— (ed.). "Children's Games and Rhymes." In *The Frank C. Brown Collection of North Carolina Folklore*, Vol. 1. Durham, North Carolina: Duke University Publications, 1952. Pp. 170–172.

Britt, Stewart Henderson, and Margaret M. Balcom. "Jumping-Rope Rhymes and the Social Psychology of Play," *Journal of Genetic Psychology*, 58 (1941), 289–305.

Browne, Ray B. "Southern California Jump-Rope Rhymes: A Study in Variants," *Western Folklore*, 14 (1955), 3–22.

Bryant, Margaret M. "Folklore in College English Classes," *New York Folklore Quarterly*, 2 (November, 1946), 293–295.

*Buckley, Bruce R. "Jump-Rope Rhymes: Suggestions for Classification and Study," *Keystone Folklore Quarterly*, 11 (1966), 99–111.

Butler, Francelia. "International Variations in Skip-Rope Rhymes," *Tennessee Folklore Society Bulletin*, 31 (1965), 1–7.

————, and Gail E. Haley. *The Skip Rope Book.* New York: Dial Press, Inc., 1963.

Calitri, Princine M. "Jump-Rope Rhymes," *Parents Magazine*, 32 (April, 1957), 53, 86.

Cameron, J. S. "Skinamalink," *Folk-Lore*, 67 (1956), 176.

Chamberlain, A. F. "Folklore of Canadian Children," *Journal of American Folklore*, 8 (1895), 253.

"Children's Rhymes, Games and Stories," *West Virginia Folklore*, 8 (1958), 36–39.

Clarke, Mary Olmsted. "Song-Games of Negro Children in Virginia," *Journal of American Folklore,* 3 (1890), 290.

Daiken, Leslie. *Children's Games Throughout the Year.* New York and London: B. T. Batsford, Ltd., 1949.

————. *Out Goes She.* Dublin: The Dolmen Press, 1963.

Davis, Arthur Kyle. *Folk-Songs of Virginia.* Durham, North Carolina: Duke University Press, 1949.

Dodson, Taylor. "Rhymes with a Reason," *Recreation,* June, 1951, pp. 172–173.

Dorson, Richard M. (ed.). *Buying the Wind.* Chicago: University of Chicago Press, 1964. Pp. 384–387, "Rope-Skipping Rhymes"; from Grace Partridge Smith (1946).

Douglas, Norman. *London Street Games.* 1st ed.; London: St. Catherine Press, 1916. 2nd ed., rev.; London: Chatto and Windus, 1931.

*Eller, Catherine [Ainsworth]. "Cinderella Dressed in Yellow," *North Carolina Education,* 10 (1944), 447, 464. *See also* Ainsworth, Catherine.

*Emrich, Marion Vallat, and George Korson. *The Child's Book of Folklore.* New York: The Dial Press, 1947.

Evans, Patricia. *Jump Rope Rhymes.* San Francisco: The Porpoise Bookshop, 1955.

————. *Rimbles.* New York: Doubleday & Co., 1961.

Fahey, Helen. "Everyone Jumps Rope," *The Journal of Health and Physical Education,* 11 (1940), 421–422.

Falk, Sam. "Chants of Childhood," *New York Times Magazine,* July 3, 1960, p. 12.

Fife, Austin E. "Rope Skipping Rhymes Collected at Greensboro, North Carolina," *Journal of American Folklore,* 59 (1946), 321–322.

————. "Two Variants of the 'Charlie Chaplin' Rhyme," *Journal of American Folklore,* 59 (1946), 532.

Ford, Nancy K. "A Garland of Playground Jingles," *Keystone Folklore Quarterly,* 2 (1957–1958), 109–111.

Fowke, Edith. "Children's Rhymes, Past and Present," *Hoot* (Toronto), September, 1966, pp. 41–42.

Frankel, Lillian, and Godfrey Frankel. *Best Games for Girls.* New York: Sterling Publishing Co., 1952.

Gibbs, Iris, and Alonso Gibbs. "Jump Rope Song," *New York Folklore Quarterly,* 14 (1958), 312–316.

Gillington, Alice. *Old Hampshire Singing Games and Trilling the Rope Rhymes.* London, 1909.

————. *Old Surrey Singing Games and Skipping-Rope Rhymes.* London, 1909.

Goddard, C. V. "Skipping Rhymes," *Word Lore,* 2 (1927), 128.

Godman, Stanley. "Good Friday Skipping," *Folk-Lore*, 67 (1956), 171–174.

*Gomme, Alice B. *The Traditional Games of England, Scotland, and Ireland.* 2 vols.; London, 1894–1898.

Gordon, David. "Rhymes," *West Virginia Folklore*, 12 (1962), 50–53.

*Graham, Cuthbert. *The Press and Journal* (Aberdeen, Scotland), November 24, 1959–January 25, 1960.

Gullen, F. Doreen. *Traditional Number Rhymes and Games.* London: University of London Press, 1950.

*Haines, Vergie. "Rhymes for Jumping-Rope," *Daedalian Quarterly*, 17 (1949), 23–30.

*Hall, Sue. "That Spring Perennial—Rope Jumping!" *Recreation*, March, 1941, pp. 713–716.

Halpert, Herbert. "Skipping Rhymes from Calgary, Alberta," *California Folklore Quarterly*, 3 (1944), 154–155.

*———. "Children's Rimes from New Hampshire," *Journal of American Folklore*, 58 (1945), 349–351 (from *Manchester* [New Hampshire] *Leader*).

Harris, Harry. "Jumpin' Jive," *The Evening Bulletin* (Philadelphia), May 30, 1949.

Haufrecht, Herbert (comp.). *More Than One Hundred Songs and Games Every Child Should Know.* Ed. Alex Kramer. New York, 1947.

*Hawthorne, Ruth. "Classifying Jump-Rope Games," *Keystone Folklore Quarterly*, 11 (1966), 113–126.

Heck, Jean O. "Folk Poetry and Folk Criticism," *Journal of American Folklore*, 40 (1927), 1–42.

Heimbuecher, Ruth. "Some Jump-Rope Rhymes," *Keystone Folklore Quarterly*, 7, No. 4 (1962).

Henry, Mellinger Edward. *Songs Sung in the Southern Appalachians.* London, 1934.

Herriman, Edith. "Children's Games and Rhymes," *West Virginia Folklore*, 3 (1953), 52.

*Holbrook, David. *Children's Games.* London: The Gordon Fraser Gallery Limited, Bedford, 1957.

Holzknecht, K. J. "Some Negro Song Variants from Louisville," *Journal of American Folklore*, 41 (1928), 576–577.

Howard, Dorothy. *See* Mills [Howard], Dorothy.

Hudson, Arthur Palmer. *Specimens of Mississippi Folk-Lore.* Ann Arbor: Edwards Brothers, 1928.

Hurvitz, Nathan. "Jews and Jewishness in the Street Rhymes of American Children," *Jewish Social Studies*, 16 (1954), 135–150.

Hyatt, Harry M. *Folk-Lore from Adams County, Illinois.* New York: Hyatt Foundation, 1935.

Ireland, Irma Thompson. "Juggling with Jingles and Jargons," *Recreation,* February, 1937, pp. 545, 564.

Johnson, Frederick. "More Children's Jumping Rhymes," *Journal of American Folklore,* 42 (1929), 305–306.

"Jump-Rope Rhymes," *Western Folklore,* 23 (1964), 258.

Kerr, John. "A Skipping Rope Rhyme," *Miscellanea of the Rymour Club,* 2 (1914), 146.

Kingston, Marion (collector). *A Folk Song Chapbook* (*The Beloit Poetry Journal,* 6, No. 2; Chapbook No. 4). Beloit, Wisconsin, 1955.

LaSalle, Dorothy. *Play Activities for Elementary Schools.* New York: A. S. Barnes & Co., 1929.

Leventhal, Nancy C., and Ed Cray. "Depth Collecting from a Sixth Grade Class," *Western Folklore,* 22 (1963), 231–238.

Lloyd, A. L. *Lilliput,* September, 1952, p. 51.

Lomax, Alan. *The Penguin Book of American Folksongs.* Baltimore: Penguin Books, 1964.

*McCaskill, Joan. "Rope Skipping Games," *North Carolina Folklore,* 1 (June, 1948), 10–12.

McCormick, Andrew. *Words from the Wild-Wood.* Glasgow and Dalbeattie, 1912.

McDowell, Kathleen F. "Jump Rope Jingles," *The New York Times Magazine,* April 14, 1946, p. 8.

*Maclagan, Robert Craig. *The Games and Diversions of Argyleshire.* London, 1901.

———. "Additions to 'The Games of Argyleshire'," *Folk-Lore,* 17 (1906), 216–217.

Maloney, Violetta G. "Jumping Rope Rhymes from Burley, Idaho," *Hoosier Folklore Bulletin,* 3 (1944), 24–25.

Mankins, Jerilyn. "Children's Games and Rhymes," *West Virginia Folklore,* 12 (1962), 53–58.

Maryott, Florence. "Nebraska Counting-Out Rhymes," *Southern Folklore Quarterly,* 1, No. 4 (1937), 39–62.

Mensing, Angela. "Jumping Rope Jingles from Bloomington, Indiana," *Hoosier Folklore Bulletin,* 2 (1943), 48–49.

Mills [Howard], Dorothy. "Playtime Verses," *Jack and Jill,* 2 (January, 1940), 18–19.

——— (ed.). *Folk Rhymes and Jingles of Maryland Children,* Frostburg, Maryland: State Teachers College, 1944.

———, and Morris Bishop. "Songs of Innocence," *The New Yorker,* November 13, 1937, pp. 32–36, 42.

Morrison, Lillian (comp.). *A Diller, a Dollar.* New York: Thomas Y. Crowell, 1955.

Mulac, Margaret. *Games and Stunts.* New York: Harper & Row, 1964.

Musick, Ruth Ann. "West Virginia Folklore," *Hoosier Folklore*, 7 (1948), 8–13.

————. "Children's Rhymes," *West Virginia Folklore*, 2, No. 3 (1952), 2, 5–7.

————, and Vance Randolph. "Children's Rhymes from Missouri," *Journal of American Folklore*, 63 (1950), 425–437.

Newell, William Wells. *Games and Songs of American Children*. Rev. ed.; New York and London: Harper and Brother, 1903.

The New York Times Magazine, "Letters to the Editor," April 28, 1946.

North, Robert. *See* Withers, Carl (1947).

*Nulton, Lucy. "Jump Rope Rhymes," *Story Parade*, April, 1940, pp. 14–16.

*————. "Jump Rope Rhymes as Folk Literature," *Journal of American Folklore*, 61 (1948), 53–67.

Opie, Iona, and Peter Opie. *I Saw Esau*. London: Williams & Norgate, Ltd., 1947.

————. *The Oxford Dictionary of Nursery Rhymes*. Oxford: Oxford University Press, 1951.

————. *Lore and Language of School Children*. Oxford: The Clarendon Press, 1959.

Ó Súilleabháin, Seán. *A Handbook of Irish Folklore*. London: Herbert Jenkins, 1942.

Owens, Florence. "Jumping Rhymes Collected in Duluth Schools," *The North Star Folk News*, 4, No. 2 (1949), 1–2.

Park, Natalie, and Helen Park. "Jump-Rope Rhymes," *California Folklore Quarterly*, 1 (1942), 377.

Petersham, Maud, and Miska Petersham. *The Rooster Crows*. New York: The Macmillan Co., 1945.

Phillips, Bluebell Stewart. "The Open Sesame," *The Dalhousie Review* (Montreal), 29 (April, 1950), 62.

Pope, Harold Clay. "Texas Rope Jumping Rhymes," *Western Folklore*, 15 (1956), 46–48.

Potter, Charles Francis. "Charlie Chaplin Rimes." In Volume 1 of *Standard Dictionary of Folklore, Mythology and Legend*, ed. Maria Leach. New York: Funk & Wagnalls, 1949.

*————. "Skip-Rope Rimes." In Volume 2 of *Standard Dictionary of Folklore, Mythology and Legend*, ed. Maria Leach. New York: Funk & Wagnalls, 1950.

Rae, Margery, and Esther Robb. "Salute to Spring," *The Christian Science Monitor Magazine*, March 21, 1942, pp. 8–9.

Randolph, Vance. "Jump Rope Rhymes from Arkansas," *Midwest Folklore*, 3 (1953), 77–84.

Reck, Alma Kehoe. "Skip and Sing," *Western Folklore*, 8 (1949), 126–130.

Reynolds, Horace. "Jump-Rope Rhymes," *The Christian Science Monitor*, July 11, 1941, p. 8.

Ritchie, James T. R. *The Singing Streets*. Edinburgh and London: Oliver & Boyd, Ltd., 1964.

———. *The Golden City*. Edinburgh and London: Oliver & Boyd, Ltd., 1965.

Roberts, Warren. "Children's Games and Games Rhymes," *Hoosier Folklore*, 8 (1949), 9–12.

Rolland, Fred. "Street Songs of Children," *New Masses*, May 10, 1938, p. 109.

Rudy, Stella M., Dorothy Mills, and Violet West Sone. "Rope-Jumping," *Jack and Jill*, 4 (March, 1942), 7.

Sackett, S. J. "Dances and Games." In *Kansas Folklore*, ed. Sackett and William Kock. Lincoln, Nebraska: University of Nebraska Press, 1961.

Sandburg, Helga. *The Owl's Roost*. New York: The Dial Press, 1962.

———. *Sweet Music*. New York: The Dial Press, 1963.

Schiller, Riva. "Jump Rope Songs and Games," *New York Folklore Quarterly*, 12 (1956), 200–206.

Scott, Alan. "Skipping Rhymes," *Singabout* (Sydney, Australia), 3, No. 3 (Winter/Spring, 1959), 4–5.

Smith, A. W. "Letter to the Editor," *Folk-Lore*, 67 (1956), 247–248.

*Smith, Grace Partridge. "Folklore from Egypt," *Hoosier Folklore*, 5 (1946), 58–60.

Smith, Winifred. "A Modern Child's Game Rhymes," *Journal of American Folklore*, 39 (1926), 82–85.

*Sone, Violet West. "Rope-Jumping Rhymes." In *Backwoods to Border*, Publications of the Texas Folklore Society, Vol. 18, 1943.

*Speroni, Charles. "Some Rope-Skipping Rhymes from Southern California," *California Folklore Quarterly*, 1 (1942), 245–252.

"Star Rating," *The Manchester Guardian Weekly*, April 10, 1958.

"Stella, Stella, Dressed in Yella—," *The Fargo* (North Dakota) *Forum*, June 23, 1940.

Stone, Charlotte. "Sidewalk Games," *Home and Highway*, March, 1958, 22–27.

*Sutton-Smith, Brian. "The Game Rhymes of New Zealand Children," *Western Folklore*, 12 (1955), 20–21.

*———. *Games of New Zealand Children*. Berkeley and Los Angeles: University of California Press, 1959.

Taylor, Archer. "Jump Rope Rhymes," *Western Folklore*, 18 (1959), 316.

Thompson, D. W. "Some Pennsylvania Rope Jumping Rhymes," *Journal of American Folklore*, 47 (1934), 383–386 (from the *Evening Sentinel* [Carlisle, Pennsylvania], June and July, 1929).

Those Dusty Bluebells. Kilmarnock, Scotland: Cumnock Academy, 1965.

Time: The Weekly Newsmagazine, May 29, 1950, pp. 19–20.

The Times (London), March 7, 1953.

Treneer, Anne. *School House in the Wind.* London: Jonathan Cape, 1944.

*Utley, Alison. *Country Things.* London: Faber & Faber, 1946.

*———. *The Swans Fly Over.* London: The Country Book Club, 1959.

Walker, Barbara K. "Folklore in the Schools: Collecting by Seventh Graders," *New York Folklore Quarterly,* 2 (1946), 231–232.

Warner, Ruth. "Come Jump With Me," *Yankee,* 30, No. 1 (January, 1966), 80–81, 93–94.

Watson, W. "Play among Children in an East Coast Mining Community," *Folk-Lore,* 64 (1953), 402–403.

White, Vallie T. "Stories and Other Lore from Second and Third Grade Pupils of Rural Schools," *Louisiana Folk-lore Miscellany,* 2, No. 2 (April, 1965), 115–116.

Whitney, Alice S. "Jumping-Rope Songs," *Green Mountain Whittlin's,* 9 (1956), 6.

Withers, Carl. "Current Events in New York City Children's Folklore," *New York Folklore Quarterly,* 3 (1947), 213–222.

——— (pseud. Robert North). *Town and Country Games.* New York: Thomas Y. Crowell Co., 1947.

———. *A Rocket in My Pocket.* New York: Henry Holt & Co., 1948.

———. *Ready or Not, Here I Come.* New York: Grosset & Dunlap, 1964.

———, and Alta Jablow. *Rainbow in the Morning.* New York: Abelard-Shuman, Ltd., 1956.

*Wood, Clement, and Gloria Goddard. *The Complete Book of Games.* New York: Doubleday & Co., 1938.

Wood, Ray. *Fun in American Folk Rhymes.* Philadelphia and New York: J. B. Lippincott Co., 1952.

Worstell, Emma Vietor. *Jump the Rope Jingles.* New York, 1961.

Yoder, Robert M. "Kids Believe the Darndest Things," *Saturday Evening Post,* October 30, 1948, p. 114.

*Yoffie, Leah Rachel Clara. "Three Generations of Children's Singing Games in St. Louis," *Journal of American Folklore,* 60 (1947), 1–51.